Analiza Quiroz Wolf

THE MYTHS OF SUCCESS:
A WOMAN OF COLOR'S GUIDE TO LEADERSHIP

*This book is dedicated to all women of color
who want to be the change they want to see,
including my daughter Scarlet.*

TABLE OF CONTENTS

PREFACE

In 2016, I went looking for the next right role and asked this question, "Do you know a woman of color CEO I can work for?" I asked this question of people I respected, top leaders in their industries. I also did some research and uncovered depressing statistics. Despite representing about 20 percent of the US population, women of color represented only 6 percent of C-Level positions in 2023, falling far below White men (56 percent) and White women (22 percent).

WHY ARE THERE SO FEW WOMEN OF COLOR CEOs?

It's not a pipeline problem. Academic institutions are graduating a high number of women of color. But only 13 percent of managers, 9 percent of senior managers, and 6 percent of top C-Suite leaders (such as Chief Operations Officer, Chief Financial Officer, and Chief Executive Officer) are women of color.

It's not a lack of ambition or confidence. One study found that 83 percent of Asian women, 80 percent of Black women, and 76 percent of Latinas want to be promoted, compared to 75 percent of men and 68 percent of White women. The pandemic and increased flexibility did not dampen women's ambition; another study found that women of color are more ambitious than White women, with 96 percent of women of color saying that their career is important to them.

Even in workplaces that we think of as female-dominated, such as education, we see a lack of women at the highest level. Women make up three-quarters of all teachers, more than half of all principals, and the majority of cabinet-level administrators. Yet, at the top, the district level, less than one-third of superintendents are women, and only 11 percent are women of color.

Despite well-intentioned efforts to advance diversity, inclusion, and equity in workplaces, these statistics tell us that there are plenty of talented, hard-working women of color, but they are not rising to the top of the ladder.

THE IMPACT OF FEW WOMEN LEADERS OF COLOR

This hurts not just the women, but the organizations themselves. Research has found that diverse companies are more innovative, produce more revenue, have happier customers, and are more productive. We know that diversity drives innovation. Which workplace comes up with more creative ideas: one where everyone thinks alike or one with many differing and fresh perspectives?

In addition, diverse employees can better connect with what customers want. For example, Latinos and members of other immigrant groups better understand their own people and have greater familiarity with niche markets so they can better create and market ideas for their community. Women, including mothers, have insight into large groups of customers too. When Indra Nooyi was CEO of Pepsi, she would conduct weekly market visits to ask herself—not as a CEO but as a mom—"What products really speak to me?" Nooyi saw that Pepsi needed new products that fit with their customers' unique needs. Pepsi created Mountain Dew Kickstart for women who wanted fewer calories in a slim can that was easy to walk around with, netting $200 million in two years.

Women leaders make for stronger teams. A Catalyst report shared that Fortune 500 companies with the most women on their executive teams provided a total return to shareholders that was 35 percent higher than that of companies with male-centric executive teams. Companies with female board representation outperform those with no women on their boards. When companies intentionally build diverse leadership, they unlock a huge untapped talent. Did you know that 70 percent of high school valedictorians are women? Their graduation rate from college is higher than men by 10 percent.

There is another reason why true diversity makes business sense. When the organization's leaders and employees are diverse, staff are more engaged and likelier to contribute their unique and diverse perspectives. Harvard Business School faculty David Thomas and Robin Ely named an approach to DEI called the "learning and effectiveness paradigm" that taps into diversity's true benefits. It's about viewing DEI more holistically—not just where an employee comes from but also what ideas, perspectives, and approaches to the work an employee brings. Leaders are open to employees' different approaches to the work, products, strategies, and culture. Employees' culturally based differences are leveraged, which results in employees feeling valued and motivated.

One of the examples that Thomas and Ely offer is of a Black woman whose manager had promoted her partly because she was an influential leader from church. Shortly after her promotion, he considered demoting her because of her poor performance. It was not until he and his manager used the learning effectiveness paradigm that they saw that there was a mismatch between how she led at work versus how she led at church. They encouraged her to draw on her cultural competencies to lead, and she began to thrive as a leader.

To incorporate the learning and effectiveness paradigm of DEI, leaders must truly value different perspectives. It means having a culture of openness where constructive challenges to the standard way of doing business are valued. It means having a culture where everyone feels empowered to bring their ideas and experiences in new ways to work and job performance.

WHAT HOLDS WOMEN OF COLOR BACK

You have probably heard of the phrase "glass ceiling." Marilyn Loden coined the phrase at a 1978 Women's Exposition to describe the invisible and impenetrable barrier preventing women from reaching the highest levels of business regardless of what they have achieved.

Victoria Sepand coined the phrase "concrete ceiling" in her 2015 thesis on the barriers and discrimination that American Black women face advancing in their career. For White women, they can see what is possible past the "glass ceiling" and shatter it. But for women of color, it is impossible to see through a "concrete ceiling." The concrete wall reflects the barriers women of color face to visualize, work around, and penetrate to upper-level and C-suite status. Concrete feels impenetrable, impossible to break through by ourselves and impossible to see through.

Women of color also face "double jeopardy." Black feminist and activist Frances M. Beal coined the phrase to describe the racism and sexism experienced by Black women and women of color more broadly. Racism and sexism promote capitalism, keep and reward those at the top (White males), and justify exploiting labor (historically, slavery and today, persistent unequal pay for women and people of color). As a result of "double jeopardy," women of color face a lack of representation, lack of management support, and lack of recognition. Women of color also face emotional exhaustion and feel invisible. On top of that, women of color get asked to do more office work and are penalized if they decline.

"Double jeopardy" also affects women and people of color, deeming them less suitable for leadership. In a 2008 study, participants read a story about a male CEO, rating his leadership effectiveness. When described as White, he was seen as more effective than when described as Black. These biases affect who is chosen to be developed and promoted.

Add to this the experience of a woman of color if she is an "only," one of the only people of her race or gender in the room. Onlys are more likely to be "othered," have their authority and expertise questioned, and be treated with disrespect. Onlys fall prey to negative stereotypes and are more heavily judged; any success or failure is carefully inspected. Women of color face even more bias as a "Double Only," a woman and a person of color. This only compounds the daily discrimination and microaggressions we face.

In *The Purpose of Power: How We Come Together When We Fall Apart*, Alicia Garza shared, "Not all patriarchy is created equal. To be racialized means that something is segregated or at least characterized by race. A racialized patriarchy allows White experiences to function as the control or the default for all experiences… It is why when we talk about the wage gap and equal pay and say that women make 81 cents to every dollar a man makes, we are actually talking about White men and White women. Black women make 66 cents to the 81 cents that White women make and to every dollar that a White man makes, and Latinas make 58 cents to the 81 cents that White women make and to every dollar that White men make. A racialized patriarchy means that White women are seen as deserving of protection, while Black women and women of color are seen as those from whom White women need to be protected."

#MeToo showed survivors of sexual abuse and harassment that we are not alone. In addition to sexual harassment in the workplace, women of color also face unwelcome environments full of microaggressions. Chester M. Pierce coined the phrase "microaggression" in his 1970 book, *The Black Seventies*. Microaggressions are commonplace daily slights that make marginalized groups feel even more marginalized. Because they are "small," outsiders might not understand the impact of their words or behaviors. Verbal examples include: "I don't see color" and "If we hire diverse staff, we dilute quality." Behavior examples include: being interrupted or spoken over, having our judgment questioned, having others comment on our emotional state, having people express surprise over our language skills or other abilities, hearing insults about our culture, being confused with someone else of the same race, feeling like we are expected to speak on behalf of all people with our identity, and having others comment on our hair or appearance. While they often aren't intentional, microaggressions are like daily cuts that add up and are painful.

The effects of the concrete ceiling, double jeopardy, and microaggressions leave women of color not only trailing behind their White peers in terms of promotion, they also have a negative impact on our mental health. Women of color are left feeling that we are "less than," "other," or never believing we fully belong anywhere no matter how hard we work. Many women of color internalize the idea that White men must be better than we are, despite evidence to the contrary. As we rise, we need to identify and call out what we can change, even as we play the game smarter.

MY PATH TO BECOMING CEO

It was with this backdrop of looking for a woman of color CEO that a Latina female mentor told me, "Why can't you become that woman of color CEO you are looking for? After all, you've been a leader since you graduated from college—first in the Air Force, then in business in brand management, and now you're a Chief Operating Officer, second to the CEO."

Up until then, I had never aspired to be CEO. I just wanted to have an impact.

I had spent my career mostly in public service as a captain in the US Air Force, then in education starting and leading schools for low-income kids of color. I wanted to help kids like me who didn't have much money and who were often dismissed because we weren't White. I wanted to build safe and good schools where teachers believed in students of color and helped to set them up for whatever career they dreamed of. I wanted to focus on leadership development and diversity, equity, and inclusion before DEI was a buzzword. I found that, partly because of my past, I was good at recruiting, developing, retaining, and advancing underrepresented talent.

Thanks to my mentor, I saw that becoming a CEO as a woman of color would make an impact. We need leaders of color at the helm—to show kids that they, too, can lead—and to bring unique experiences, perspectives, and ideas that help make changes at the system level.

With this encouragement, I turned my attention to CEO roles and decided to apply to one role in particular. A White male leader had recommended me for a CEO role leading a small charter school network in New York City. The board chair urged me to meet with the board to interview for the role. There were several rounds of interviews, including one in-person interview with half a dozen board members. Throughout the process, I was surprised to find that the interview questions were not difficult because I had experienced similar leadership situations. I realized I was more ready than I thought. Two weeks later, they offered me the job. I became a CEO.

WOMEN OF COLOR RISE

Eventually I did find other women CEOs of color. I started a podcast called *Women of Color Rise* and interviewed over 80 women, many of them women of color CEOs from all over the country. I hoped to discover:

- How did these women beat the odds? What made their ascent possible?
- How did managers, mentors, and community play a role in their career?
- What do they wish they had done differently?

- What held them back, and how did they overcome these challenges to succeed?
- What myths did they find were untrue?
- What did they wish they knew earlier to help them rise in their careers?
- What were their lessons learned, mindsets, and tools that helped them get to the top?
- How did they decide on the right career path?
- What could we do to share these lessons learned and change organizations for others who came after us?

I wanted to point to these inspiring women and say, "We did it, and so can you." This is that book. We share inspirational stories of many women of color who faced discrimination and challenges and still rose to the top.

I acknowledge that this book is a work in progress. Of the 53 women of color interviewed in this book, only three are Indigenous. Also, while the interviewees are from different industries, including for-profit, start-ups, and one who took her company public, the book skews nonprofit and particularly education. Company sizes range from yearly budgets of $500K to $1.38B, with the average size being $54M. In addition, women of color are not a homogeneous group and have vastly different cultural, economic, and immigrant circumstances. Many of the women I interviewed grew up poor. Part of the "old boys network" is class as well as race and gender. Not having resources and having the additional burden and trauma of insecure food, housing, or safety makes rising to the top even more challenging. Additionally, while this book is positioned as a book for women of color, much of the content will feel familiar to all women, especially White women immigrants. For example, while there is an element of privilege in White skin, White immigrants with an accent can also face discrimination and experience "otherness."

That said, there is much we can learn from each other. Seeing women who look like us at the top gives us hope that it is possible to rise. Our experiences are real, and we are not alone. Current workplace structures are not set up to successfully support us to reach top leadership roles. But we can still take action and crack the concrete ceiling—for ourselves and for those who follow us. Together we can build a world where we don't have to adapt ourselves to White male privilege and assumptions, where everybody is valued equally.

SHATTERING MYTHS

To empower women of color in leadership, we must confront the outdated narratives, or myths, that hinder our progress. This book focuses on dismantling 10 such myths that I, along with many of the women leaders of color whom I interviewed, personally experienced.

I first learned about the myths and how to shatter them because I had to live them. I had to test out different ways of thinking, believing, and embodying so that I could be a better leader, entrepreneur, mother, friend, and citizen. Shattering these myths has helped me fulfill my potential.

For women of color, this book serves as a guide to dispel the myths the system has led us to believe. By addressing these myths, we can position ourselves to achieve our goals and drive meaningful change. This book delves into the barriers we face, including our beliefs, attitudes, and actions that push us backstage despite our inherent strength. It also provides practical advice on overcoming challenges, communicating our desires, building confidence, and fostering relationships to advance in our careers.

For organizations, this book challenges misconceptions about women of color. The final section is aimed at leaders shaping DEI within their organizations. We debunk the myth that if we fix women of color and their behavior, then they could rise to leadership roles that have long eluded them. Instead of a "fix-the-women" mentality, this book offers strategies to change our workplaces so that more women of color are able to rise to top roles. This includes everyone, especially White male leaders, addressing and fixing the problem so that they can be better advocates, managers, and workplace leaders. We can change workplace dynamics, foster new networks, and create clear pathways to leadership for women of color who have long been overlooked in the past because they aren't part of the club.

While this book includes a synthesis of research and academic support, my hope is that this book is an operating guide, focusing on the most impactful ideas that are actionable and achievable. I am grateful to the many researchers who have come before me and the women leaders of color who have generously shared their stories.

I hope this book will help women of color gain power, not only to combat prevailing myths and stereotypes but also to level the playing field and lead in more equitable and inclusive ways. Though it might seem self-serving as a woman of color to champion the leadership of others like me, representation matters deeply. As Heather McGhee shared in her book *Sum of Us*, "We need leaders who see color, who recognize the profound impact social hierarchies have had and continue to have on our national well-being, and who create new visions for how we can recognize our American diversity as the asset that it is."

We need more women leaders of color making big decisions, shaping our laws, overseeing government agencies, and heading nonprofit and for-profit companies. It is not the responsibility of women of color to eradicate the pervasive racism and sexism ingrained in our society. Nevertheless, it's possible to bust through the concrete ceiling and drive change. This requires all of us. I hope this book helps women, men, and organizations better understand the challenges faced by women of color and inspires them to help. Thasunda Brown Duckett, the second Black woman to serve as the CEO of a Fortune 500 company in the United States, aptly stated, "My hope is that corporate America realizes that talent is equally distributed, but opportunities are not, and we all acknowledge that there is still more work to be done."

We are stronger together.

HOW TO USE THIS BOOK

This book serves as a dynamic tool to empower women of color in advancing their careers and leading with authenticity, impact, and purpose. Throughout the chapters, you'll discover a wealth of resources, guides, and prompts. As you read through each myth, consider which one or two most speak to you at this point in your leadership journey. Focus in on these areas, and take the accompanying action steps. Here are some tips to enhance your learning experience.

A JOURNAL

In this book, there are reflection prompts. I suggest grabbing a journal and taking some time to answer these questions. It will help you understand your leadership journey and craft your own career roadmap.

THE BOOK BONUSES' QR CODE

Have you ever wanted to participate in an exclusive coaching and mastermind program but faced financial constraints? The opportunity is now available to you through the information shared in each chapter. I am providing access to worksheets featured in my Women of Color Rise: Next Level Leadership Course. These are not ordinary worksheets; rather, they encompass practical frameworks, proven systems, and step-by-step guides to assist you in formulating your career growth roadmap.

The Book Bonuses encompass links to additional resources such as books, articles, and podcasts. Within each chapter, you'll find personal narratives from women leaders of color, predominantly CEOs. Exploring these resources provides a more in-depth perspective on the factors that contributed to their remarkable success.

The Book Bonuses also feature a summary list of strategies designed for organizations aiming to bolster support for women of color in their companies.

All these resources can be accessed for free via the QR Code provided below. This compilation represents over two decades of invaluable knowledge acquired by women of color leaders, enabling them to ascend to the C-Suite and make the positive changes they envision for the world. We trust that these resources will aid you on your journey to elevate yourself and contribute to making a positive impact on the world as well.

MYTH ONE
The workplace is a meritocracy

Growing up, my parents would tell me, "You can do anything in America! Just work hard!" They were determined to give me opportunities they never had.

My dad grew up as one of 10 children in a one-room shack in the Philippines. His father did not value education, and told my dad when he was six, "Make yourself useful and get a job!" So the next week, my dad woke up at 4 am and carried a sack of *pandesal*, warm bread, through his barrio. He met the American gate guards at the US Air Force Base half a mile from his home, and each day he would sell them bread and practice his English. Although he did not know it at the time, these daily visits would provide him with enough English so that he could pass the tests to join the US military. He was one of only a few who passed. My dad had won the golden ticket to become an American.

My mom's family was also in the Philippines and poor but had a different view on education. Her father told her, "There is no need to work. Just focus on school." Even with their meager income, her parents insisted that my mother, her two sisters, and brother get a good education. Instead of the terrible public schools, they scraped enough money together for their children to attend Catholic school. My mom sometimes feared she would not be able to take her exams because her tuition was not paid, but her parents somehow found the funds, sometimes begging to borrow money from relatives.

My mom dreamed of being an engineer, but her mother wanted her to be a nurse. So become a nurse she did. Good thing too because this was my mom's golden ticket to move to the United States. America needed nurses, and my mom jumped at the opportunity.

Both my mom and dad had big goals. When they met in San Diego, California, and married six months later, they vowed that their children would have a good education and be able to have any career they dreamed of. My parents did not know that being in America did not guarantee good schools for their kids. We lived in a low-income neighborhood in San Diego with gang violence as the norm. My younger brother and I went to the neighborhood school, which was lousy and unsafe.

One time in third grade, I was playing four square, a game that over the years, I felt I had developed Wimbledon-like skills with drop shots and fierce poundings. Except my skills got the best of me. I got the wrong boy out. He spat at me, "I am going to beat you up after school." He was twice my size. If an 8-year-old could have an ulcer, I felt like I had one—my stomach grinded with worry the entire day. I plotted my escape.

Once the dismissal bell rang, my plan was to run as fast as I could home. But I did not think about his friends. As I ran out of the classroom, trying to take a shortcut by the garbage bins, his two friends caught up to me and grabbed me. The boy arrived and glared at me, "I'm going to teach you a lesson." He shoved me, my head hit the metal bin, and it crashed to the ground. Thank goodness for the loud noise. We heard footsteps. I didn't need to see what would happen next. I ran.

I never told anyone what happened. Not when I came home crying, and my mom dried my tears. Not when I insisted I needed a new school. Not when we arrived at the new school, almost an hour away, and the teacher asked me why I left.

So why I am sharing now? Because moments like these helped shape who I am. It helps explain my deep commitment to education and making sure that every kid has access to a good and safe school. It was a turning point for me. My mom found my brother and me a better public school in a White neighborhood, and I was on a different educational trajectory. I attended Stanford for my BA, then Northwestern Kellogg School of Management for my MBA, and then the Broad Center (now at Yale) for my Master's of Educational Leadership. This turning point helped set up a 25-year career as a captain in the US Air Force, CEO of a charter school network in New York City, marketing leader at Fortune 300 Colgate-Palmolive, and an executive coach for leaders of color.

It seemed as if I had achieved the American Dream my parents had hoped for me.

Fast forward years later, and I am getting my annual job performance review.

My manager says, "You are liked by your team, but I'm not sure about your leadership."

I was baffled by my manager's feedback. I had worked hard, exceeded my goals, and achieved strong 360 reviews. I was sure I would get promoted. Where was the issue with my leadership? I broached the question, "Can you please share some examples of where I could have led differently?" My manager looked down at his notes and then began shuffling his papers, "Um, well, what I am talking about here is what people think of you. As a leadership team, we sit down and discuss not just a person's current performance but their potential. The team wasn't sure you could take on more responsibility. We all agreed you are nice and well-liked. But we're not sure you have what it takes to take on bigger teams or challenges where your personality can't win them over."

THE MYTH

If we work hard, we will be rewarded. The American Dream relies on the idea of meritocracy, a system that rewards merit (ability and effort), where everyone follows the same rules and has the potential to rise. Success is determined by individual achievement, intelligence, hard work, and talent.

WHICH OF THESE EXPERIENCES RESONATE WITH YOU?

- ☐ Even after stellar performance reviews, you were passed over for recognition, a promotion, or raise, and were given vague feedback that you needed to be less "emotional," more "fact-based," more "confident," or more "strategic."
- ☐ The opportunity above was given to a man who had less experience than you.
- ☐ If you ask a question about a project, colleagues describe you as a "control freak" or "emotional." But this same behavior by a man would be described as "prudent," "passionate," or "proactive."

> - You are asked to do office work such as planning the holiday party, a task that will not help you rise in your career or that you will be compensated for. However, if you do not help, you know that you will be frowned upon as not being a team player.
> - You have questioned whether being authentic or vulnerable is a strength or a weakness when leading.

Sound familiar? Situations like these are common for many women of color I interviewed and coach, where their hard work and outstanding results are ignored and the path to advancement is unclear.

THE REALITY

Our American capitalist system is not a meritocracy because the playing field is not level; people do not start on equal footing. The problem isn't with lack of individual effort but lack of access to resources due to systems of oppression. In short, it is still a White Man's World.

Women of color are not in the boys club, specifically the old White boys network that rests on inherited wealth, Ivy League fraternities, and Whites-only country clubs, among other exclusive structures. The club is where decisions are made. Promotions, hires, and other big decisions are rigged by implicit male bias and networks. Our workplace cultures and professionalism standards were defined by White, heterosexual, cisgender men. The system was built by White males for White males.

There are White men who like their unquestioned power. There are also well-meaning leaders who operate out of unconscious bias. Hiring decisions are too often based on who the bosses like, who they're comfortable with, and who is most similar to them. The more like the decision makers a person is, the more likely this person will be rewarded. These patterns prove resistant to diversity, equity, and inclusion campaigns waged in offices across the country in the wake of George Floyd's murder and the resurgence of the Black Lives Matter movement.

Instead of being a meritocracy, the workplace is more of a mirror-tocracy, with an unconscious bias and comfort level to recruit those who are similar (White male) and dismiss many talented employees, especially women of color. Research shows that humans are all biased to some degree. Our brain makes quick judgments of people, influenced by our personal experiences, culture, and background. Each second, our brains receive 11 million bits of information. But our conscious mind can handle only 40 of those pieces. To process the remaining 10,999,960, our brains help us filter information through mental shortcuts. But these shortcuts often use instinct, not analysis, and introduce unconscious bias, the information, attitudes, and stereotypes that lead to errors in our decision-making. It's impossible to choose the best people for a role if our unconscious mind narrows the field due to unrelated, biased reasons. Most people don't mean to discriminate, but this unconscious bias keeps discrimination in place.

People don't tend to examine why they think, "This person must be more qualified or less qualified." People also don't tend to examine why women and people of color are often deemed "less qualified" and that it may be because the White man deciding whether to hire us isn't used to seeing us in corner offices. Women are told to "be more confident," but that doesn't offset interviewers' unconscious bias. In fact, showing more confidence may alienate men who prefer women to be less challenging and more pliable and pleasing.

HOW UNCONSCIOUS BIAS PLAYS OUT IN LEADERSHIP

When we think of a leader, why do we picture a male? Likely, it's because most publicly recognized leaders belong to dominant groups in both race (White) and gender (male), and there is an unconscious assumption that White men are effective leaders. Second, what makes a great leader is based on qualities stereotypically associated with men: being confident, tough, aggressive, ambitious, and decisive. Women, on the other hand, are seen as having supporting-role qualities: helpful, modest, collaborative, service-oriented, empathetic, and caring.

So a man who displays leadership qualities will confirm people's stereotypes about him and rise to leadership positions quickly. If he makes a mistake, he'll be given another chance. But when a woman displays leadership qualities, she will need to repeat this over and over again because she does not match the masculine stereotype of what people see as a leader. If she does get a leadership position and makes a mistake, she is less likely to be given another chance.

Men can point to other men who are CEOs and find many personality types—awkward geek, party animal, sexist slime ball, ruthless capitalist. Compare that with the very limited range of leadership styles available to women. Women have few role models, and if they presented as awkward geek, party animal, sexist slime ball, or ruthless capitalist, they would have been fired early in their careers.

WELCOME TO THE DOUBLE BIND

Because our culture has an unconscious bias of how each gender should be, women are caught in a double bind. When we're caught in a double bind, doing one thing we need to do will undercut another, equally important thing. In this case, if we act in ways consistent with gender stereotypes and are modest, collaborative, service-oriented, empathetic, and caring, we will be liked but not seen as a leader and not seen as competent. If we display leadership qualities like being confident, tough, aggressive, ambitious, and decisive, we might be seen as a leader, but we will also be seen as cold, unlikeable, and unlikely to reach a top leadership role.

Let's think of a few examples of the double bind. When Hillary Clinton became First Lady, she became involved in health care policy. The public thought she was overreaching and bitchy in part because she voiced strong (informed) opinions. Sixteen years later, Michelle Obama faced sexism and racism. She was deemed unlikeable in the beginning for sharing any opinions. She had to give up much of who she was and focus on acceptable First Lady topics such as healthy food for children, exercise, and gardening.

The gender box isn't limited to politics. Carly Fiorina, former CEO of Hewlett Packard, was the first woman to run a Fortune 20 firm. Upon her hiring, she publicly said that she hoped that "everyone has figured out that there is not a glass ceiling." Five and a half years later, she was fired, and she blamed sexism.

NYU Professor of Psychology Madeline Heilman's research on gender stereotyping found that women are not expected to be good at traditionally agentic (take charge, get things done, confront conflict) leadership roles, so they are passed over and put into roles that undervalue them.

Professor Heilman found that even when women are in traditionally agentic roles, their successes are explained by something outside of their ability; perhaps someone helped them or the task was not as difficult. Even if women are recognized to be successful, they should not take on a directive leadership style, be tough negotiators, speak with authority, or express ambition. Otherwise, they will be described as abrasive, untrustworthy, manipulative, selfish, and cold.

Professor Heilman also found that women are expected to be helpful, but helping makes little difference to how they are viewed. Not helping was seen as horrible. If a man helped, he was perceived as amazing. Not helping had no impact on how he was viewed.

HOW THIS APPLIES TO WOMEN OF COLOR

As women of color, we face the double bind not only from being female but also from the whole array of unexamined biases against people of color. This includes doubts about our intelligence, competence, and skill—doubts unrelated to our actual performance. Babson College professor Dr. Tina Opie specializes in workplace discrimination. She reported, "Black women are the first ones to get laid off. We're the last ones to get hired. We get paid far less than White women do. Our behavior and our appearance tend to be policed much more stringently." Black women are also often called "intimidating" or "angry." Latinas face stereotypes that they are illegally in the country. Asian American women face stereotypes that they are not "leader" material. They also face misunderstandings from the model minority myth, which says that Asian Americans have overcome all the barriers to success, and thus don't need support. As a result, Asian Americans might not be included in discussions about workplace discrimination or be able to participate in diversity or mentoring programs. But this doesn't take into consideration the wide disparity among different Asian communities and the discrimination Asian Americans face.

These stereotypes prevent women of color from being seen, heard, and valued. Women of color, especially Black workers, need to be twice as good and work twice as hard as others to succeed, often taking on projects that are outside of our roles and leading to burnout. This impacts not only our careers but also our sense of belonging, mental health, and psychological safety.

Stereotypes also prevent women of color from advancing in our careers. We are less likely to be given credit for our work, less likely to be promoted to top leadership positions, and less likely to negotiate for the roles and salaries we deserve. Our hard work, top performance, and technical skills do not keep us from crashing into the concrete ceiling.

This isn't fair, but there are things we can do, and as we rise, we can bring others along with us. We have the advantage of seeing unconscious bias, even though we must still work not to internalize it.

STORIES FROM WOMEN OF COLOR

These stories share the myth of meritocracy and how racism and sexism continue to be embedded in workplaces and society. Yet we can take action, lead differently, and create more opportunities for people who are often overlooked.

SHARHONDA BOSSIER
Black, CEO of Education Leaders of Color (EdLoC)

As a self-described rebel child who got her first tattoo at 12, Sharhonda channeled her beliefs in justice and became a public school teacher and activist. Sharhonda shares her experience pushing against a White supremacist system and leading EdLoC, an organization for and by people of color. While she has always valued her independence, Sharhonda knows that her true strength comes from supportive networks and communities like EdLoC. There is power when we stand together.

My family had deep roots in the south so I knew what overt racism looked like and felt like. But I didn't know what it meant to sit across from someone and have them say something and for me to think, "Was that racist? I don't know. They voted for Obama. Can they also be racist?"

Then you realize that even if your interests overlap in this one place, they probably don't in many others. You're constantly confronting this while trying to be in community and solidarity with someone who probably doesn't actually share your worldview.

The other lesson I learned is how people will leverage your skills, experience, and proximity for their own credibility. I hadn't thought about the ways in which my presence as a Black woman who grew up poor and had to navigate a really terrible public education system lent credibility to other people who would not have otherwise been able to organize or mobilize those same people. I hadn't thought about what it meant to come to the realization that what you were doing wasn't what you thought you were doing.

I got into the work because I wanted to push back against a system, and we slowly got co-opted by a different system. Confronting that and walking away from something that I had built from the ground up left me pretty wounded. I was unsure about the seat of relative power that I thought I sat in given all of those things that happened to me. It's been three years of processing not just as a professional but as a Black woman who cared deeply about the families we were working with.

Now as the CEO of EdLoC, I started to figure out who were the folks who could support me, even if they couldn't see themselves in me. I learned that part of the reason that some of my White male peers in particular were successful was because people could sit down with them at lunch and say, "Oh, I see myself in you. You remind me of a friend of mine. Or you remind me of my own kid." It was unlikely they were going to have a similar experience with me. But I could figure out where there was that point of connection and be very clear about what my needs were.

Sometimes you're sitting down with a funder or a potential mentor or potential coach. At the end of the conversation, they ask you, "So why me?" I learned that I just need to get clear and say, "Here are the places I think you can be helpful. Also, I want to name what you are probably sensing. Here are the places and ways in which we are different. And I'm cool with that, as long as you're cool with that." It has really helped me build relationships with people who might not be, at first glance, folks who you would think would be supportive of me, my career, my work, and my aims. The trick to building a relationship with a person is finding places of overlap, where they could be helpful, and naming the potential awkward sticking point so that we can just get that out of the way.

I found myself sitting across the table from people who worked at hedge funds, who make hundreds of millions of dollars. For whatever reason, they were interested in what's happening in some remote corner of a city that they've never been to. It was the first time that I had to confront what racism looks like with people who voted the same way I did.

My current executive coach is a White woman. I told her, "There are some experiences you've had in your career as a woman that are going to be helpful for me. As long as you and I can both name that there are some experiences you have not had because I'm a Black woman or you are a White woman, that's cool. Are you willing to help identify other folks who might be able to lean in as additional sources of advice and counsel on these particular questions?" I've learned to name the thing. I've learned to be explicit about where I think someone could be of value to me.

I think what's been beautiful about EdLoC is that it has been an organization for us. We've been able to create a vision for what a collective can look like if we are all focused on each other. We've been able to get support and resources to do that work. This was the first time I didn't have a White boss. It was the first time I didn't have White board members. It was the first time that the only people around the table making decisions about our collective work – aside from some of our funding partners – were people of color.

It's been a significant shift. Before, my belief was that if you want to be really successful or live a certain standard of life, you're going to have to work with or for White people. You cannot be who you are or represent where you come from. I've learned that this doesn't necessarily need to be true. The idea that you can create a successful organization and have it be all people of color is something that I'm fighting to prove day in and day out.

While I've always valued my independence, I know that my true strength often comes from the supportive networks and communities I've been fortunate to be a part of. I've found incredible empowerment and solidarity within these communal bonds, proving that being independent and embracing community support can go hand in hand, amplifying each other's impact and significance.

There is power when we stand together. EdLoC is a reflection of this philosophy: together, we are a collective power, shaping solutions and driving progress on some of the most pressing challenges in American life.

There are too many elements in our society that seek to divide us. But we are building a collective power through our Network, a network of values-aligned leaders of color across the country, to remove the systemic and institutional barriers that continue to deny opportunities for all young people of color.

We are successful because we help each other to be successful. A community for us, by us—EdLoC acts as a safe, supportive, and catalytic community that leaders of color are often looking for. We are a Network that supports one another, innovates on ideas together, and invests in each other's work. This is the dynamism inherent in community-based work.

JESSICA SANTANA

Afro Latinx, Puerto Rican, Co-Founder and CEO of America on Tech

Growing up in East New York, Brooklyn, Jessica saw what the criminalization of her neighborhood looked like. She attended Syracuse University as one of the few women of color with degrees in Accounting and Information

Technology. Jessica shares how she came to realize that meritocracy is a myth.

In high school, we started as a class of 118. Only 54 graduated, and only about 18 of us pursued a two-year or four-year college university degree program. You start to ask yourself a lot of questions. How did I get here? Why do so many people where I'm from not have these same opportunities? What are the systemic barriers that leave people out of the spaces that I'm currently occupying?

Before entering college, I used to believe that through hard work and dedication, I could make something of myself. If I worked hard and I applied myself and I did what I had to do and I pursued an education and I got good grades, there was no way that I would fail because we have a system based on meritocracy. If I worked hard and excelled, then I would be rewarded by this system.

But in my university program, I realized that I was sitting next to peers who were from economically prosperous communities who did not work that hard to get to the place where I was. They had access to things like their mother and father being legacies to the university who could pay their way into accessing this college campus where I actually had to put in a massive amount of work to get here.

The myth was this. It's not about working hard. For us, it's about money. So when I think about the first narrative shift for me, it was, "Wait, I worked so hard to be here, and you still don't think that I deserve to be here. But you didn't work hard at all to be here; you actually paid your way to get here and had a connection of some sort."

I told myself that money matters. I planned to set myself up to make sure that after I graduate school, I get a high paying job. If the [legacy students] didn't work that hard, and all they did was have mom and dad donate in order to get into the university, then that means that I need to make sure that I center my influence on building capital, so that I can access things and make it easier for my children to take advantage of institutions and programs and SAT prep and all these things that I didn't have access to.

When I started my career in the private sector working in tech, it became very evident to me that I had entered a phase in my life where I did everything that I was supposed to do, in order to get a good paying job that could lead to economic empowerment for myself and for future generations.

But sitting in your cubicle, you look around, and no one else looks like you. You talk to HR, and they say that there are not a lot of Black and Latinx people that they can hire because they're just not interested in tech. Or you're having conversations with your best friend who is from where you're from, who's experiencing a series of microaggressions in his workplace, while you also are experiencing microaggressions in your workplace as a woman of color.

You start to realize that there are narratives and beliefs that don't challenge systems to change in order for the creation of opportunities for people that look like you. So it's not that you were the lucky one. It's that the system is actually working, and is designed in such a fashion that leaves you and your people out.

As you continue to climb up this ladder, you have to lift as you climb. We had a sense of frustration that we were not seeing people who looked like us in this industry and at the same time, seeing the growth of technology happening in New York City and seeing really big companies in New York City be centered right next to subsidized housing where there is a myriad of amazing young people. We said no. The proximity of these companies to the students and the communities that we care about, it's not justified that this pipeline of talent can't thrive in these spaces as well. We should not create an environment where students are from places that they can't *thrive in because of lack of opportunity. We took that grief, and we channeled it into what is now America on Tech.*

What we've learned is that genius is equally distributed. Opportunity is not. Narratives that are incorrect about our communities plague the opportunity for us to create more opportunities. There are policies and systems in place that prohibit young people of color, specifically Black and Latinx people, from achieving their highest and fullest potential, as they seek to build skills that have the opportunity to empower them economically.

JENISE TERRELL
Black, CEO, Public Allies

Despite being a single mother, Jenise's mom continued to pursue her education. One time, she needed to go to class, but her childcare plans for Jenise and her sister fell through. How did Jenise's mom solve the problem? She brought her two young girls to class, telling them to sit quietly in the back. Her mother would go on to get her associate degree. Jenise would go on to graduate from Marquette University. Jenise shares how even with a degree and ambition, she lacked a network and access to opportunity. Her story shows the myth of meritocracy.

I was deeply pulled to be of service to my community. I wanted to take these skill sets that I had been gifted and the knowledge that I honed in school and apply it to my community. But the nonprofit sector operated very much like the private sector. To get a break, you had to know people, and I didn't know anyone. I had my degree, I had my ambition, I had goals, I had insights, and I had passion. But I didn't know anyone.

Oftentimes, young people like me who have ambition, who have tenacity, who have familiarity because of where we come from with the very issues that the nonprofit sector is seeking to address don't often have an entry point to the sector.

So Public Allies was my entry point. It was the program that saw beyond who we were, what degrees we held, or in many cases, the degrees that we did not hold. They saw our ambition, our drive, our desire to be of service, and gave us the opportunity to hone our leadership skills and a platform to exercise leadership.

When Public Allies invited me in to participate in a program, they said, "We're not looking for diamonds. We're looking for diamonds in the rough. This program is about giving to those who have been overlooked because they don't fit the traditional definition of a leader." It spoke to me in a way that was very deeply personal because I had experienced the truth of what they were saying.

When I participated in my 10-month apprenticeship at Public Allies, I found my tribe. I found people who were not like me in terms of background, in terms of socioeconomic status or race or gender or sexual orientation. What I found was a group of people who commonly believed in the power that we each held to build something together for the future of our city and for the future of our country.

These experiences have informed my leadership. I seek opportunities to open doors, to give others a chance to be heard. I see beyond what is traditional and truly see folks for what they have to offer and give them an opportunity to demonstrate that.

Growing up as a poor Black female in the deep South, Tequilla shares how her grandparents and teachers instilled in her high expectations, the value of education, and that she can choose her own path. She applied to two colleges, including Yale, because her uncle and guidance counselor had recommended it. After graduating from Yale, Tequilla was a researcher, school social worker and then an administrator at Memphis City Schools (MCS). Towards the end of her tenure in MCS, as a result of a district merger, she found herself front and center of an historical and present-day racist context. Tequilla asked herself, "Should I stay or go?" Tequilla's story illustrates how racism persists and that "the workplace is a meritocracy" is still a myth.

At Memphis City Schools, we were doing some major reform work around teacher effectiveness and quality. The Memphis district I worked in, the big urban poor district, merged with the more middle class, affluent, suburban district. Merging two districts of two different identities was a monumental task. This was in Memphis, which is not without its own history and legacies of racism. Focusing on how to merge these districts together really distracted from the work we were trying to do, focusing on kids and teacher effectiveness. It shifted from the work that I love—strategizing around where we needed to innovate—to becoming more political and focused on power between adults with the undergirding presence of race, bias, and people with choice, i.e., more affluent parents.

It was the first time in my life that I felt, "This is what it was like for my grandfather." My grandfather was born in 1910 in the heart of the Mississippi River Delta in Clarksville, Mississippi. My grandparents raised me, and I grew up watching my grandfather as a man say, "Yes, sir. No, sir," to a 12-year-old White male.

My experience in Memphis City Schools felt like I had been catapulted back into the Jim Crow South. It was so in my face in a way that it was hindering me from not only doing my job but from sleeping at night. I had to make the very difficult choice to leave, knowing that the work was not done. It was definitely a rock bottom moment.

Looking back, I send a thank you card to that moment. It catapulted me professionally and personally.

What would I recommend to others in a similar situation?

STEP 1. Have the self-awareness that you have choices.

You've got to be confident enough to know that you do have a choice here. Otherwise, you could act out of fear. Your decision needs to be guided by your beliefs, your values, what you want, not as a response to fear. I worried, If I don't do this, will I land in a good job that is mission aligned? I had to put that aside and stand in the confidence that if I were a 20-year-old White male, I wouldn't have that doubt. I would know that I can add value, and someone will recognize that. I had to abandon that fear and that lack of self-confidence.

STEP 2. Reflect.

The second step took seven months. I'm blessed that because my work aligns with my personal mission, it doesn't feel like work. I'm getting paid to do the thing that I love to do. I asked myself, Am I feeling gratified? Am I continuing to learn and grow?

STEP 3. Find the right environment.

One thing that I tell all of my mentees is, "Never work for a person or an organization that you don't feel has your best interests at heart." Because if you don't, you're always in the back of your *mind wondering, Is my manager or this company going to do something to me? You need to work in an environment that you have absolute confidence that your manager and this company has your best interests at heart. They don't have to be mutually exclusive. You can work in a mission-driven organization and environment that also wants to see you thrive as a human being.*

That is what I found in TNTP. When I started here, the CEO at the time used to ask me, because I was so full of joy, "Did they beat you at your former job?" I responded, "Almost." That is what has kept me at TNTP. For nine years, I've continued to grow and learn, while serving a mission that I wholeheartedly believe in. I also believe that every manager I've had at TNTP and the organization at large have my best interests at heart. For me, as an employee, as a woman, as a Black woman, I'm able to bring all of that to the table. I have the psychological and personal and mental and emotional safety to just focus on the work.

WHAT WOMEN OF COLOR CAN DO

Women of color can be more aware of the challenges of a workplace where structural racism, sexism, and patriarchy are alive and well. If we face bias or unfair treatment, don't let the company undermine our truth or cross a boundary. Know that what we are facing is real and we have the power to respond, know where our line is, and manage the double bind without compromising our values.

PRACTICE 1. FIND WAYS TO NAVIGATE THE DOUBLE BIND.

It is unfair that women must navigate the double bind, which takes an enormous amount of emotional intelligence (EQ). That said, here are strategies to manage the double bind.

In 2018, Wei Zheng, Ronit Kark, and Alyson Meister interviewed 64 top-level women leaders from 51 different organizations in the US to investigate what strategies women used to manage the double bind challenge.

The team identified four kinds of paradoxical balancing acts that the women needed to perform:

DOUBLE BIND 1 - BE DEMANDING AND CARING

Women were expected to demand high performance from others while also caring for them. One strategy women used to address this double bind was that at some meetings, she would sit at the head of the table to show authority and decisiveness. Other times, she would sit amongst the team. In addition, a "tough on tasks and soft on people" approach helped women leaders keep debate and disagreement separate from relationships. Along the same lines, they suggest maintaining awareness of the little girl inside us who wants to be liked by everybody all the time and pinpoint how this need to be liked serves us. There is a difference between being liked and being respected.

DOUBLE BIND 2 - BE AUTHORITATIVE AND VULNERABLE

Women were expected to project authority to establish credibility. But to prevent from being seen as arrogant, women needed to quickly acknowledge their own weaknesses and ask others to collaborate. One strategy that women used with this double bind was to start with being caring and collaborative to build relationships and trust and then move to being tough and directive to achieve goals.

DOUBLE BIND 3 - ADVOCATE FOR OURSELVES WHILE SERVING OTHERS

Women were expected not to be too aggressive in pursuing their own goals. Being seen as too ambitious or self-serving could come with major backlash. But at the same time, not pursuing personal goals was career stifling. One strategy that women leaders used was creating win-win goals. They would learn the goals a person they were hoping to influence wanted and would tie a goal they were trying to achieve with something that person wanted to personally achieve too.

DOUBLE BIND 4 - MAINTAIN DISTANCE WHILE ALSO APPEARING APPROACHABLE

Women were expected to maintain an impersonal professional leadership presence but at the same time not be too stiff or egocentric. To address this paradox, women shared that they deliberately worked to share a human side that was warm and easy to connect with. One CEO shared that she was able to do this with her clothing. She dressed more formally than employees except on Fridays when she dressed informally to show that she was approachable.

For all of these tensions, women need to be aware of the double bind, adapt, and mindfully choose strategies based on the situation and who they are with. Women may need to use hard power (being tough) or soft power (being collaborative). Neither power is good or bad, they are tools in the toolbelt.

PRACTICE 2. BE PREPARED FOR MICROAGGRESSIONS.

Unfortunately, women of color are highly likely to face microaggressions, whether it's being talked over, ignored, or told inappropriate things. So many times, I have been shocked by a microaggression, and in the moment I'm unable to defend myself. Then I beat myself up later for not sticking up for myself.

So what do we do?

STEP 1. Practice self-compassion and self-care.

Remind ourselves that we are worthy and strong and do not deserve bad treatment. At the same time, tell ourselves that what is happening isn't personal. This is not about us. This is about them and their bias.

STEP 2. Consider having a conversation with the person.

This may be hard for some of us. For example, I was raised with Asian values of harmony over conflict. But don't assume that the other person's reaction may be negative. They may appreciate our feedback.

As an example, I attended a meeting with other nonprofit leaders only to be greeted by the wrong name (that of another Asian woman leader). This same White leader said to me, "You can take our meeting notes." There were other leaders at the table who were my peers, so I wasn't sure why he singled me out. I guessed that it had to do with me being the only female and one of the few people of color.

My follow-up conversation looked like this, "Hi Joe, yesterday afternoon, you called me Lynn. That's the name of the other Asian woman leader. I don't think it was intentional on your part, but I wanted to talk with you about it. My name is Analiza, so when you called me Lynn, I felt disappointed and not seen. I also noticed you asked me to take our meeting notes. I decided to do it, but as a woman of color, it's important for me to ask what made you ask me specifically."

Joe apologized, and we ended up discussing ways to rotate note-taking responsibilities.

If Joe had responded with, "I didn't mean it. You're being a bit sensitive" or something else inappropriate, know that this is not a concern of ours. We are standing up for ourselves—and others who struggle with microaggressions—and that is the equity movement we are part of.

STEP 3. Report, if needed.

If after sharing our feedback, the issue continues, report the microaggression to HR. If we see something, say something. We need to face the beast of sexism and racism so that together we can slay it.

BOOK BONUSES

Explore the Book Bonuses for this chapter:

- List of books for further reading
- Podcasts with the full interviews of the women leaders spotlighted in this chapter

MYTH TWO

We're not worthy

After graduating from Stanford, I joined the military to follow in my dad's footsteps. He had served for 22 years in the US Navy and advised me, "Serve your country. But do it in the Air Force. You'll be treated better there as a Filipina."

But my military career did not start out well. During ROTC training, I was often yelled at by senior cadet officers. My uniform was never ironed enough, my shoes never shiny enough. Before my summer boot camp training began, a senior female cadet took me aside, "Analiza, the leadership team has been talking about you." My heart ballooned with pride. But then she continued, "We're worried you will fail. The bottom percent gets kicked out. We think that could be you." I wasn't sure what made the leadership team feel that way. It seemed to me that I was scruffier than other cadets, but otherwise, my classwork and athletic performance weren't any worse. But I was one of the few females and even fewer women of color. Maybe that had something to do with it?

When I showed up at bootcamp, I lacked confidence and was overwhelmed with the fear that I would be kicked out. But soon that fear was replaced by concern for others. There was Peter whose glasses fogged with sweat during an obstacle course where we walked on uneven tree trunks twenty feet above the ground. I saw him in front of me trying to wipe his glasses in vain. He muttered to himself, "I can't see!" He had stopped during the timed obstacle course, and if he didn't go soon, he would be singled out and punished. I made a snap decision. Even though we weren't allowed to talk to each other, I called out to him, "Lean down and touch the tree. Use the tree as a guide to keep moving. Nice and slow, but keep moving." Peter paused to consider but then leaned down and took a step forward. He made it through the obstacle course, and we gave each other a high five.

At the end of bootcamp, I no longer worried that I would be kicked out. But during the awards ceremony, I was shocked. I won the Distinguished Award, the highest award at military training. I had also won a top athletic award.

As much as I was shocked, the cadets back at my training program were even more shocked. One member of the leadership team came up to me with his raised eyebrows, "Was this really you?" Later, the same female cadet who had warned me I would fail sat me down and said, "The leadership team sees a lot of potential in you. They would like you to lead everyone, our entire team, next year." I was baffled by the invitation and declined. There had never been a woman of color at the helm, and I was worried about being the first.

Even though I've experienced successes like these, throughout my life, I have struggled with self-acceptance and self-worth. I was a model people pleaser, trying to prove I was worthy of their time and attention. I tried to live up to what people expected of me and would bury my own dreams and feelings. As I've gotten older and wiser, I've learned that time is limited, and if I want to go after my dreams, this starts with believing in myself and my worth.

As women of color, we hear messages—from teachers, our family, our community, society—that we are less than. Sadly, many of us internalize these sexist and racist messages. We then spend our lives believing that we have to be perfect to succeed, that there is no room for error. We believe that failure is bad and is to be avoided at all costs. Asking for help is a signal that we are weak.

WHICH OF THESE EXPERIENCES RESONATE WITH YOU?

☐ You worry that you are not smart, skilled, qualified, or good enough. You are afraid you'll be judged, fail, or are unworthy of respect or admiration.

☐ You overprepare or overdeliver.

☐ You get caught up in what others are thinking.

☐ You are reluctant to speak up in meetings or groups. Or you present expertise with caveats ("This is just my opinion").

☐ You code-switch or adjust your style, demeanor, or presentation to please or impress others.

☐ You obsessively check your work, thoroughly considering every scenario to avoid mistakes.

☐ You hesitate, second-guess, or overthink decisions, continually seeking additional input for assurance.

☐ You are averse to taking on new things that are out of your comfort zone. Or you have a fear of failure or a fear of taking risks and learning new skills.

> ☐ You take things personally. Or you people please or have a fear of not meeting people's expectations or letting your manager or your company down. You have a fear of conflict/offending others.
> ☐ You don't reach out for support or help because you feel people won't have time for you.

THE REALITY

We can overthrow this internalized racism and sexism and find self-confidence to speak up.

Most of us don't choose our beliefs. We inherit them from the world around us, our family, media, and culture. And yet, these beliefs direct our life's path. Some beliefs propel us forward, while others hold us back.

For women, the beliefs that hold us back often relate to imposter syndrome. Imposter syndrome is the feeling that we are faking it, that we alone are not smart, competent, perfect, or worthy enough, while others know what they are doing. As girls, our American culture (family, school, media) taught us to be compliant, obedient, quiet, clean, and not stand out. Boys, on the other hand, were raised to be rambunctious, dirty, silly, and speak their mind. Obedient, "perfect" girls got positive feedback from teachers, coaches, and parents; boys got more praise for thinking outside the box.

By the time we are adults, women are held to impossible standards: stay feminine, humble, thin, and make it all look easy. University of Houston Professor Brené Brown says, "The real struggle for women—what amplifies shame regardless of the category is that we're expected (and sometimes desire) to be perfect, yet we're not allowed to look as if we're working for it." It's no wonder it feels shameful to ask for help or to fail. No matter what we do, it doesn't feel like enough.

This lack of self-confidence holds us back from raising our hands in meetings and asking for promotions and raises. Katty Kay and Claire Shipman, authors of *The Confidence Code: The Science and Art of Self-Assurance—What Women Should Know* explain, "Compared with men, women don't consider themselves as ready for promotions, they predict they'll do worse on tests, and they generally underestimate their abilities." A 2011 gender report by Europe's Institute of Leadership and Management showed that women reported lower confidence in their careers: Half of women managers admitted to feelings of self-doubt about their performance, but only 31 percent of men reported the same. In striving for perfection, women would work long hours to perfect even the smallest detail, were reluctant to delegate work, and were seen as worker bees instead of leaders. The result is that women's hard work isn't recognized, and we keep getting passed over for promotion.

Why do women have such a low sense of self-worth? Girls are conditioned to be "less than" boys. Then as women, we have internalized that we are less valuable than men. Dr. Cecilia Ridgeway, a Stanford University sociologist who studies status by gender says that women are considered to be "low-status" and men, specifically college-educated White men, are considered to be "high-status." High-status people set the agenda, talk a lot, and make decisions, while low-status people follow the agenda, listen, and make sure high-status people have the support they need.

With this internalized lack of self-worth, many women don't consider becoming a CEO. For those women who do consider it, they tend to wait until they feel they have enough experience. A Korn Ferry study found that female CEOs worked harder and longer to get to the top. They were on average four years older than male CEOs and had worked in a higher number of leadership roles, functions, and companies prior to securing the top role. In contrast, men tend to throw themselves at all sorts of opportunities, without regard to whether they are qualified. Their confidence makes sense in an "old boys network," and it allows them to rise to the top with less angst.

Many women of color struggle with self-doubt and confidence due to not seeing ourselves represented in the workplace or leadership, which leads us to feel like we don't belong or that leadership roles are not attainable for us. Women of color may feel the need to "prove ourselves" and outperform so that we can be valued.

However, years of being marginalized exacts an "emotional tax" on women of color where we feel "different from peers at work because of gender, race, and/or ethnicity and the associated effects on health, well-being, and ability to thrive at work." As women of color, we may constantly feel we have to be "on guard" and ready to armor up for potential discrimination, being stereotyped, or feeling less than.

In February 2021, *Harvard Business Review* published "Stop Telling Women They Have Imposter Syndrome" where Ruchika Tulshyan and Jodi-Ann Burey point out that the problem is not individual women lacking self-confidence but the workplaces where women work, especially for women of color. (If you are unfamiliar with this concept, I encourage you to check out the full article in the resources provided in the Book Bonuses.) These workplace issues include biases in recruitment, compensation, promotion, and leadership.

STORIES FROM WOMEN OF COLOR

These stories show how so many of us struggle with not feeling enough. Yet it is also possible to take risks, embrace successes and failures, and feel confident that we deserve to be at the table.

> **Melisha "Mel" Jackman**
> Black, Executive Director of Brooklyn Kindergarten Society

As a daughter to Caribbean immigrants and a first generation high school and college graduate, Mel realized that her story that she was not worthy was a myth. Mel shares her journey to feel worthy and lean into vulnerability as strength.

I felt like I had to have this Superwoman cape on all the time, that I must fix every problem, know every solution, and never make a mistake. The amount of pressure that puts on you. It's unfair. Leaders don't know that all leaders learn by doing, just like everyone else.

Self-love and validation were important for me in advancing in my career. It helped me build my confidence, which I found to be more important than the technical skills as I became more senior. I received my principal certification three years before I became a principal. Even though I went through the training, and I had all the extra degrees, I wasn't ready. I realized my emotional fortitude still needed more development. Technically, I could do the job. But until I tapped into my confidence and felt secure, and I had the right mindset, it wasn't going to happen. ... For me, it was very much emotional. I had to believe in myself first before everyone else believed in me.

I started asking myself some really hard questions. What does Mel bring to the table? What are some areas that I want to get better at? What do I need to work on? I had about 50 or so little micro questions that I worked on for months. I would do the same questions month after month, and the answers started changing. I had to go through a really deep reflection process and not keep it surface to get to the core of what I was afraid of.

What I was afraid of was rejection, and that stemmed from what happened in my childhood. Wanting to be perfect and not wanting to get that negative response because I didn't do the thing the way someone else wanted me to do it. I worked with a therapist and got to the core of my fear which was rejection, and I started working through that. What will I feel if I were rejected? Then I would sit in that feeling.

When I did get rejected, I realized, "Oh, I didn't die and fall apart." It was a feeling, it was an emotion, and it worked itself out. Then I started digging deep—how long did these feelings of despair last when they came? For me, it was two weeks, and then I started to feel better. I started to normalize rejection and failure.

Once I realized this perfection wasn't needed, this pressure to get it right, life and the work started to become more enjoyable. I now know that I'm not supposed to know all the things. I will make mistakes. Perfectionism is not the end goal. Trying my best is what I should value.

It helps having a community of people who are vulnerable and share trials and tribulations. It helps to normalize that there are other people who are having these emotions. It's a shared experience. I can give myself ease. I can forgive myself for mistakes because we're all in this together.

This is when I knew I could become a principal. I knew what was at the root of my fear—rejection. It's very important to understand that software and to continue to nurture it, because that's your inner child work. We all get that childhood amnesia, but you have to address it because that subconscious will have you doing things you're not even aware of. The goal is to become more self-aware and to catch it when it's happening.

One time where I was able to catch myself was during my first year at Brooklyn Kindergarten Society. I had a banner year despite the pandemic. But I was still worried about how everybody perceived me. In my end-of-year review, I shared areas where I felt that I could do better.

I was very hesitant to share a weakness. I was afraid they wouldn't see me as a strong leader or successful. My boss responded, "We can actually help you with this. You don't have to be the bearer of this burden." Being vulnerable to say what's on my mind helped me get the support I needed.

Understanding what you are afraid of and then sitting with the discomfort when you are afraid, asking for what you need, releasing perfection, getting clear on your why. All of this plays a role in setting yourself up for a top position. You no longer get stuck in your thoughts or hold yourself back. You can address it and move forward.

Aimée (pronounced ah me) Eubanks Davis was raised in Chicago's South Side. Tragedy struck her young life when her father died when she was two and her mother was unemployed and without a financial safety net. Her life could have gone in many different directions but, after her mother met her stepfather and they built a fledgling real estate business together, she and her sister experienced economic mobility in their teen years. She went on to Mount Holyoke College and a career at Teach For America. Later, she became an entrepreneur, founding Braven in 2013. She encourages others, especially women of color, to embrace the learning opportunity in failure and "step into the gray" in a black and white world.

I think women and people of color often second-guess ourselves. Almost by accident I started running the Summerbridge (now known as Breakthrough) program in New Orleans at 23 years old. I was so young. I had no business running a full-scale summer school and after school enrichment program. Nonprofits are businesses. It took me a while to realize that I was running my own "mini-school", let alone a business. My real focus was to make sure these young people reached their academic goals.

I could have thought, "I'm not ready." But that program wasn't going to see another summer if I hadn't stepped in. That would have been tragic for the students. You could say the same about your own career. If there is an area of gray, step in and figure it out.

As Summerbridge continued, she made herself more and more valuable to the organization, asked new questions, and found outcomes in order to leave things better than she found them.

I ran the program for a total of five years. By the time I was on my way out, it was one of the highest performing Summerbridge/ Breakthrough sites in the country That set me up to meet Wendy Kopp, the CEO of Teach For America, who said to me, "I don't understand why you haven't come to work at TFA."

In what some would consider an ill-advised comment, Aimée told Kopp TFA had a diversity problem. Kopp agreed and asked the young educator to consider coming to work alongside her. Aimée knew that to work alongside one of the most successful educational entrepreneurs in history was a professional development opportunity to accept. She thought she would be there for two years and go to business school to learn about running a nonprofit business but instead, she ended up staying at Teach For America and becoming a key leader in the organization's catalytic growth and impact.

When I worked for Wendy, I received a lot of feedback, including when I wasn't doing things well, which built me into a better leader: setting vision, direction, goals and closely tracking impact. People encourage others to avoid failure, but I think there's a lot to learn from getting knocked down, getting back up, and saying, "Here's how I'm going to do it differently next time." Usually, it is through the hardest moments that you learn what you are made of and also get more understanding of what it will take to make something successful the next time. Wendy taught me to strive for excellence.

As her former students and thousands of young people from their demographic backgrounds started graduating college, Aimée noticed they struggled to find quality jobs.

That led her down the path to start Braven, an organization devoted to providing young people of color and low-income backgrounds the skills, confidence, experience and networks to enter the job market stronger.

I never set out to be a CEO. I accidentally became a CEO and founded Braven. I've watched some very inspiring leaders in the field become CEOs of organizations; it's especially awesome if they are women and women of color. I think they succeeded because they stepped into the gray and asked for constructive feedback. We need that to build skills for whatever role we find ourselves in.

MELISSA WU

Taiwanese American, CEO of Education Pioneers

Melissa grew up with privilege, attending strong public schools. As one of the few people of color in her school, she often felt "othered," and that belonging was conditional on not making mistakes. She counters the myth that we should avoid failure at all costs. Melissa shares how deliberately seeking out and embracing failure helped her to build confidence, be successful, and lead.

My first job at a start-up organization, I was responsible for editing our newsletter and sent to print a newsletter that had typos in it. My boss was wonderful, but she was so disappointed and angry at me. It was one of the first times I had made a real mistake with real consequences. I really damaged her trust and faith in me. That was hard.

It was the two of us at that point, the founder and me sitting in the basement of a school trying to start this organization. Our primary means of generating income was sending this newsletter to people who might support our work and send donations. There was no choice but to pick up the next day and pay the extra money to reprint the newsletter. I did the editing, carefully fixed all those mistakes, and got it back out to the printer. I think that was an important experience. I got through it and recognized that I was going to have to work twice as hard to do that work well.

Experiences like that were humbling but helped me grow. With that start-up, I was around young people in our TEAK Fellowship who were going through their own learning experiences, failing, and being brave to get up again. That's part of what pushed me to go to Harvard Business School (HBS). I ran for Section president at HBS. I thought, "I should try this. I've never run for office, but I feel like I have something to contribute, and I can be good at this job." I did not win.

There were a bunch of experiences like this that were challenges I deliberately took on, knowing there was a chance I would fail. For example, I made a decision to go into consulting. The career counselor said, "This is a hard path. It's very competitive. You don't have a background that's going to make sense. You're going to have to work twice as hard." I wanted to prove to myself that I could put in the work in something that I wasn't expected to be successful at.

Some of the experiences were successes, some failures, but many of them were more in the middle. Whether it was a clear success or a clear failure or something in the middle, I realized I could handle it, I could survive it, I could learn from it, I could get better.

Meralis grew up with loving parents and was outwardly successful. At 16, she graduated high school with straight A's. At 21, she graduated from Marquette University. She became a successful teacher, being named Teacher of the Year.

But Meralis struggled with anxiety, panic attacks, and self-harm. She found herself hospitalized and forced to do therapy. Meralis credits these dark moments and being at rock bottom with why she is fearless today. Meralis dispels the myth that we are not worthy. She shares how she learned to believe in herself and get over imposter syndrome.

Growing up, my mother would say two things, "First class. This is what I need from you—first class behavior, first class grades, first class everything." And, "You're the head, not the tail. You're a leader." That was something I heard every day since I was a little girl. So I thought, "I have this responsibility, I better work hard and serve others."

As a young person, specifically through my teens and early 20s, I struggled with self-harm, depression, and extreme anxiety. I was having panic attacks daily. When I was 27, I started to get help and therapy. But I really had nobody to talk to about it. Certainly not in my family where it wasn't the culture to talk about that.

I was excelling at work during this time, leading teams, and working really hard. I was able to hide a lot of my struggles behind those external successes like Teacher of the Year awards. But I was also very guarded as a leader and not vulnerable. I had very little patience for anybody who wasn't meeting my standards because I thought my standards were perfect. I didn't have any real relationships because

I wasn't able to be vulnerable with anybody. I wasn't in relationship with anyone, not even my own husband.

I had to have this perfection and facade and hide my real feelings. Anytime that I would fail was a big struggle for me. A flat tire could throw me into a panic attack that would last days because I would feel like such a failure, like I was just doing life wrong. I ended up going to therapy because I harmed myself to the point where I didn't really have a choice. That actually saved my life.

In the last 15 years of therapy, mindfulness, prayer, meditation, self-reflection, and building of emotional intelligence, I've become a better leader.

First, I'm not afraid to fail. I'm a pretty fearless leader because I feel like we can try anything. I've already hit rock bottom. I've already hit the point in my life where I was hospitalized against my will. Everybody in my family, including my husband, had to know my big dark secret, which was that I've been struggling with these kinds of ideas of harming myself, and I have actually tried to harm myself several times. And I have kept it a secret. I also didn't have much hope for the future, so I didn't make any financial plan, and I lost my house. Realizing how far I've come and the different life I have now, there's no reason for me to be afraid. I've been through the worst of it, and it didn't break me. It actually helped me get better in so many ways.

I tell my team, "Let's not be afraid if there's something that we want to try. Right now we serve 500 entrepreneurs a year. Let's try to take that number to 50,000." I also believe in others. I trust others. I'm a better delegator.

Being fearless means I'm not afraid to be vulnerable. I'm not afraid to say, "I really messed that up. Sorry about that." Before I struggled with overthinking. After a conversation, I would review it over and over, inventing a narrative about what the person thinks of me. They probably think I'm such a weakling. I've had to learn how meditation helps me to be in the moment and be present. I've learned how to have healthy boundaries.

Lastly, getting over imposter syndrome is about believing in myself. I think that the biggest mindset for me to know every day, and especially as a woman of color, is that I belong in this role and that I'm good at it. It's okay to say that I'm really good at my job, and I'm a good leader. I have weaknesses for sure. But I'm really clear on what my strengths are. Connecting with people is a strength. Being a strong manager is a strength. Setting goals and reaching them has always been a strength.

I've earned this position. I've earned the right to be here and the right to be at the table. Many years ago when I was struggling with imposter syndrome, a mentor told me, "Minorities, you don't feel like you belong. How can you create spaces of belonging for others?" I realized that belonging is such an important part of our diversity, equity, and inclusion work. If our people feel like they don't belong in spaces, you can't even get to equity. If I care about social justice and creating inclusive and diverse spaces and getting to a point of equity in our society, that starts with me recognizing how I belong so that I can create spaces to show you belong too.

Growing up on the Rosebud Indian Reservation, Cheryl's parents were forced by the US government to attend boarding schools, places where Indigenous children were taken to subvert their identity and strip away all of their family connections. Despite this, Cheryl's parents raised Cheryl and her siblings in a community-grounded extended family that valued their culture. This upbringing inspired Cheryl to help her own children and Indigenous young people across the country connect to their culture and identity. Cheryl counters the myth that we are not enough. She shares strategies to not only overcome imposter syndrome but to also aspire to lead in the top CEO role.

I realized, at one point in my career, that the glass ceiling was on top of my head. My boss, the president of the college, was not going to retire or step aside. He was a young man. This was his career, his love. Being CEO in this organization wasn't really realistic for me.

So, I did go to my tribal school and serve as the CEO there for a while, and then a tribal college presidency came open. This is what I tell young Native people and what I would tell women, "You get to aspire to be an executive, you get to aspire to take what you've learned, and apply that in a leadership role." That was hard to do. Because we often as women, as people of color, are told by society that you're not good enough. It's imposter syndrome, that people are going to find out that you're not really that good. That has a lot of power. And that happened to me.

And I told myself, "You know what? You can be that good. You can take your vision, and apply it." Giving myself that permission was very powerful.

WHAT WOMEN OF COLOR CAN DO

PRACTICE 1. DEVELOP AWARENESS OF WHY WE THINK OR ACT THE WAY WE DO.

Many of us float through life on autopilot without asking ourselves why we do, think, or act the way we do. Zig Ziglar tells a story about a newly married couple. The wife would cut the end of the ham off before baking it. The husband asked why she did that, and her response was that her mother always cut off the end of the ham, and that's "the way it was supposed to be." Then the husband called his mother-in-law and asked why she cut off the end of the ham. Her response was that her mother always cut off the end of the ham. The husband then called the grandmother and asked why she cut off the end of the ham. She told him that her oven was small, and to fit the ham, she had to cut off the end of it. While the grandmother had a reason for cutting the end of the ham, the wife and her mother did it because it was "the way it was supposed to be."

The ham story can remind us to question our thoughts, beliefs, and actions. What beliefs are serving or not serving us? Where did these beliefs come from?

PRACTICE 2. QUESTION BELIEFS OF NOT BEING ENOUGH.

One specific belief to question is the feeling of being unworthy, which comes from the White patriarchy that has deemed "feminine" qualities as not enough and not leadership material. Schools base our worthiness on grades and tests. Parents teach us that accomplishments like success and winning awards means we are worthy of love. Ads tell us to buy things so that we are more accepted. Social media makes us feel like our worth is based on how many followers we have. It's understandable why we would believe that our self-worth is tied up in achievement, possessions, and approval. When we lose any of these, it's easy to see why we experience low self-worth.

In a February 2023 New Yorker article, Australian scholar Rebecca Harkins-Cross shares her past struggles with imposter syndrome as a college student. Today, she is suspicious of how impostor syndrome serves capitalism: "Capitalism needs us all to feel like impostors, because feeling like an impostor ensures we'll strive for endless progress: work harder, make more money, try to be better than our former selves and the people around us."

When we lift the hood on the system that has women believe we are less worthy, we can overthrow that socialization and be smarter about how to take action and rise. We can shed what does not serve us, release others' expectations, and let go of old programming. We can believe in ourselves, our worthiness, that we have what it takes. We can feel confident that we have the skills, talent, and potential to move toward fulfillment and self-actualization and to become a top leader. This includes reinforcing our worthiness, asking for help, and building a community of support around us.

PRACTICE 3. RELEASE DISEMPOWERING STORIES.

Whatever stories we create for ourselves determine our life's course. Marissa Peer, author of *Tell Yourself a Better Lie*, says that all disempowering stories break down to three themes:

1) I'm not good enough.
2) I'm different therefore I don't belong.
3) What I want is not available to me.

Who would we be if we stopped believing these stories about ourselves? What if we were always enough, no matter what we do or don't do? What if we didn't have to worry about being good enough anymore? What if being good enough was our base assumption?

Reshma Saujani, founder of Girls Who Code, shares, "It's never about whether we're qualified, whether we're prepared, whether we're ready. We've really never dissected all of the undeserved, unearned privilege that so many people have. And that we have literally bought and been fed, basically this propaganda, that we're not good enough, that we're not smart enough, that we don't belong. And the real resistance in this moment is saying … I'm not buying into that bullshit. I'm here. And I can lead too."

PRACTICE 4. TRADE LIMITING BELIEFS FOR AFFIRMING ONES.

Author of *A Confident Mind*, Dr. Nate Zinsser, a human performance psychology expert, dispels the misconception that confidence is innate. Instead, he emphasizes building confidence through practicing belief in our self-worth.

One suggestion Dr. Zinsser offers is to trade limiting thoughts for affirming thoughts. We need to stop being our own worst enemy and instead treat ourselves like our best friend. When an internal voice threatens our confidence, we need to substitute that voice with affirming thoughts. Practice this often to boost performance.

We've got to make a conscious decision to embrace our full selves. It's our job to see our value. Goodness knows the workplace isn't going to send us love notes. We've got to be intentional and decide to take ownership of our thoughts and make sure they are consistent with the person we want to be. Replace that self-criticism with lots of self-love. Make the conscious decision to have a positive mindset. We've got to be mentally fit so we can climb the career mountain.

Practice reframing your mindset. For example, instead of, "I'm not good at finance," think, "I'm working on getting better at finance." Every time I think I'm not good enough, I remind myself about my inherent worthiness, that feeling unworthy is falling into the system's sham, and that it just isn't true. Loving ourselves is a way to fight the system. We need to talk to ourselves with more self-compassion. We tend to be more compassionate toward others and more critical of ourselves. Rather than beating ourselves up when we make a mistake, we can talk to ourselves as we would to an unconditionally loving friend. For example, imagine that you called me and shared, "Today was terrible. I didn't get that job I really wanted." I would try to empathize and comfort you, "I'm sorry to hear this. It makes sense to feel sad. I know that you've been disappointed before, and you've used these moments to learn and find even better opportunities. I believe in you. You've got this." Why not talk to ourselves that way too?

PRACTICE 5. BUILD UNCONDITIONAL SELF-WORTH.

As an antidote to low self-worth, we can practice unconditional self-worth, the sense that we deserve to be alive, to be loved and cared for, and to take up space. Unconditional self-worth is a way out of self-criticism, shame, and unhealthy behavior. It is a way out of depression, anxiety, and substance abuse. It is time for us to base our worth on the fact that we are human and to cultivate self-confidence even when life does not go as we hope.

In her TED talk, clinical psychologist Adia Gooden shares steps to help us feel unconditional self-worth.

STEP 1. Forgive ourselves.

Many of us have a hard time accepting and forgiving ourselves for past mistakes. Being angry with ourselves keeps us from feeling worthy. To move forward, we accept what has happened, acknowledge the pain, and reflect on what we learned. Mistakes are normal—the average US worker makes 118 per year. The key is to learn from them and forgive ourselves. We say to ourselves, "I forgive you."

STEP 2. Practice self-acceptance.

We receive so many messages that we are not okay the way we are. This leads us to believe we need to look and be different. Rather than believe these thoughts, release them. Focus on what makes us different—our body shape, loud laugh, awkward dancing, or leadership style. These all make us unique and special. We are worthy, just the way we are.

STEP 3. Comfort ourselves and share our struggles with those we trust.

When life gets tough, we tend to get tougher on ourselves. But what we need most is for someone to see us and our pain and comfort us. We can do this for ourselves. When we face a challenge, we can acknowledge our pain and offer ourselves comfort. We can also connect to our support group, instead of isolating ourselves. We are not alone in struggle, and struggling does not make us unworthy.

The journey to unconditional self-worth takes courage to change the beliefs we've placed on our worth. While not easy, the journey will help us know that we are worthy. Imagine what we would dare to dream if we already knew we were worthy.

PRACTICE 6. CREATE A DAILY MANTRA.

Create an affirmation and practice it daily. This affirmation could be: I am strong, I am confident, I am bold, I am enough, I am perfect as I am, or I earned my place here. It's about taking small actions and making them into a habit, a self-fulfilling prophecy.

There are two things I practice. Each morning, I do a power ritual of three things I am grateful for, three mantras (in my case, "I am enough"), and three deep breaths. This might sound "woo," but when we look at Oprah, Tony Robbins, and successful leaders and Olympians, they practice rituals similar to this to prime their mind and self-confidence. We can do this even if we don't quite believe in our mantra. When we execute this consistently over time, we'll start to believe.

PRACTICE 7. EMBRACE SUCCESSES AND FAILURES.

Instead of beating ourselves up and focusing on our failures, focus on our successes. At the end of each day, reflect on our successes and what went right. We can also write a list of our top success moments from the past. The goal is to keep these successes top of mind to boost our confidence for the next task.

We are taught that failure is bad, and if we fail, to take it personally. Add to this that research shows that negative feedback and bad news has a much stronger impact on our self-concept than positive feedback and good news.

Imagine that we can create our own definition of failure. Consider that the Chinese word for "crisis" means "danger" but also "opportunity." What if we could see failure as an opportunity to learn? As Malcolm Forbes once said, "Failure is success if we learn from it." If we didn't achieve a goal, was that failure? Or was it a learning moment that is part of life to help us course-correct, bring us one step closer to success, and form a foundation to win later? What if we saw that on our journey to success, failure was intrinsically included?

To get to a goal, we usually experience some setbacks. People we admire have failed miserably. Thomas Edison failed 1,000 times before creating the light bulb. Theodor Seuss Geisel's (Dr. Seuss) first children's book *And to Think That I Saw It on Mulberry Street* was rejected by 27 publishers before it went on to sell six million copies. J.K. Rowling's book was rejected 12 times. In her 2008 Harvard commencement address, Rowling shared that her biggest failures (a failed marriage, being jobless, a single parent with little money) led her to the international bestseller, *Harry Potter*. "Why do I talk about the benefits of failure? Simply because failure meant a stripping away of the inessential. I stopped pretending to myself that I was anything other than what I was, and began to direct all my energy into finishing the only work that mattered to me... And so rock bottom became the solid foundation on which I rebuilt my life."

Failure teaches us grit, which researcher Angela Duckworth describes as a combination of passion and perseverance for an important goal. From her research of West Point cadets, National Spelling Bee finalists, and teachers in America's toughest schools, Duckworth found that "a significant predictor of success ... wasn't social intelligence. It wasn't good looks, physical health, and it wasn't IQ. It was grit." Passion and perseverance, picking ourselves up by the bootstraps, and getting up after a fall.

Success often relies heavily on failure. It's a chance to reflect and adapt, a chance to re-evaluate our plan and figure out what went wrong. It's a chance to do our best to fix it and spark a new direction. Failure brings "aha" moments to help us define what success means, redefine priorities in life, and do the self-work to align our time with what really matters.

PRACTICE 8. RELEASE PERFECTION.

Society teaches us we need to be perfect, which drives a fear of failure and making mistakes. This can get us stuck in a place of indecision because we can't know 100 percent what the right decision is. This can also make us more risk averse and not able to take risks or go for roles that would allow us to rise.

The reality is that we do not need to be perfect. Here are steps to release perfection:

STEP 1. Reflect on the costs of perfection.

Women who need all things to be perfect sometimes set themselves up to be passed over for promotion. Perfectionism often results in debilitating indecision and excessive time spent on tasks that lack importance in the grand scheme of things. Perfectionism can also be demotivating for our teams if we insist on personally handling tasks because we believe that no one else can do them "correctly." These are red flags that can impact decisions from leadership about who should be promoted.

STEP 2. Clarify what is most important.

Sometimes, the situation calls for checking every detail, and there can't be any mistakes. But as we become more senior, we need to be less focused on micromanaging the details and more focused on the big vision. We need to focus on what most matters to the organization.

STEP 3. Discern what needs to be good versus great.

We need to differentiate that not everything has to be the best. Sometimes, good enough is good enough. If this feels challenging, practice with low-stakes work. For example, at a weekly meeting, we can practice saying something immediately instead of hashing it out perfectly in our head before sharing our thoughts. We can also raise our hand for a project that needs skills we don't quite have. Get feedback from peers or other stakeholders on their expectations and use that to calibrate whether our work is "good enough."

STEP 4. Delegate.

Decide what work we need to do and delegate the rest. Develop our teams so that they can run the day-to-day, and we can focus on the strategic direction of the organization. If there is a tendency to do things on our own instead of delegating to our team, work on letting things go. This is our chance to strengthen our leadership skills and give our team a chance to shine. Tell them our expectations, standards, and priorities, and check with them to ensure these guidelines are clear so that they are able to execute. They won't do the work exactly the way we do, but they can still get the job done.

STEP 5. Schedule our work.

Set a concrete time block to work on a project instead of open-ended work time. Knowing we only have an hour to write a report will force us to get it done in an hour. If we find ourselves overpreparing or doing a third revision of a presentation, ask ourselves if this is good enough. If we're not sure, reflect on what was asked of us and whether we got the job done. If so, let it go—we're set. Often the difference between 80 percent and 100 percent perfection won't be noticed by most people, and we can shift our time to other important work.

STEP 6. Embrace the learning and normalize mistakes.

The next time we find ourselves stuck trying to get things right, we can release procrastination, self-protection, and perfection by seeing it as a learning process. Focus on one thing to do now. Think of how we can feel safe while taking action. Aim for doing our best rather than perfect work. Focus on one lesson learned from our mistake. See each step and mistake as a way to get more information to help us take the next action. Share our mistakes with others to help us realize how common failures are.

STEP 7. Release feelings of failure from our bodies.

Take five deep breaths and as you exhale, imagine your failure being released. If we view failure as a pathway to growth and learning, our mistakes will help us perform better next time. This allows us to be more empowered instead of stuck in indecision and inaction.

PRACTICE 9. SPEAK UP.

Speaking up is necessary, but some people (often men) talk too much and listen too little. As part of releasing perfection, make sure that we are speaking up and being visible at meetings. We might lean toward waiting until others have a turn or want to craft the perfect, insightful question. Instead, jump in and share a question or thought so that others know we are engaged and have a point of view.

If we tend to be quiet, introverted, or shy, before a meeting, we can plan what to say and practice beforehand. Even though it's tedious, this rehearsal will help us to feel more confident when we are in the meeting.

One Black woman I coached struggled with speaking up at meetings. She was an introvert at heart and also a perfectionist. At meetings, her tendency was to take time to formulate a response before opening her mouth. But she found that she was not able to have her voice heard, and her manager gave her feedback that she needed to participate more. I recommended that she rethink her role in meetings. Instead of trying to be the most insightful contributor in the group, she decided she wanted to show her care for her teammates by being an active participant and getting to know others personally. I also encouraged her to take baby steps; at every meeting, her goal would be to make one comment, even if that comment was agreeing with the person who had just spoken. She began speaking up and also learning about others, which made meetings more interesting and fun. Today, she is much more comfortable sharing her thoughts at meetings, including large meetings with over 100 people. She says that as a result, senior leaders have reached out asking her thoughts on important decisions for the company, and she is better primed for senior leadership.

PRACTICE 10. VISUALIZE SUCCESS.

People often have a mistaken notion that visualization is magic. But it's actually science. Visualization is a powerful process to boost confidence, performance, and success and manifest our desired future outcome. "When you visualize, the brain doesn't differentiate very much from a real event," Dr. Tara Swart, author of *The Source* explains. People who imagine themselves flexing a muscle achieve actual physical strength gains because they activate the same pathways in the brain that relate to the actual, real-life movement of the muscle. Visualization activates our creative subconscious to generate ideas to achieve our goal, programs our brain to recognize resources, increases confidence as we see ourselves accomplishing our goals, and sets us up for success as we "practice" success in our minds.

There are two kinds of visualizations. Outcome visualization places the focus on our desired future. For example, we imagine what it is like to get a promotion, how we spend our time, and we feel it in our body and mind. We can do this by envisioning ourselves in a role we aspire to, the more details and senses the better. Perhaps it is in the corner office, and we see ourselves at the desk gazing at the beautiful skyline outside our window. Process visualization places the focus on the steps needed to reach the desired outcome. Think about where we are and what we want to happen from beginning to end, including the celebration when we are successful.

For example, Olympic ice skater Kristi Yamaguchi handles the pressure of competing through process visualization. "The day and night before competitions, I would visualize my performance. I would run it through in my mind and watch the routine on the floor. I'd tell myself I'd trained and I was ready. Still, every single time, I'd be nervous, no matter what competition it was."

Even though we're not competing in the Olympics, we can use this strategy in our daily lives. We can envision ourselves networking with senior leaders, delivering our elevator pitch, championing ourselves for the promotion with our boss, getting the good news that we will be promoted, and celebrating with family and friends.

We might think we don't deserve a great opportunity and back down from applying. We might look at being a senior leader and not see people who look like us and think we don't belong. We might think that we're not worthy of a high salary. When that imposter syndrome raises its ugly head and we feel scared, we can beat it down with our affirmations, mantras, visualizations, and embracing of successes and failures.

Explore the Book Bonuses for this chapter:

- List of books for further reading
- Articles
- Videos
- Podcasts with full interviews of women leaders spotlighted in this chapter

MYTH THREE

Women are too emotional
to be good leaders

One day, when my son was 7, I chatted with his friend's mom.

Within earshot of my son, she told me, "At my parent-teacher conference today, the teachers told me that my son is struggling. Not just with reading but with behavior too. Apparently, he doesn't listen and is rude to the teachers and to other kids. He's been talking back to me at home, but I didn't realize this was also happening at school."

She seemed on the verge of tears, but then turned her attention to me, asking, "Is this something you're facing with your son?"

Actually, my son loved school and adored his teachers. He was an avid and enthusiastic reader, and one of his favorite places was the library.

But I wasn't about to bust her dam of waterfall tears. Instead, I reassured her, "My son can be a lot sometimes. At first, school was a tough transition, but it's getting better. I'm learning that these are just phases. You're doing your best, you're a great mom, and your son is lucky to have you."

Later, when it was just my son and me, I said to him, "You might have heard me talk to your friend's mom about you being a lot?" I was ready to tell him about being aware of other people's feelings and how we can help by choosing our response.

He replied, "Yes, but it's okay. I know you were trying to be nice, and you didn't want her to feel alone."

I didn't need to say another word; instead, I gave him a hug.

THE MYTH

In the workplace, being seen as too emotional is negative. Although emotional intelligence (EQ), the ability to understand, manage, and convey emotions, is important, it is less important than conventional intelligence (IQ). EQ is still a "soft," "nice to have" skill compared to "hard," essential technical skills. The myth continues that EQ is also innate, not a skill that can be learned and deliberately developed.

WHICH OF THESE EXPERIENCES RESONATE WITH YOU?

- ☐ You are an expert at your field, but you get passed over for recognition or a promotion and you aren't sure why.
- ☐ You avoid expressing your emotions at work.
- ☐ You are not able to recognize your emotions at any given moment or describe them easily outside of mad, sad, and glad.
- ☐ You see being vulnerable as a sign of weakness.
- ☐ In your daily life, you don't tend to rely on your emotions to guide your decisions.
- ☐ In difficult moments or when you experience adversity, you sometimes lose your composure or get caught up in dwelling on it instead of moving on.

- ☐ When you make a mistake, you tend to be hard on yourself and spend time rehashing all the ways you could have acted differently instead of practicing self-compassion.
- ☐ When you are with others, you are not consistently aware of their emotions or how your emotions affect them.
- ☐ You lack an understanding about how others perceive you (for example, not speaking up in meetings gets translated into ignorance, arrogance, or lack of interest in the business).
- ☐ During your day, you don't have a consistent practice to take time to quiet your mind or reflect.

THE REALITY

Which candidate would you choose for a leadership role?

- Candidate 1: Good technical skills (but lacks industry expertise) and strong communication and relationship building skills.
- Candidate 2: Expert technical skills, below average communication, and lack of confidence.

Which candidate would make the better leader? The reality is that most hiring managers would choose the candidate with the stronger EQ skills (candidate 1).

At an early job in my career, I received a top percentile performance review. Despite praise from my manager for exceeding expectations and having the strongest technical skills, when promotions were announced, my name was not called. What went wrong?

EQ explains why I was not promoted. While I was a hard worker, had delivered strong results, and had strong technical skills, I was lagging with my EQ. I didn't want to play into the stereotype of being a woman who was emotional or weak. I had worked hard to keep from showing my feelings and connecting with the feelings of others. As a result, when my name was discussed at the promotion table, people did not have a sense of who I was as a person; they only knew my work. I had not built connections to senior leaders or shown them my EQ and leadership skills. I had not shown them that I could listen and persuade or that I could influence or lead. While my peers might not have had my technical chops, they were able to establish themselves as leaders in the organization because of their relationships, communication, influence, and EQ skills.

EMOTIONAL INTELLIGENCE

I remember when I first learned about EQ. I read psychologist Daniel Goleman's book, *Emotional Intelligence: Why It Can Matter More Than IQ*. His research showed that EQ accounts for 67 percent of the abilities needed for superior performance at work, mattering twice as much as IQ and technical skills. He said, "Without [EQ] a person can have the best training in the world, an incisive, analytical mind, and an endless supply of smart ideas, but he still won't make a great leader."

Even though EQ is thought by many to be a "soft skill," it is an essential skill with Goleman labeling EQ a "must have." EQ is not innate but a skill to be developed through "extended practice" and feedback from others.

Goleman's EQ model includes:

1. Know our emotions.
2. Manage our emotions.
3. Motivate ourselves.
4. Recognize and understand other people's emotions.
5. Manage relationships by understanding the emotions of other people.

These are broken down into four EQ quadrants:

EQ QUADRANT 1 - SELF-AWARENESS: Self-awareness is about knowing ourselves, our strengths and limitations, having confidence, and being aware of our emotional state and the thoughts and beliefs behind them.

EQ QUADRANT 2 - SELF-MANAGEMENT: It's not enough to be aware of our emotions. We need to be able to channel these emotions effectively and control ourselves in difficult situations. Developing self-awareness and self-management means understanding our triggers and trauma. Many women of color have experienced personal and societal abuse. Abuse from childhood, racism, sexism, and sexual harassment are traumatic. What can hold women of color back is not understanding triggers or not working through related emotions. Whether we like it or not, we bring our whole, wounded self to a workplace that often applauds strength and emotionlessness. Self-management means taking care of ourselves so that we can heal.

EQ QUADRANT 3 - SOCIAL AWARENESS: This is the ability to relate to and empathize with others. We can listen well, understand how others feel, see others' perspectives, and be actively interested in others' concerns.

EQ SKILLS IN ACTION

In the beginning of our careers, it's important to develop a strong technical foundation. Know that as we rise in an organization, success will be less about what we know and more about our EQ skills. This includes building a broad network of relationships who see our value and cultivating support from and influencing our team.

Looking at Catalyst's research, we can understand why emotional intelligence (EQ) is important. In 2020, when organizations faced challenges due to COVID and George Floyd's murder, those with leaders who were understanding and more empathetic (had strong EQ) gained the trust of their employees. This trust was built around the belief that the organization's COVID and racial equity policies were sincere. On the other hand, organizations with leaders lacking in EQ couldn't establish this trust. This shows why EQ matters; it can make the difference in fostering genuine connections and credibility in the workplace.

STORIES FROM WOMEN OF COLOR

These stories show the range of EQ work—from healing trauma to being vulnerable—that allows women of color to become centered, impactful leaders.

ZAWADI BRYANT

Black, Founder and Former CEO of Nightlight Pediatric
Urgent Care and Former President, Acute Care Pediatrics
for Pediatrix Medical Group

Zawadi faced food and housing insecurities growing up with four siblings in Austin, Texas. Her father suffered trauma connected with being a Black man in the US. But her mom always encouraged her education and dreams. She worked for successful women of color and connected Zawadi with them. Seeing these professionals, Zawadi set her sights on becoming an engineer and attending Cornell University. Years later, she co-founded and became CEO of Nightlight Pediatric Urgent Care and later became President of Acute Care Pediatrics. Zawadi debunks the myth that technical skills are more important than emotional intelligence. Through her journey and healing from childhood traumas, Zawadi emerged as a resilient leader.

To be the best leader and person you can be, facing trauma is very important for self-care and healing. Without that, you tie a piece of yourself up. In order to show up completely and freely, you need to release yourself from that bondage. For a long time, I had this hostility with my dad. Over the years, I sought out help to understand how that was showing up in my life. This had effects on how I was relating to my husband. It helped to have tools in our toolkit because we don't have ways of maneuvering around trauma.

A lot of times, trauma is generational. I know my dad did the best he could with what he had. He was a Black man who grew up in a very segregated society that did not recognize his brilliance. He was frustrated that he didn't reach his potential. That didn't have to prevent me from having a very healthy relationship with my husband or with myself or feeling that I was lacking my father's love. That didn't mean that I wasn't deserving of all the love that I was capable of receiving.

In working with a therapist, I reflected on the good things that I experienced. As kids, we had lots of love. My mom taught us grit and determination. She had three jobs and was always working. I wouldn't have my love of books if it weren't for my father, making us get up every Saturday and Sunday, read books, analyze them, and have debates. My critical thinking comes from my father. Some of the other stuff, I'm going to scrap. I have released my father as well as my mother from what I experienced, just understanding that they did the best they could with what they had.

Toward the end of his life, my father and I reconciled. I also learned how to set boundaries, what is safe, and what protects me. This was key to understanding that I can have a relationship with someone on my terms that is good for me to be a healthy, thriving individual.

I learned that I can only change what's in my sphere of control. I can't change other people. I can only change myself. For me, getting help supported me with having a set of tools, talking about it, releasing things, and learning to be kinder and gentler to myself, my spouse, and my children. I didn't realize I was manifesting and perpetuating things that my parents did. I spent time unpacking this, understanding, How can I do things better? I know better, so I should do better.

ELAINE MILLER-KARAS

Latina, Co-founder and the Director of Innovation of the
Trauma Resource Institute

Elaine's family immigrated from El Salvador to California, where she grew up. When she visited El Salvador at 11, she saw poverty and felt a strong urge to help others. Becoming a social worker, she created the Community Resiliency Model (CRM) from research done through the California Mental Health Services Act. CRM teaches people, including children, to understand their emotions and regain balance in body and mind. Elaine's book, *Building Resiliency to Trauma*, gained recognition from the United Nations. Her work has impacted people worldwide, in schools, hospitals, and war-torn areas. Elaine emphasizes the importance of EQ over technical skills, focusing on self-awareness and self-management.

I have three generations of women in my family. Magdalena never married my great grandfather even though they had children together because she was a Mayan from Guatemala, and my great grandfather was a Spaniard. Later, my grandmother ended up having my mother out of wedlock. Then my mother had her first child out of wedlock. So when you see generations of this pattern, I think it has to do with colonialism and who was entitled and who was not.

Growing up in families where there are secrets, there was a lasting imprint on our family. I think that shame is part of what propelled my mom to leave the little village in El Salvador and come to the United States where she could start afresh. But she didn't leave the shame behind. It got translated to, "Make sure that you're always dressed well. Make sure you're always using proper language."

But then you feel you're not good enough. You're always striving to show that you belong. I think it starts with colonialism, the conquering of the Spaniards. We internalize not being good enough. I remember talking to one person who had just finished their third PhD, and they told me they don't feel good enough. I said, "How many PhDs are you going to need to believe that you are smart enough or good enough?"

Part of my work is to help leaders and educators develop resilience. As a trauma therapist, I was trained to talk about your trauma in order to heal. Since then, I have learned that's not the case. For some people, they may have told the story so many times that they don't want to tell it one more time. Or they could be a soldier in war who doesn't want to tell someone what they did, because they're ashamed and may get retraumatized in sharing.

Talk therapy also doesn't necessarily change the nervous system. For example, something happened to us when we were little, and there was a person with a certain kind of cologne who attacked us. Later, as an adult in the grocery store, someone with that same cologne walks by you. You're actually in a safe place, but all of a sudden, your heart starts to beat fast, you're terrified. It's because we have multi-sensory reminders that part of our body holds to remind us of when we were having existential events. Our nervous system reacts as if the trauma could happen in the present moment.

Part of how I heal myself has been learning more about how my body is connected to my thoughts and my feelings. We intercept these experiences of trauma and notice what's happening in our body. We learn that we can choose what to pay attention to and have better control of our emotions and have better impulse control. For me, when I am triggered, I feel my ears getting hot. So now when I sense the hot ears, I know immediately to practice a Community Resiliency Strategy such as feeling my feet on the ground or my hand or doing a Help Now strategy like having a glass of water. All of a sudden, my ears cool down, I'm back into my zone of well-being and my nervous system has settled.

When you say you're not good enough, what do you notice happening inside? There might be a tightness. There also might be a little bit of lightness. Now, if I decide to focus on the tightness, it actually expands. But if I pay attention to the lightness, it has the amazing possibility of letting go of the tightness. I take a deep breath and can feel myself as a whole full body person, mind, body, spirit.

This not only affects how we feel and sense ourselves but what we think about ourselves. We realize, "I am good enough. I'm a really good friend. I'm a good parent." We notice what else is true. We have more compassion and forgiveness for ourselves and others. If you're not in your zone of well-being, it's very hard to be compassionate. The Community Resiliency Model helps you learn wellness skills that you can share with your children and with the elders in your family to build a community of well-being.

I use a garden metaphor. If you plant vegetables and you want to have a hearty harvest, if you only water the weeds in your garden, would your vegetables grow in the same way? No, because we're not putting enough nourishment in that part of what we want to grow.

KATHY KUO
Taiwanese American, Founder and CEO,
Kathy Kuo Home

Kathy, born in Taipei to a diplomat, moved eight times in her childhood. This taught her how vital having a home was and later inspired her to start her own company, Kathy Kuo Home. Instead of believing the myth of placing more focus on technical skills, she believed in the power of emotional intelligence. When she pitched an online market concept at a previous job, it got rejected, and she lost her job due to the recession. But Kathy's strong EQ helped her persevere. In 2012, she founded Kathy Kuo Home, her own online store. Today, she leads her company by modeling vulnerability and embedding "radical candor" into the culture.

As part of the Asian culture, my options were a doctor, lawyer, and engineer. Of course, I decided to be an artist. Also, an entrepreneur. That was horrifying to my parents. These careers were like being unemployed. But creating Kathy Kuo Home was not just about great home design, it was also about creating environments where everyone could thrive.

For example, we created the company so that parents could work and raise children without having to make a choice. We pioneered working from home before working from home was a thing. We also wanted a place where women could thrive. A large part of our executive team and our company are women of different ethnic backgrounds. It's remarkable to see what women can do when you put them together in a room. We solve so many problems together. There's an innate understanding that we can build this together and check our egos at the door.

As part of creating the workspaces we want, we have created a culture of radical candor. This means making sure that everyone in leadership is excellent, that we can trust what we say, that we are values-aligned. It also means that we are vulnerable. Our leadership team spends two to three hours each week to meet. We always start with gratitude and vulnerability, then move to unpacking one difficult topic. We ask ourselves whether we will be above the line or below the line. Being above the line is being empathetic, curious, maintaining a positive outlook, and assuming positive intent.

Being below the line is opposite of this—closed off, judgmental, and defensive. It's okay to be below the line, but you want to be aware of where you are and name it so that you can take time to move above the line. I set expectations and model calling out for myself and others when we are below the line.

This shared vulnerability helps us to hack through really difficult problems. All of our problems have nothing to do with, Can we do it? It has more to do with the politics around, Should I do it? Who am I going to offend? Is this my responsibility? With shared vulnerability, you can say the thing and mean what you say.

As part of radical candor, this means each of us owning our 100 percent and making sure the rest of our team does too. This means taking 100 percent ownership and responsibility, even when what we are talking about is not in your realm of work. If each person were to lean in 100 percent—for example, it's an issue on customer service damages, what can I do in ops, in service, in trade?—when one person owns their 100 percent, this sets up other members of the team to own their 100 percent. It shifts the culture to unpack issues and find solutions.

MARCELLE FOWLER

Black, Chief Coaching Officer, C-Suite Coach

Marcelle's mother taught her about the importance of authentically connecting with people, especially people with different experiences. This led Marcelle to become a coach. Marcelle shares that it's a myth that EQ is not essential. She points to how developing EQ has been important in her career and the careers of others she coaches.

We're seeing a trend in the learning and development space where they're no longer calling EQ by the name of soft skills. They're calling them essential skills. It's a recognition that emotional intelligence is essential, not a nice-to-have as may be implied by soft skills. In order to rise in an organization, you have to be able to work effectively with others and demonstrate that you can rise to the challenge in a situation without burning bridges as you go along. This includes communications, relationship management, self-awareness, and self-management.

For self-awareness and self-management, it's important to notice our feelings and manage ourselves. A lot of times we judge our emotions and think of them as good or bad. Instead, an emotion is what it is; we need to know what that emotion is telling us.

When I'm getting ready to give a big speech or have an important meeting, yes, I feel nervous. But that's okay. It just means that this is important to me. Rather than judging it, "I'm feeling nervous, this is horrible, and I'm going to fail," I can instead manage myself by thinking, "I'm nervous. That makes sense. I've been here before. That's okay." So that's an important aspect of getting over impostor syndrome or anxiety—just leaning into that emotion, being okay with it, and not judging it.

In terms of social awareness and management, it's about connecting with others. For me personally, I remember when I worked on a team for the chief auditor of a major corporation. One of the things I recognized was, I'm not an auditor, I can't even play one on TV. If I'm going to be effective, I need to be able to get to know people. These were auditors and corporate security professionals, neither of which I had any knowledge about. But I knew how to connect to people. I knew how to get to know them and their stories and their backgrounds and to see them as people, which also made it easier when conflict arose.

Often we, especially as women of color, feel we have to make everyone else feel comfortable. It's difficult for us to be able to have uncomfortable conversations, but it's one that's necessary to not let people off the hook. To help with these conversations, it's helpful to have a structure.

- *Here's the behavior.*
- *Here's the impact that it had on me.*
- *Here's what I'd like to see differently.*

You can do this without being apologetic about it or feeling like you need to internalize it, which is so empowering for women.

TINA FERNANDEZ

Latina, Former Executive Director, Achieve Atlanta

Tina, the eldest child of Mexican immigrant and Mexican-American parents, fulfilled her father's dream of attending Harvard and becoming a lawyer. After achieving her AB at Harvard and JD at Columbia, she practiced corporate law for five years. However, Tina realized the importance of embracing her whole self at work—mind, body, and spirit. This realization led her to shift her career toward helping others, particularly in education. Tina challenges the myth that intellect should override emotions. She advocates for considering not just the mind but also our emotions and body when gathering information and making decisions.

As a woman of color, assumptions are going to be made about your intelligence, your abilities, your capacity to lead. One of the ways that we counteract negative assumptions is by going above and beyond. You can't just be good, you've got to be great. You can't just be great, you've got to be the best. These are White supremacist structures. What is privileged above all else is cognitive analysis, the analytical mind, the verbal expression, and taking out feelings. Don't talk about gut.

I really bought into that for a long time because it is what you need to be successful. I ignored those pits in my stomach, the churning in my chest. I've always been a person of faith, and I would pray, but they were more anxious prayers trying to find comfort when I was feeling uncomfortable.

What I've learned over the years is that the body has a wisdom to it, and that we are spiritual beings as well. I read The Body Keeps the Score, which is about how we hold trauma in our bodies and how that impacts our physical health. That's very real. My daughter was diagnosed with an autoimmune disorder tied to chronic stress. Many of the women in my family have autoimmune diseases. What we're seeing is that these are caused by being in a state of constant stress where hormones rush through your body when you're in fight or flight mode. Your brain is in the limbic system. We don't have access to the prefrontal cortex, which helps us make rational decisions when we are feeling threatened.

How do we soothe our bodies? How do we bring down our nervous system when it's in that fight or flight? I've done a lot of research while I've been at Harvard on the vagus nerve, meditation, and mindfulness, and how all of these things can help you stay connected to your body. Listen to the signals that your body has given you. It has been a game changer.

When those big emotions come up, once you have the tools to settle in, to breathe, to not clench every muscle in your fiber, you create this openness that allows you to see and feel what's happening around you. Only a very small percentage of what we know is through reading or the rational and analytical side of the brain. So much of what we know in this world is what we take in through *our senses, through the way that our bodies feel when we're with other people.*

I've always been aware of my body but I ignored it because I felt it would undermine my credibility to talk about that. Now I'm on the other side where I accept and value those ways of knowing, insights, awareness. I tap into that wisdom because it's really powerful. For so many of us, we've denied it for a really long time.

SARAH WHITE
Oglala Lakota and Executive Director of the South Dakota Education Equity Coalition

Raised in a community that valued spirituality and education, Sarah observed the widening achievement gap with Indigenous communities falling further behind. Motivated to make a difference, she founded the South Dakota Education Equity Coalition (SDEEC), dedicated to fostering diverse, equitable, and inclusive learning environments for future generations. Along the way, Sarah experienced burnout as she pursued achievements to cope with trauma and find self-worth. She realized that if she wanted to heal her community, she needed to start by healing herself. Sarah counters the myth that focusing on EQ is a nice-to-have. Instead, Sarah encourages focusing on ourselves, embracing personal healing, and honoring Indigenous values to drive genuine transformation in our personal and work lives, as well as in DEI.

There have been a lot of policy attacks on our people and Indigenous education, especially in South Dakota. At what point are we going to quit swimming upstream? Because that's what education reform has felt like. Swimming constantly upstream in survival mode to the depletion of self.

If I look at that through the language of love and the spirit of forgiveness, we can recognize that we do have power. What can we honor that we already have to create pathways and alternatives that both create a sense of accountability for existing systems and create a pathway for healing to occur within those systems? We can think innovatively outside of the box. Yes, there is a sense of urgency around the active resistance to these political threats. But there's also this notion that we have inherent genius. We have tried and true solutions. Before America was colonized, this land was all Indigenous. We can come back to the spirit of those values based on stewardship of the land and values based on relationships. We could start thinking of innovative ways to get these ideas more exposure and more immersed in our spaces. We're never going to reverse the wrongs that happened. So how can healing begin? How can we be the catalyst for that healing?

My response to coping with trauma has always been achievement because I was seeking self-worth, believing it's going to make me happy. I wanted prosperity for my community so much that I offered so much of myself. Ultimately, what I found was that at the pinnacle of success, I was the furthest from myself and from the Creator when I was in that space.

I realized that I need to come back to me. I need to find my own source and be close with that source. That has helped me with healing. Self-care is critical. When I think about the moments where I'm under the most stress, I'll skip meals or not drink enough water. We overlook that as something minimal, but that's a literal survival skill. I was denying myself survival.

I feel like women overburden themselves with this more than men in that we will suffer and martyr ourselves to our own detriment, falsely believing that it's going to contribute to prosperity. But that's not ever going to be sustainable. A model of sustainability is taking care of ourselves, nurturing our spirits, focusing on healing, and recognizing that this is synonymous with the healing that we need to see within our professional work as well.

WHAT WOMEN OF COLOR CAN DO

We can't rely on organizations to build our EQ skills or direct our career paths and learning. Research shows that less than 40 percent of companies have an organizational strategy that actively supports career development and only 22 percent of companies have clearly defined career paths for employees seeking more responsibility in management roles. Instead, we need to take the lead in our careers and development, which includes strengthening our EQ skills.

EQ SKILL 1. BUILD SELF-AWARENESS.

Self-awareness is about knowing ourselves, our strengths and limitations, welcoming criticism, having confidence, and being in tune with our emotions and how they affect our performance.

Shawn Ginwright, author of *The Four Pivots: Reimagining Justice, Remaining Ourselves* writes that becoming the best leaders we can be and improving our communities requires personal change. "So much of our efforts for social change have been outward looking. We have focused on changing systems, laws, and policies in our society that create inequality and suffering. ... Social change is also an inside job, and there is a relationship between our individual healing and social transformation, and the two cannot be separated."

PRACTICE 1. BE AWARE OF OUR CULTURE'S INFLUENCE.

Be aware of our culture and how this influences how we behave at work. For example, one of my clients is an Asian American woman who struggles with making decisions that she knows are better for the organization but are unpopular. We discussed how her Asian culture could be impacting her leadership. One Asian value she embraces is harmony, which shows up in her leadership as prioritizing what her team wants over what the organization needs. Now with this self-awareness, she continues to solicit input from her team but ultimately bases her decision on a balanced approach. She considers both her team's wishes and what is best for the organization and makes a decision, even if it isn't the most popular option.

Understanding how our culture shapes our work behavior allows us to consciously decide how we want to lead instead of being in our default mode. When we are aware of our patterns, such as keeping our head down and not making our voice heard, we can disrupt the way we work and challenge and influence authority.

PRACTICE 2. UTILIZE THE WHEEL OF AWARENESS.

Dr. Daniel J. Siegel, author of *Aware: The Science and Practice of Presence*, offers a tool called The Wheel of Awareness.

Our mind can be pictured as a bicycle wheel, with a hub at the center and spokes radiating toward the outer rim. The rim represents anything we can pay attention to or become aware of: our thoughts and feelings, our dreams and desires, our memories, our perceptions of the outside world, and the sensations from our body. ... The hub represents part of what's called the executive brain, because it's from this place we make our best decisions.

Figure 1: Wheel of Awareness

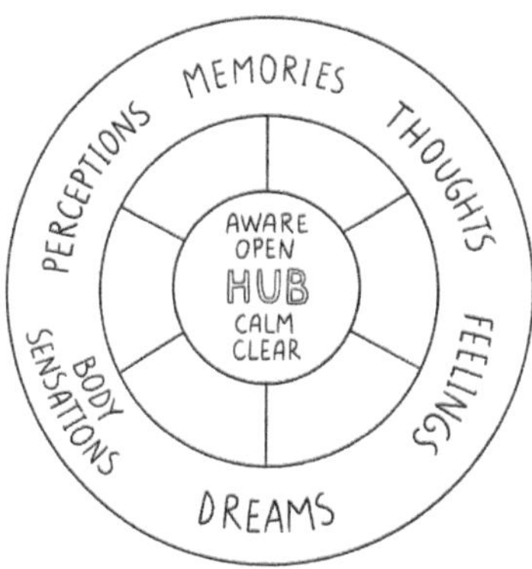

As you can see from the figure above, the Wheel of Awareness can help us better understand that what is happening in our mind (our feelings, thoughts, perceptions) does not define who we are. When we practice mindfulness and are aware of what's happening in our own mind (the rim), we can return to our hub, our executive function, to calm down and focus our attention on beliefs that support us. The wheel of awareness helps to see ourselves as a multifaceted person, preventing us from fixating on only one part. We may have parts that are insecure and other parts that are confident. If we can find acceptance of our many parts and experiences, even if they share conflicting narratives about ourselves, we can create space to access a wiser "center" that allows us to make decisions.

Figure 2: Analiza's example with the Wheel of Awareness

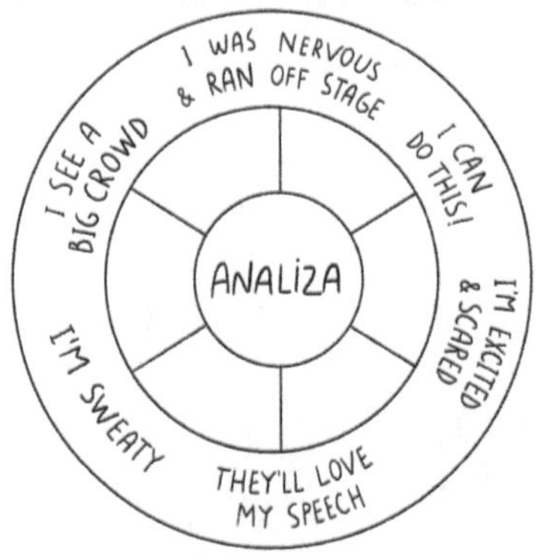

Here is an example of how I have used the Wheel of Awareness. I used to be petrified of speaking in public. I once was so nervous that I ran off stage. With the Wheel of Awareness, I was able to identify what was happening on the outer rim. For example, I saw that running off stage was a memory. I recognized my thought, "I can do this!" I also noticed that I was scared and also excited at the same time. I saw that there was a big crowd and that I was sweaty. I also saw that I had a dream that they would love my speech. With the Wheel of Awareness, I realized that all of this was part of my outer rim. I could focus my attention on beliefs that would support me. I began to focus on my thought, "I can do this!," feeling excited, and my dream that the crowd would love my speech. The Wheel of Awareness has allowed me to not only strengthen but also enjoy public speaking.

PRACTICE 3. LISTEN TO OUR BODY'S WISDOM.

At some point in our careers, many of us have been exhausted and have pushed our bodies to the limit, sometimes experiencing a breakdown. As Tina Fernandez shared in her earlier story, instead of ignoring our bodies and using just our minds, we can listen to our gut and inner body wisdom.

Martha Beck, Oprah's coach, shares an exercise which can help us be more attuned to our bodies' wisdom.

STEP 1. Think of a time when we said yes and agreed to something we later regretted.

What were we feeling physically when we were making that choice? Did our gut churn or our hands get cold? Even small sensations are significant.

STEP 2. Think of a time we said no to something and later wished we'd said yes.

What physical sensations did we experience when we were making that choice?

STEP 3. Think of a time we said no and were later relieved that we'd passed on what would have been a bad experience.

What physical sensations did we experience when we were making that choice?

STEP 4. Think of a time we said yes to something that turned out to be a great choice.

What physical sensations did we experience when we were making that choice?

STEP 5. Now that we are more attuned to our bodies, notice that our bodies will give us a consistent yes or no, a consistent "body truth" that can help us with current decisions.

For example, a client of mine struggled to decide if she should stay in her current job or look for a new one. When she imagined staying in her current job, her stomach tightened and her jaw clenched. When she imagined looking for a new job, she had a lightness in her chest and a release in her shoulders. The choice was clear. We worked together on finding a new job, and six months later, she secured a promotion, 50 percent pay raise, schedule with fewer hours, and more time to be present for her family.

For a worksheet on body wisdom for you to fill out on your own, check out the Book Bonuses.

EQ SKILL 2. BUILD SELF-MANAGEMENT SKILLS.

It's not enough to be aware of our emotions. Self-management is about channeling these emotions effectively and keeping ourselves in our resiliency zone. It is the ability to go from a triggered state back to our resiliency zone.

PRACTICE 1. STAY IN OUR RESILIENCY ZONE.

Combine self-awareness and self-management skills to stay in our resiliency zone. Our resiliency zone is where we are calm, focused, and functioning as our best selves.

Here are steps to stay in our resiliency zone:

STEP 1: Recognize our triggers.

We get out of our resiliency zone when we are triggered, such as with a microaggression. For women of color, many of us are constantly on guard, which makes it difficult to be in our resiliency zone and at our high-peak performance.

Work with a therapist to understand how past hurt, anger, shame, and fear may trigger hot buttons today. Reflect on how family models have shaped our views and get clarity on where we would like to change. Instead of burying this pain, wrestle with it and heal.

STEP 2. Get comfortable with uncomfortable emotions.

Most people don't want to feel sad, angry, or scared. We avoid these emotions because we feel that there's something wrong with feeling them. Most of our lives are spent resisting these emotions. What if we just allowed ourselves to feel sad or angry or afraid? Going through these emotions is unpleasant. But these emotions can also be places of learning and wisdom.

STEP 3. Identify and practice a Community Resiliency Model (CRM) strategy.

Developed by author of *Building Resilience to Trauma* Elaine Miller-Karas, CRM is an evidence-based practice that explains how stress affects our nervous system, emotions, and behaviors. CRM offers strategies to help us stay in our resiliency zone.

Here are three core CRM skills and one non-CRM strategy to bring our body, mind, and spirit back into our resiliency zone when we are triggered. For more information on CRM strategies, check out the Book Bonuses.

CRM STRATEGY 1. TRACKING – Tracking is about noticing sensations within the body.

Learn to focus our attention on pleasant or neutral sensations. Where our attention goes, energy flows. When we pay attention to pleasant or neutral sensations instead of unpleasant ones, our body calms down, and we shift toward our resiliency zone. For example, I notice at this moment that my upper back is tight, and I feel a lightness in my arms. I choose to focus on the lightness in my arms and notice that my back relaxes, and I feel more calm.

CRM STRATEGY 2. RESOURCING – Identify a potential resource that brings calm, peace, or joy.

After identifying this resource, track the resulting positive sensations that occur when we think about this resource. Add more details to the resource to deepen the positive sensation connected with this resource. For me, I think about a specific beach I used to go to when I was a kid, adding details like the ocean breeze, sea smell, and gentle wind in my face, which relaxes my body and brings me a sense of calm.

CRM STRATEGY 3. GROUNDING – Notice what is supporting our body.

Notice the direct contact of our body and the solid surface that is physically supporting us in the present moment. For example, I bring my attention to my feet on the ground, which gives me a sense of security.

NON-CRM STRATEGY 4. ALLOWING – Allow the emotion to pass.

While this is not an explicit CRM strategy, the practice of allowing our emotions to pass can be helpful. After noticing the emotion, give ourselves love, some breath, and some space. Feel and trust our feelings and ourselves. Then notice how the emotion passes. We don't have to spend so much energy resisting and suppressing. Invite greater ease around our emotions.

STEP 4. Choose our response.

When we are ready, choose how to respond and act in alignment with our values.

EQ SKILL 3. BUILD SOCIAL AWARENESS.

Social awareness is the ability to relate to and empathize with others. It is the ability to listen well, understand how others feel, and see others' perspectives. This is a critical skill, particularly given the Center for Creative Leadership's research, which found that the most common reason why executives fail is not being able to grasp other people's perspectives. Social awareness also includes organizational awareness and understanding room dynamics and how decisions are made.

PRACTICE 1. CREATE A RELATIONSHIP MAP.

Michael Watkins' *The First 90 Days* shares tips for starting a new role that improve our social awareness. Create a relationship map of our organization to understand the political landscape—which people have influence, decision-making power, and who is most likely to resist our agenda. How are decisions made and by whom, and how does influence happen?

To do this, arrange one-on-one meetings, even as brief as 15 minutes, with team members and peers in cross-functional groups such as technology, finance, and HR. The goal of these meetings is to build relationships, understand how to work well with their team (e.g., their preferred way to communicate and collaborate), and learn how decisions are made and how to go about achieving results.

Build our ability to read situations so that we are aware of what's going on around us. This means being able to walk into a room and understand who is influential and what everyone's agenda is. It's also about being able to read between the lines in emails and meetings and understand what people are really thinking. To do this, we'll need to get to know people through meetings and informal conversations and watch verbal and non-verbal cues.

By being more socially aware, we will be able to understand how to be smart and strategic about achieving results and how to rise in our organization.

EQ SKILL 4. MANAGE RELATIONSHIPS.

The fourth EQ skill is about building relationships and doing it authentically.

One woman leader of color I coached told me that she hated politics at work, saying, "It feels dirty and fake!" She was frustrated that she had delivered a strong proposal to the executive team, but they decided on another project that was more risky and not as well thought-out. We worked together to uncover that even before proposals had been pitched, the decision had already been made through pre-meetings and alliances. The winning project was led by her male peer who had met individually with the executive team and had built alliances with key decision makers. These key decision makers then rallied the rest of the executive team to go along with them. I worked with my client to reframe what politics means—being smart about how to get things done by building relationships and understanding how decisions are made.

PRACTICE 1. BUILD AUTHENTIC CONNECTIONS WITH STAKEHOLDERS.

Women generally tend to be relationship builders. Whether this is a strength of ours or not, build authentic connections with stakeholders, including decision makers and senior leaders. Become politically savvy—know who to persuade and how to persuade them to help us move forward with our work. Leverage pre-meetings (the meetings before the public meeting) to get people on board with our ideas, and build consensus and address any issues beforehand.

One of my clients told me, "I don't have time to schmooze. I've got too much work!" We discussed how making time to cultivate relationships, especially with senior leaders, could help her with her work. She could get to know stakeholders personally and build trust. In addition, she could get feedback and support with her projects. Convinced, she quit working through lunch and began having lunch outside with colleagues and clients each day. These relationships helped her build a network of support, which helped her projects' success and her reputation as a leader.

PRACTICE 2. STRENGTHEN COMMUNICATION.

To be seen as a leader, we need strong communication skills. We need to express ideas so that our message resonates while being sensitive to others' feelings. We need to know when to listen and when to speak—even when what we have to say is controversial or we are the only woman or person of color in the room. We need to be able to adapt our communication style so that our message resonates, balancing the key points with details. We also need to persuade, especially when research shows that the most important trait for entrepreneurs is the ability to persuade. Finally, we need to be able to give and receive feedback.

PRACTICE 3. BE VULNERABLE.

In managing relationships, create spaces where people feel psychologically safe and can be vulnerable. Model this by being vulnerable ourselves—for example, asking for help. Show that asking for help is not a sign of weakness but a sign of strength. Even if we are the CEO, it's not possible to know everything. Asking for help and sharing our vulnerability is a way for people to connect with us and to build trust and emotional bonds that create spaces of belonging.

BOOK BONUSES

Explore the Book Bonuses for this chapter:

- Body wisdom worksheet
- Resources on CRM Strategies
- List of books for further reading
- Podcasts with full interviews of women leaders spotlighted in this chapter

MYTH FOUR

Be humble. Our work will speak for itself

Growing up, I wanted to make my parents proud and be a good student and a good Asian.

In the beginning, I wasn't particularly great at either. I was a bad student and therefore a bad Asian. It wasn't until fourth grade when I brought home a history test that I had failed that I turned it around. The teacher told me, "You need to show this test to one of your parents and return it back to me with their signature as proof." My dad was out to sea in the US Navy, so I only had my mom as an option. I was relieved because my dad was a tough disciplinarian who was not above spanking. Not that my mom was going to be a cake walk. I guessed that she would yell and tell me what a disappointment I was. I considered folding my test and asking my mom for an "autograph." Instead, I wrote her a letter that began, "Dear Mom, I'm sorry..." I left the letter and the test on her bed.

Later when my mom came home from work, I held my breath. It did not take her long to call out, "Analiza, come here." I was prepared for the worst. I dragged myself to her room, and she gestured to the chair in front of her.

"Sit down... Is this your test?" I quaked in my seat and nodded. She sighed and said, "I only have one question for you. Did you try your best?"

I couldn't answer. I was so nervous.

I shook my head, and I started bawling, "I'm so sorry mom!" She continued, "Listen. I don't care what grade you get. All I want to know is that you tried your best. That's enough for me. Will you promise to try your best next time?" I nodded, and she wiped my tears away.

From then on, I kept my promise. I tried my best.

On the next tests, I got the highest scores in the class. I learned that if I worked hard and focused on my schoolwork, I could do well. I eventually graduated at the top of my class, going from failure to valedictorian. School felt like a meritocracy. I worked hard, and I became a good student.

I also became a good Asian. I embraced the idea of keeping my head down and trusting that my hard work would speak for itself. The idea of sharing my accomplishments was the antithesis of what I thought made a good Asian—humble, self-deprecating, behind the scenes, loyal, and focused on the collective group above myself.

Throughout my career, I worked long hours, focused on work in my own lane, got strong at the technical skills in my role, stayed on budget, and met deadlines. I said yes to every extra project that was given to me. I said yes to nights and weekends. I said yes without additional pay or promotion. Surely with all of my extra work and stellar performance reviews, my organization would recognize me.

One time, when I knew that promotions would be publicized the next day, I announced to my family, "We'll be celebrating tomorrow!" I booked a reservation at my favorite restaurant.

But when promotions were announced, I did not hear my name. Instead, a junior (and White male) colleague got promoted. I could run circles around him. What happened?

I eventually realized that what wins in school and what makes a good Asian are not necessarily strategies that win at work. At school, what is scripted out—the syllabus, tests, homework, and projects—makes up the bulk of decisions about who rises to the top. But at work, what is scripted out—job descriptions, performance reviews, technical skills, and feedback surveys— makes up only a small part of the decision.

It wasn't until getting passed over yet another time that I went to my boss. I brought a list of my accomplishments to share with him. To my shock, he said, "I had no idea." I had assumed that he had been keeping tabs on all of my impact to the organization. I was wrong.

Having now been at the decision-making table, I know that leaders gather around the table, and they talk about us. We might be loved by our team, but if people in other departments and senior leadership don't know us or our skills and contributions, then we have become too insular. That means we're relying on our boss or our boss's boss to champion us. This is why it's possible to have weaker performers chosen over stronger performers. The people who tend to get chosen have built relationships with decision makers; they have tooted their horns and made themselves, their leadership, and their work visible to decision makers.

I learned that no matter how uncomfortable it felt, I needed to toot my own horn. We can't assume that our bosses will look out for us. We need to network and seek opportunities that will make us visible. Our careers are too important to stay humble and hope someone will notice our work and skills. If we don't tell leadership what we've accomplished, we won't get rewarded.

THE MYTH

I had specific programming as an Asian woman, but women in general are conditioned to be modest, to keep a low profile, not stand out, and not take credit. We are told, "Do a good job, and trust that your work will speak for itself."

WHICH OF THESE EXPERIENCES RESONATE WITH YOU?

- ☐ As a woman of color, you believe that your work (you may be working twice as hard) should speak for itself.
- ☐ You believe it is your manager's job to share your results with others.
- ☐ You have been at a job for a long time with strong performance but get passed over for promotion by people who have been at the company for less time or have weaker performance.
- ☐ You don't talk about your good work or ideas. Someone else may be taking credit for your work.
- ☐ You sit down in a meeting and introduce a new idea, but you are interrupted by a male colleague. You try to speak again but get cut off. A few minutes later, another male colleague shares the same idea you just brought up, and everyone nods and thanks him for his idea.
- ☐ Few people outside your department know the quality of your work.

We may think that our work will speak for itself, that doing good work alone should be enough to get recognized. But this is a myth. While quality work is important, it is not enough to guarantee success. I've heard women say that they don't care about getting credit; they're more focused on contributing to the mission and the bottom line. But being humble and not taking credit for our accomplishments can prevent us from getting the opportunities we deserve. We need to be confident and promote our work, while also being respectful and collaborative with others, so that we can advance in our careers.

Women may be more humble because we are implicitly and explicitly socialized to be nice and nurturing. Research shows that this conditioning starts early. Though roles are changing and gender binaries are less confining, girls often still play "house" or "school" while boys beat each other up or play sports where one team always loses. Girls playing with other girls learn to be less confident. They avoid sharing that they are a leader in the group or that they're great at something. If they do, the other girls will call them "bossy" or "full of herself." As women in the workplace, this behavior then translates to lack of confidence and lack of a desire to further our careers.

In contrast, boys are taught to take public credit, to share what they're good at or that they are a leader. When they become men in the workplace, they have been naturally groomed to toot their own horn, setting them up for opportunities and promotion.

Harvard psychologist Carol Gilligan's gender studies research found that women see the world as a web of cooperation while men see it as a place to beat others for the best spots. Women tend to nurture, often putting others' needs first instead of advocating for ourselves. While men move from job to job, women have a tendency to plant roots in a job, sometimes driven by having young children and not having the extra time and headspace to switch jobs. Women also tend to be loyal because we feel appreciated by our boss and team as the go-to person for our organization. Of course, some of us do find the right fit, but don't assume that our sacrifice and service will be rewarded. Know that when we stay too long and don't grow in an organization, we pass on opportunities to rise in our careers.

Culture plays a role in our beliefs. For example, Asian values include hard work, modesty, and avoiding anything that draws attention such as self-promotion. This explains why many Asians feel uncomfortable with taking time from work to network and share accomplishments. We assume that we don't need to brag; others will take care of us and do it for us. But putting our heads down instead of self-marketing stunts our careers.

KNOW WHY TAKING CREDIT MATTERS

Women of color need to strategically bring attention to ourselves and take credit for our achievements. A 2011 Catalyst study confirmed that the most powerful tactic for a woman's career advancement is to call attention to accomplishments. This was the only factor associated with bigger raises.

Strategically bragging is not just important to do inside the company we work for, it's also important to do outside of the company. Since 85 percent of all corporate workers get their job by networking (based on a 2016 survey), it's critical that people outside of the company are aware of our work accomplishments too. The reality is that people aren't hired because of their resume. They are hired because they were recommended to the people doing the hiring.

For hires and promotions, it's not what we know but who we know and whether they speak on our behalf. We need to get noticed and be "top of mind." In marketing, "top of mind" means that when people are thinking about possible people to promote, hire, or consult, we come to mind. If we are not promoting ourselves, we will fall into being "outta sight, outta mind." Executive coach Kathy Lockwood hammers this point in a 2018 Forbes article: "Being 'quietly competent' is not going to get you promoted; you need to promote yourself first."

STORIES FROM WOMEN OF COLOR

These women of color show us the importance of tooting our own horns and doing it in a way that feels authentic, purposeful, and community-oriented.

KIANTI BROWN WHITNEY
Black, Vice President of Marketing and Communications at the Relay Graduate School of Education

Kianti's parents saved for all four of their children to attend private school instead of public school. Kianti attended University of California, San Diego for her BA in Communications, then Rice University for her MBA in Marketing. Kianti worked at advertising agencies, then finance institutions, and finally education, where she brings together her passions of education, stories, and marketing. Kianti used to keep her head down, but as she learned her own worth, she grew more comfortable acknowledging her excellence.

As a Black woman, I learned not to outshine anyone because that makes things so much easier. I work in White institutions. If I am to highlight my excellence, that can intimidate my bosses who are likely White and would make my job harder. So if I'm humble and let them shine, then I'm deemed more valuable and not intimidating.

As I get older and evolve and grow, I'm less afraid of the alternative. I know my worth. If you're so intimidated by me that you beat me out the door, I have full confidence that I will toot my own horn based on my skills, my talents, and my experience. I can get something else. Maybe that means I'm not working for an institution anymore. Maybe that means I'm working for myself. But I'm not willing to dim my light out of fear of intimidating or hurting someone else's feelings. I'm just not willing to do that. That's been the biggest shift in my life.

CAROLINE CENIZA-LEVINE
Filipina American, Founder, Dream Career Club

Caroline's Filipino family told her to study hard, get good grades, and get a good job—which meant being a business person, lawyer, or doctor. Instead, Caroline decided to study piano at Juilliard and then become a recruiter, Senior Contributor to Forbes, author of *Jump Ship: Career Change: 10 Steps To Starting A New Career*, and Founder of the Dream Career Club. Caroline addresses the myth of being humble and shares how important tooting her horn was to her career.

I had gone after the media to establish credibility. I encourage all leaders and aspiring leaders to do the same. You have to establish your thought leadership and your expertise in a way that people will believe and remember you. I reflected on my experience, what people cared about, and where the area wasn't too crowded so that I could create a name for myself. I decided to focus on career transitions.

Then I put myself out there. I started with my community newspaper guest blogging about career transitions. I started with journalists I happened to know who were regional reporters on a regional channel. I tried to be as helpful as I could to as many people as possible.

I've been writing for 11 years now for Forbes. They reached out to me because you can't apply to be a contributor. I was one of the first contributors. I asked the editor, "How did you hear about me?" She said, "Everywhere." At that point, I knew I was starting to get some traction. It works to be in different places so that people will recognize your work. That's the media part of it.

Someone invited me into my first book project, an anthology of essays about fear. I wrote about fear and career change because I wanted to own that career change space. Having experienced career change myself and found happiness, I knew from being a recruiter that there is room to write about people changing careers. It isn't like looking for another job. It is a different animal.

The editor of that book happened to have worked at a company I had worked at. We didn't know each other at the company, but I reached out to her and I played on that affinity. I said, "Hey, we both were there, and now we're both here. It would be great to work together again." Even though we hadn't technically worked together, I established that affinity.

The second book project came when the publishers reached out to me. They had seen my work, and they were looking for someone to *write a textbook on job searching for college students. The third book,* Jump Ship: Career Change: 10 Steps To Starting A New Career, *was through Forbes. Forbes and Amazon had a partnership to release a number of "how to" books on Kindle, and they asked me to write the career book.*

RHEA WONG

Chinese American, Founder of Rhea Wong Consulting, Former Executive Director of Breakthrough New York

Author of *Get that Money, Honey* and aspiring stand-up comedian, Rhea counters the myth that we should let our work speak for itself. Rhea shares how tooting her own horn has allowed her to build a strong brand and business as a fundraising consultant.

I don't think any Asian American kid says, "I'm going to be a consultant." To this day, my parents don't actually know what I do. I was a 26-year-old Executive Director (ED) in New York. My first day on the job I did two Google searches. One was, What does an ED do? Google Search two was, How do you fundraise? Twelve and a half years later, my team and I built up the organization to serve over 500 kids a year in New York, and I was raising $3 million a year in private philanthropy. I didn't know that I was destined to run my own company.

After I left Breakthrough in 2017, I joined a tech firm for about two and a half months. I realized that was not for me. I left and felt like I was adrift because I had been a very good Asian, got all the A's, went to the right schools, and got a job after college. It was really the first time in my life that I didn't have a next step. Leaving that job was a big crisis moment for me because I had identified myself with what I do, and going to work was my identity.

Breakdown to breakthrough, I realized, "Wait, that means I can do anything." I became an accidental consultant because I had lots of ED [Executive Director] friends and did projects for them. Then mid-pandemic is really when I transitioned to focus on fundraising, the number one problem all nonprofits have. I provide training around major gift fundraising.

Did I know that this is where I would end up? Not at all. Did I know that I had a book in me? I did. I thought it was the great American novel. Turns out it was a fundraising book.

The stand-up comedy was a lifelong dream. But there is nothing more soul crushing than bombing on stages throughout downtown Brooklyn and downtown Manhattan. I bombed everywhere. One time, I was doing an open mic in a little dive bar in San Francisco where I live, and my whole family was there. My brothers came, my parents came, my best friend and their parents came. My set was not super clean. I thought, "Oh my God, I am telling sex jokes in front of my parents. This is terrible. The nightmare is complete. I just need to be naked and have a calculus test." But there's nothing better than stand-up comedy to get you ready to do anything. Because if you can bomb a set in front of your parents and not die, you feel like you are bulletproof and can do anything.

One important skill that has helped me is building my brand. I approach this not from a place of, "I'm so great; look at me," but rather, "I figured out some stuff, and if it's helpful to you, cool, and if it's not, that's cool too." I'm a recovering people pleaser. That's my Achilles heel. I want everyone to like me, but the truth is, not everyone's going to like me. I'm just going to be okay with some people thinking I'm obnoxious and not wanting to engage with me. That's fine. There are lots of people in the world. But there are other people who are going to be really into my message and want to be in my community and my weekly emails. Those are my people.

For me, getting out there and building a brand is about being helpful to people. It's more hurtful to me for someone to say that I was not helpful versus they didn't like me or my personality. I don't care if you don't like my personality, but I really pride myself on being helpful and adding value to people.

When I think about people I most admire, they have very strong personalities. They're not in the middle trying to please everybody. They are strong people, strong flavors, and have strong points of view. I asked myself, "Do I want to be for some people and not for others? Or do I want to be beige?" I don't want to be beige. It's also getting older and realizing that it doesn't matter what people think about you. I'm growing into my own skin.

LISA SONG SUTTON
Korean American, Former Miss Nevada, Entrepreneur, Investor

Lisa's journey challenges the myth of staying silent about our achievements. Raised in South Korea by an American military family, her confidence was instilled by her determined mother. Starting in law, Lisa later founded successful multimillion-dollar companies. In 2021, she became a General Partner of a $20M pre-seed venture capital fund, The Veteran Fund, supporting veteran and military-spouse-led businesses. Named a Top Ten Social Entrepreneur by Inc. Magazine, Lisa embraced public roles as Miss Nevada and a Congressional candidate for Nevada's 4th district, showcasing the importance of self-promotion and confidence.

Pageantry was not part of the plan growing up. But my mom was a former Miss Korea. In the fall of 2013, my mom called me and asked, "Are you competing for Miss Las Vegas?" I said, "I just started a business. I'm busy. What are you talking about?" She said, "You're getting ready to age out."

Back then, the age cutoff for Miss America was 24, Miss USA was 26, and Miss United States was 29. So I had one last chance to win a state title before aging out. And I guess you fall off a cliff if you're not married by 29.

To compete, I had to buckle down. I was racing against the clock. I hired a pageant coach. I was definitely the underdog. I was the shortest contestant. I was the oldest in the Miss Division. I had a lot of perceived strikes against me but still pulled out the win.

I think any time you take on a public endeavor, whether it's pageantry, whether it's politics, you're making a conscious choice to actively participate. You have to understand why you're doing this in the first place because it's not always going to be roses. Especially with Miss Nevada, my purpose was to connect with the community on a nonprofit level. I did nearly 500 community appearances during my time as Miss Las Vegas and Miss Nevada. I spent time volunteering in schools reading, visiting hospitals, and working with countless nonprofits.

That was eight years ago, and to this day, I still have tremendous relationships from that time period. I hear from kids who I met when they were in elementary school, and now they're going to high school. They're finding me on Instagram and telling me, "You came to my class when I was in fourth grade." The impact you can have on a kid, when you go to their school with this shiny crown to talk about education, college, and opening your own business plants seeds to dreams they may have never heard of. What a great platform, a great microphone to amplify a message. I think I gained the respect from the community for the work that I did.

Politics was also not in the plan. When I ran during the 2020 cycle, I felt very moved to run. Like many first-time candidates, I had this very altruistic view because I genuinely wanted to help the community. I genuinely felt that I was a better choice than the incumbent who I was running against.

This all came about by being a small business owner. I own some shipping stores, and one of them is outside of Nellis Air Force Base in North Las Vegas. When I opened up that store in 2018, I was attracted to the area because the rent was cheap. I found out that it was completely vacant on all sides. Walmart had pulled out of the area because of shoplifting and crime. There's a Reddit thread on this Walmart called Stab Mart. The community is low-income, predominantly African American, and there's nothing over there, no resources.

I was advised by Metro Police, "Please don't open up here, you're going to get robbed." But I'm hard-headed and optimistic. So I said, "No, I'm going to try this." We opened up a mailbox pack and ship store. The very first customers we had the day we opened were two Black ladies who lived in the apartments across the street. They were so happy to have a place to buy stamps. Without us, they would have needed to take a bus to the closest post office, which was 40 minutes away. To this day, we have not been robbed or vandalized. We have brought business into the area.

So that got my brain ticking, "How does this pocket exist in a city with so much abundance?" I learned that the congressman for the area lives in Virginia even though he's a Nevada congressman. That wasn't right. I called around telling people, "Someone needed to run against this guy." Everyone said, "Lisa, you should run." I said, "You know what? I'll do it."

It was the craziest 10 months of my life. It felt like starting a new business. During the campaign, we had tremendous support to raise donations from all 50 states. I raised the most in a primary election in Nevada. I was the first Korean American candidate. I was the first woman candidate under 40. I had national leadership come off the sidelines and endorse me. Similar to my time as Miss Nevada, I was out talking to people. I traveled the entire district I ran in talking to people.

I'm grateful that I ran. My parents were so proud of me. God works in mysterious ways. I'm used to being rewarded for my hard work, and I worked really, really hard. I lost the primary election in June of 2020. That was really hard. Then my dad was diagnosed with cancer, August of 2020. He passed away in October 2020. Had I won, I would have been full speed ahead to prepare for the November 2020 general election and not be able to be there for my dad. Things truly do work out the way that they're supposed to do. We think we're in control, but we're not.

RENATA SOTO

Latina, Founder and CEO, Mosaic Changemakers

Raised in Costa Rica, Renata was inspired by her grandmother's and mother's dedication to education and moved to the US at 21. Working at United Way, she defied the myth that we should stay silent about our work and accomplishments. Renata emphasizes the importance of speaking up, taking a seat at the table, and promoting our own work and others'.

Working at United Way in Nashville, I was one of the few people who spoke English with an accent. I questioned, "Do I really belong here?" I was fortunate to work with two women at United Way who were supportive and mentored me. With their encouragement, I didn't shrink when maybe I would have.

I understood that I was one of the first Latinos for some people to interact with professionally. I understood the danger of being seen as a representative of an entire community. I also understood that it would be a missed opportunity for me not to be at the table, and I wish more people like me had it.

I decided to make sure that people understood that I didn't represent the whole community. I also decided to bring more people along. I saw that I had a great responsibility to make sure that my one voice counts when I'm at the table. Also to be unapologetic that I can be here because I have something to say, and I have something to offer. So I never shied away from being the spokesperson.

I have loved that in the last few years, I have not been the one speaking about education and Latinos. We have colleagues who are the experts and can offer their own experience, both personal and their work. We have spokespersons for many issues, and we are experts collectively. Growing and supporting other leaders is about uplifting our expertise and being more visible as a community of leaders of color. There's not one single story for any community. We are growing our leadership ranks on all levels, in organizations, in public institutions, in philanthropy, in business. Many more of us are occupying and owning that space and bringing other people along with us.

Born in Michoacán, Mexico, Viri grew up in a small town where she only had access to an elementary education. Her father decided to make the trek up north to America so that he could find better schools and opportunities for his four girls. The summer before starting middle school, Viri, her sisters and mother made the trip north to reunite with their father. During their trip, they almost got lost while walking in the desert. In America, Viri's undocumented status prevented her from going to college. Viri's experiences shaped her decision to found ImmSchools, a nonprofit that seeks to close the gap between immigration and education by working with schools to create safe and welcoming classrooms for immigrant and undocumented students. She counters the myth that we should not seek attention for ourselves and our goals. Viri shares how sharing her story changed her life.

I was so heartbroken and angry. I felt like I was being fed a lie. I thought that if I worked hard in school, got good grades, became president of the student council, did all of these things, I could get a chance to go to college. I could pursue my dreams that we risked our lives to achieve. But I was being told, "No, none of that mattered." I needed this nine-digit social security number, and I did not have it.

I spent three months asking myself, "What's the point? I can't do anything about this."

I am so grateful that I was surrounded by supportive people, including one mentor specifically, who asked me, "What are you going to do about it?" I responded, "You dare me? Of course, I want to do something about it. I'm going to take this on."

That question ignited something in me. I reached out to a newspaper in Dallas. I said, "This is my story. I want to go to college." They put my story on the front page. The headline was, "There are two young sisters seeking the opportunity to go to college, but they can't because they're undocumented." There were pictures of us holding a book. A random reader reached out to me and said, "I'm an undocumented student in college. You can go to college. Here's how, here's the law, here's the process, here's what to do."

This random person that read my story is the reason why I'm even here, why I have a college education. My education let me see the power that I had and that I was more than my immigration status.

Starting ImmSchools has given me the opportunity to uplift my own lived experience as a former undocumented student. It was unjust what I experienced as a student, especially not getting the support from educators that I deserved and needed. Through my work at ImmSchools, I help teachers and educators understand that there are so many students like myself in their classrooms and schools who need their support.

WHAT WOMEN OF COLOR CAN DO

I raise up my voice not so I can shout, but so that those without a voice can be heard. — Malala Yousafzai

PRACTICE 1. PREPARE TO PROMOTE OURSELVES.

Along with Asian and other cultural norms, many women have internalized sexist ideas and been socialized to be humble, to not brag. Remember that environments have been designed to keep us quiet. Holding our tongue keeps us from speaking up for what we believe in. We can be smarter about how to push ourselves forward. We need to overthrow some of that socialization and instead self-promote, speak up, take credit, be bold, and seize opportunities. Even though it's uncomfortable, self-promotion is important for our career. So here's how we do it.

STEP 1. Determine a personal brand.

What are we best known for? What do we want to be known for in our organization and field? This sets us up to be tapped for relevant assignments and stand out.

STEP 2. Create an elevator pitch.

It's story time! We love stories because they are powerful tools to engage people so they'll remember us. Once we are clear on our personal brand, develop an elevator pitch that explains how our previous skills connect with and add value to what we're doing now, as well as one or two key accomplishments. Make that connection explicit, rather than hoping others will figure it out on their own. Be concise, and don't repeat our resume.

Peggy Klaus, author of *BRAG! The Art of Tooting Your Own Horn Without Blowing It* shares a "Take-12" Self-Evaluation Questionnaire to create our elevator pitch. You can get the worksheet to fill out yourself in the Book Bonuses.

- What would we and others say are five of our personality pluses?
- What are the ten most interesting things we have done or that have happened to us?
- What do we do for a living and how did we end up doing it?

- What do we like/love about our current job/career?
- How does our job/career use our skills and talents, and what projects are we working on right now that best showcase them?
- What career successes are we most proud of having accomplished (from current position and past jobs)?
- What new skills have we learned in the last year?
- What obstacles have we overcome to get to where we are today, both professionally and personally?
- What essential lessons have we learned from some of our mistakes?
- What training/education have we completed and what did we gain from those experiences?
- What professional organizations are we associated with and in what ways (member, board, treasurer, or the like)?
- How do we spend our time outside of work, including hobbies, interests, sports, family, church, and volunteer activities?
- In what ways are we making a difference in the lives of others?

For example, to create my elevator pitch, I would consider my path in the military, corporate marketing, education leadership, and now executive coaching. How do these fit together? I might say, "Service is a core value of mine. After Stanford, I followed my father's footsteps and served in the US Air Force. This is where I developed strong leadership skills and was able to lead people very different from me. I decided I wanted to apply my leadership to the nonprofit sector and attended Northwestern's Kellogg School of Management to focus on marketing and nonprofit management. After graduation, I honed my leadership in the corporate world in brand management at Colgate-Palmolive. Then I applied my leadership and marketing skills to my passion of leading schools for young people of color. Today I'm a leadership coach and facilitator focused on women of color and diversity, equity, and inclusion."

An elevator pitch is helpful to share our unique talents and experiences and how valuable we are. It's not just job searches, it's also for when we meet new people at happy hours, parties, or on the soccer field watching our kid play. We never know when an opportunity might arise. Before going to an event, consider what might be most interesting to the people we will meet. Sometimes, I will emphasize my military background, that I was a military brat, or that the best leadership training I ever had was from the military. Or I'll emphasize my international relations background and talk about what it was like as the junior desk officer in the US Air Force for China, Taiwan, and the Philippines. Or I'll emphasize my passion for diversity, equity, and inclusion and women of color, and I'll talk about my podcast called *Women of Color Rise*. The key is to convey what makes us special in a thoughtful, targeted way.

Tooting our horns isn't about becoming something we aren't. It's about becoming more of who we are and sharing ourselves with pride and authenticity. It's about sharing our story to highlight our strengths and how we can bring value to others.

STEP 3. Self-promote strategically.

Begin tooting our horn within our organization. Start with our supervisor, mentors, and sponsors, and then include senior leaders. Rather than call attention to ourselves as an individual, connect our results to the organization's goals and needs. "I'm proud about my team and this quarter's results. Sales increased by 10 percent, on top of the previous 10 percent. This is the biggest gain in our organization this year." We can also make singing the praises of ourselves or others a team norm by setting aside a few minutes during team meetings to celebrate someone for their extraordinary contribution or completing an important project.

STEP 4. Go beyond the work environment.

Spread the word even wider in social media. By marketing ourselves and making ourselves visible, we set ourselves up to be seen as an expert in our field. A strong reputation can put us on the radar for exciting career opportunities. This includes publishing an article on LinkedIn, being interviewed on a podcast, and doing guest lectures on a topic.

PRACTICE 2. TOOT OUR HORN WITHOUT GETTING SHAMED.

How does a woman of color share her accomplishments without feeling like a braggart?

STRATEGY 1. SHARE STORIES.

Sharing stories is a natural way to share what we have done so that others can connect with us. People tend to remember stories more than our specific skills. So when a problem comes up that we have experience with, we can share a story of how we handled it and what we learned that could be helpful in this situation.

STRATEGY 2. ACKNOWLEDGE OUR TEAM.

Subtly self-promote by congratulating our team in front of senior leaders. By acknowledging our team, we present as a strong leader and at the same time give deserved praise and build loyalty from our team.

STRATEGY 3. AVOID BEING INTERRUPTED.

When we promote ourselves or speak up during meetings, maintain our power and ensure we are not interrupted. If we are interrupted, maintain a neutral expression, speak slightly louder, and gesture for the person to wait. If they continue to interrupt us, speak with them privately and share feedback.

STRATEGY 4. ADD VALUE.

Promote our expertise by adding value. For example, we can write an article for the company newsletter or volunteer to host a "best practice" lunch session on a project that could be helpful for others.

STRATEGY 5. ACCEPT COMPLIMENTS.

Finally, as we toot our horn, stop with the self-deprecating comments. When someone gives us a compliment, just say thanks. My favorite responses to a compliment used to be, "It really wasn't anything," or "You could have done it too." It was a way to move the spotlight away from me. But it undermined my contribution and wasn't necessary. One time, because of my "it wasn't anything" comment, I had a hard time requesting more staff on my team. Now, when I get a compliment for my team's performance, I respond with, "Our entire team worked incredibly hard to get the job done. I'm proud of our team and glad you see our hard work." When I get a compliment for my individual performance, I respond with a simple, "Thank you."

Explore the Book Bonuses for this chapter:

- Elevator Pitch Worksheet with "Take-12" Self-Evaluation Questionnaire from Peggy Klaus
- List of books for further reading
- Podcasts with full interviews of women leaders spotlighted in this chapter

MYTH FIVE
Women who negotiate are greedy

Growing up watching my parents' careers, I thought I should be grateful and loyal, just like them. My dad retired from the US Navy after 22 years, and my mom was a nurse at Kaiser Permanente for 38 years. They both were able to come to the US through the Immigration Act of 1965, which encouraged educated immigrants to fill a shortage of American workers in fields like engineering, medicine, and the military. My parents were part of this wave of immigrants and came to the US in 1972. Seemingly each week, they reminded my brother and me, "You're lucky to be born in America. You should be grateful for all the opportunities you have."

I ended up making more transitions than my parents. I began my career in the US Air Force, then changed to corporate, then to nonprofit, and then entrepreneurship. Throughout that time, I said yes to the first offers that were given to me, I never negotiated, I never asked for a raise or promotion. I assumed that my hard work would get the attention it deserved, and the company would take care of me.

I remember when I was hired to lead a 50-person team. It never dawned on me to negotiate. I happily signed my letter of agreement because I was grateful to find a role that I was passionate about. I thought, "It's not about the money. To focus on money and myself is selfish. It's about the mission."

It wasn't until later that I realized my mistake. A peer asked me how I was going to approach salary negotiations with my team. I responded, "We never negotiate. The salary is the salary. It's standard for everyone." She shook her head, "C'mon. That's what they say, but it's rarely true. I always negotiate." That's when I found out she was making 25 percent more than me—with less experience.

Now with 25 years of work experience under my belt, I see how that mentality held me and other women of color back. We often don't negotiate, say no, or advocate for ourselves. Thank goodness for my mentor who said, "Even though you don't think you're ready, you are. Trust me." He helped me see that I could go for a big role.

I learned that no matter how uncomfortable I felt, I needed to train myself to ask for what I want. I remember the first time I did it. I knew when salary decisions would be shared with employees. Then I made sure to have a conversation with my manager a few months beforehand where I shared my accomplishments and results. I created a bullet list of my impact to the organization pointing to quantitative measurements such as dollars earned and saved. I made sure to include my strategic projects, organizational impact, strong performance reviews, and results that showcased my contribution to the bottom line. I was also explicit that I believed my impact set me up for a salary increase. I communicated my impact not just with my boss but my boss's boss and as many senior leaders as I could. Did it feel uncomfortable? Oh, hell yes. But it's much better to have many people at the decision-making table who know us and will champion us.

Based on this experience, I learned that if I want the title, salary, promotion, or position, I need to ask for it. They might say no now, but it puts me on the radar for future opportunities. It also sets me up to get feedback and understand what I specifically need to do to address concerns. I use this information to plan and prepare for a more senior position.

THE MYTH

Women who negotiate are greedy. Women of color should be grateful for what we have. Pushing for more money or recognition is selfish. We should accept what is offered and not negotiate. It's not worth hurting our boss' impression of us. It's more important that we are polite, reserved, and selfless, not aggressive or outspoken. We need to be focused on others and not ourselves. If we work hard and do our work well, we will get our fair share. Our managers will look out for us and make sure that we are getting what we deserve.

WHICH OF THESE EXPERIENCES RESONATE WITH YOU?

- ☐ It has been over a year since you got, or asked for, a raise or promotion.
- ☐ You don't tend to negotiate or if you do, it feels icky.
- ☐ You ask for what you think you can get instead of what you really want.
- ☐ You don't take initiative to tell others what you want and need. This could include a specific project that will help your career, a raise, more vacation days, or professional development.
- ☐ You work later than anyone else. You meet or beat every deadline. But when there's an opening higher up the career ladder, you are passed over for someone who achieves less than you do.

> ☐ You have been at a job for a long time with strong performance but get passed over for promotion by people who have been at the company for less time with weaker performance.

THE REALITY

Asking for what we want is not about being greedy but about advocating for ourselves and achieving a fair outcome. Women who negotiate effectively are not asking for more than they deserve. They are standing up for their worth. Gender stereotypes unfairly paint women who assert themselves as pushy. In truth, negotiating is necessary for success at work and in life. Women of color can feel empowered to negotiate for what we deserve without fear of being labeled as greedy or selfish.

WHY WOMEN DON'T ASK

A friend who is a corporate recruiter told me that throughout her 15 years of recruiting, she's noticed a trend. When she recruits Black and Latinx candidates, they tend to accept the first offer, while White candidates with less experience tend to negotiate, which gets them salaries of 20 percent more.

This salary gap widens for women of color. For every dollar that White men earn, White women earn 79 cents, Black women earn 64 cents, and Latinas earn 57 cents. Structural racism and sexism are obviously a big part of these depressingly persistent statistics. Another reason is that women are less likely to negotiate their salary and thus get paid less. Why?

For one thing, negotiation sets women up to be in conflict, something we are raised to avoid. Women also have lower expectations about our salaries. We are socialized to feel grateful for whatever we get. Otta, a job search platform with one million users in 2023, found that women of color set minimum salary requirements 40 percent lower than those of White men, while White women's requirements were 25 percent lower than those of White men. These disparities were evident across every role and every level of experience. Negin Toosi, professor at California State University, East Bay, and diversity expert commented on Otta's statistics as "disheartening but not surprising. ... This is really about who has status in this society, whose work is valued more, and who gets to ask for a larger salary without having to deal with backlash. It's not about something inherent to women or people of color, but how they are treated."

Studies back up the real possibility of backlash. In Linda Babcock's book, *Women Don't Ask: The High Cost of Avoiding Negotiation and Positive Strategies for Change*, research shows that when women push for higher pay, people are less likely to want to work with us. For men, there is less of an effect. That said, asking outweighs possible backlash. If we don't ask, we don't risk getting rejected, but we also won't get what we want. One study found that 36 percent of women asked for a raise and of those, 74 percent were successful. We don't make any of the shots we don't take.

When we compare men and women and their approaches to negotiation, we see why there is such a big wage gap. One study of graduating MBA students found that half of the men had negotiated their job offers as compared to only one-eighth of the women. Because of this and the other factors we've discussed in this book, men were paid 7.6 percent higher on average than women. Tory Johnson, CEO of Women for Hire said, "Men are four times more likely than women to negotiate the first offer." One study found that the impact of negotiating less over the course of a woman's career leaves up to a million dollars on the table.

To compound matters, women are more likely to wait for or pass on opportunities, resulting in longer tenure in jobs. An internal report from Hewlett-Packard found that women tend to pass on opportunities if they don't have 100 percent of the skills necessary, while men tend to apply if they only have 60 percent.

Research shows that this applies to going for a CEO job as well. In one research study for women in the construction industry, 41 percent of the male respondents reported knowing very early on in their careers that they wanted to achieve a CEO spot compared to only 23 percent of women.

So not only are men applying for more promotions and higher-level jobs than women, the system is biased so that men are getting these promotions and top jobs more quickly and easily than women too. Why? Dr. Cecilia L. Ridgeway, a gender researcher at Stanford University, found that while men are not better at their jobs than women, they are seen as safer bets and more competent than women. So if there is a position at a company, and a male and female compete, the male has better odds. To add to that, men get a shot at the top spot earlier in their careers than women. If a woman does get a shot at the top spot, she is more than twice as likely as a man to not be promoted from within and instead hired from outside of the company.

Here, women of color share their experiences and advice about negotiation.

MELISSA NG GOLDNER
Chinese American, Partner at Prophet Consulting

Melissa addresses the myth that we should not negotiate. She shares how she was able to negotiate for what she wanted and land a leadership role, despite her cultural upbringing to be loyal and content with what she had.

When I was at my last company, I got a promotion. But my mentor told me, "You didn't get a promotion. You've got a title to do more work with the cost of inflation. Go back to your boss and ask for more money." I told my mentor, "No way! As an Asian woman who grew up with my cultural norms and also as a recovering people pleaser, these are not discussions that you have. You don't negotiate, you accept what is given to you." But my mentor gave me the accountability to have that discussion.

I remember it very well. I was sweating and felt like I was going to faint or throw up. But I said to my boss, "This isn't a promotion. This is more work for the cost of inflation." At the time, they said that there wasn't anything they could do about it. But then I ended up getting paid the highest bonus. That made me realize that if you don't ask for it, you're not going to get it.

So fast forward, and I was recruited by Google and Prophet Consulting. Prophet Consulting offered me a partner level position. It felt really scary and different from what I was currently doing. I had recently given birth to my daughter, Emily, and I wanted to lead by example and reach for the stars. In my gut, I believed that people learn by putting themselves out there even though they might be uncomfortable or afraid.

In negotiating this Prophet offer, I made the ask that doubled my salary. I also made the ask for Prophet to pay for the stock that was given to me in my last company. The last thing I asked for was for the North America President to be my executive sponsor. She happens to be an Asian woman, the first Asian woman in my entire career of seven companies whom I've seen in an executive leadership position. I said to the executive recruiter, "This is a wonderful offer. Thank you so much. But I would like this woman, the president, to be my executive sponsor." He responded, "We could try. But most likely it's not going to cut it." I told him, "If you could get me a yes in writing, I will put pen to paper on the offer." Thirty minutes later, I got the offer with her as my executive sponsor.

KIANTI BROWN WHITNEY
Black, Vice President of Marketing and Communications at the Relay Graduate School of Education

Dispelling the myth that negotiating makes us greedy, Kianti shares what two mediocre White college mates taught her.

It's a faux pas particularly for families of color to talk about money. I think that's because money is a source of shame. I didn't grow up talking about it at all. One myth I've believed and perpetuated is you take what you're given. This can be very damaging, especially as women of color who go into the workforce. In negotiating salary, there is a starting number. That number is certainly not the cap, and there's a lot of room for negotiation. But I wasn't taught that. It was something that I learned over time.

I think a lot of White people know this. I remember in undergrad when I overheard this conversation with two White dudes whom I had classes with. They were mediocre at best. They were talking about the salary they were offered and how they were asking for more. Before I heard this conversation, I had no idea you could ask for more.

I thought to myself, "If they can get more money, then why not me too? I'm bright, I'm smart, I'm intelligent. I'm a quick study. There's no reason I can't."

So when I got my first job offer, I knew to ask for more money and said, "I deserve 10 percent more." What's interesting is that I was told no. They said, "This is the number in advertising. Nobody gets paid more money than this." I held my ground and said, "I'll just find something else. Don't worry about it. This is my number. I'm not moving." And guess what? They matched my number. That gave me the confidence to keep negotiating successfully throughout my career.

Now, do I always hit the number that I want? No. But I've learned over time to ask for more than I actually want to get, and then usually we meet somewhere in the middle.

CAROLINE CENIZA-LEVINE

Filipina American, Founder, Dream Career Club

Caroline exposes the myths about negotiating. As a negotiation expert, she shares the necessity of negotiation and tips on how women of color can get the salary they deserve.

I don't have rose-colored glasses. Racial discrimination, age discrimination, and gender discrimination happen. But I will tell you what has served me really well: Do the best that you can. Then when you get to the top, help other people.

When I'm in a negotiation, I don't think, "I'm a woman in a negotiation." I think, "Okay, what do I need to do? What is the other person saying? How can I work off of that?" I don't assume that I'm in a tougher position because I'm a woman or older or Filipina.

I've always gone into situations thinking, "Hmm, Why not me?" I just assume that it will be okay. This isn't to diminish things like the double bind, which is to say that if a man negotiates hard or asks for what he wants, he's being assertive, and that's a good quality. But if a woman does it, she's being bossy. If a person of color does it, they have to be careful not to come across as angry or asking too much. At the end of the day, people hire people, people promote people. It is about relationships that we develop, and we have to do the best we can.

As a woman of color, the key is to think of negotiation as not a one-time event, but actually a process. Then you will be ahead of the game. Most people think that negotiation is sitting at a table across from the other person talking about the job offer, the raise, or whatever it is that they're negotiating. In reality, negotiation is a process that starts before you get to the table. It starts with your preparation, the other person's preparation, and thinking about what they want. Sitting down at the table is just one part of that. After you sit down at the table, you follow up with that person, and you're continuing the conversation. It's a lot of little conversations. It's a lot of action in between. There are a lot of things that you do on your own well before you talk to anybody. So if you can think of it as a longer game than right now, you can take some of the anxiety off.

There are many levers you can pull, many factors you can influence. You don't have one chance and that's it. So think of it as a process and prepare. When I coach people on their negotiation, sometimes *they say they're not 100 percent clear on what they want. They'll say, "I'll know when I see it." Or they think of a job offer as one thing, when a job offer is dozens of things. Compensation isn't just salary. It includes growth, sign-on bonus, profit-sharing, equity, title, vacation, etc. Then there is your work environment, your resources, and your relationships with other people. There are so many things to negotiate. You have to be really clear. That's all part of the preparation.*

Finally, remember that the reason you're negotiating is because you want to work together. You really do want to make a deal. They're there for that reason too. So you start from a place of agreement. I think people hear the word negotiation, and they think hostile and conflict. That's actually not true because if you really didn't want to work together, you would just not negotiate. Both of you are looking to build longer-term genuine relationships.

MICHELLE PALMER
African American, Executive Director of Breakthrough Greater Philadelphia

Growing up with a single mom in Philadelphia, Michelle felt imposter syndrome and didn't feel confident in herself. Michelle was the first person in her family to attend college. After graduating from Temple University, Michelle tried several different jobs. She found her fit in a development role at a nonprofit. Throughout her journey, Michelle realized that key to being the leader she wanted to be was believing in herself. She discredits the myth that asking for more means we are greedy. Michelle shares that asking for more is connected to her own confidence in herself.

Negotiation has not always come easy. For me, it came when I started to believe in myself and to believe in my self-worth. I deserve to have a seat at the table. When I was younger, I had impostor syndrome. I had worked in many nonprofits over the years on the fundraising side and questioned, "Who wants to give to a Black woman?" But at the end of the day, I deserve to have a seat at the table just like anyone else.

I now see that negotiations are really just conversations. I believe in myself, no one is better than me. We're all human beings. I deserve to ask and challenge something if I feel like it's necessary. The biggest part of negotiation is believing in yourself. Then go for it. Base your argument on why this would or would not work. For salary negotiations, I write down every single thing of why I feel like I deserve it. I include the new things that I've implemented and the time and the values and results that I've had. Sometimes you win, sometimes you lose. But if you don't go for it, then you'll never know.

Just recently with a donor, there was a negotiation that was going on back and forth. I've always been taught that the donor is right; you want to make your donors happy. I had to go back and challenge her, "We need to talk about this some more." She was amenable to talk, but I didn't win. You don't always win with negotiations. But I gave it a try. You have to be willing to take a risk, be willing to ask. Hopefully it's a yes. But if you don't believe in yourself and why you're asking and put yourself out there to ask, then it will never happen.

The donor ended up saying no, but she offered something else that was valuable. If I didn't make that call, I wouldn't have gotten that second win.

SAU-FONG AU

Asian American, Director of Brooklyn College Women's Center

Sau-fong was born in Hong Kong and went to college at the Chinese University of Hong Kong. She followed her boyfriend to the US and for the first time felt like she did not belong and something was wrong with her. Sau-fong has led Brooklyn College's Women's Center for 23 years and has noticed that many women and particularly women of color share this lack of self-worth, which leads us to not ask for what we deserve. Sau-fong debunks the myth that negotiating is greedy. She shares practical tips to ask for what we deserve.

Coming from Hong Kong, a very homogenous society, to the US was a cultural shock. It was the first time I thought about myself as a Chinese woman. When I was in America, I heard, "You're not American." That is code for not being White. It changed the way that I see myself and see the world. My identity got stripped away.

In my 20+ year career, I have noticed for women of color, especially first generation college students, college is often perceived as something you're not supposed to have, and you should feel grateful or lucky. This feeling makes it virtually impossible to ask for more. Yet the reality for women of color is that we don't have as much social capital compared to our White counterparts in the upper middle class. These people got exposed to college and professional life, how to dress, when to raise your hand, and all those nuances never experienced by women of color.

Women of color also feel inadequate. Building self-esteem takes years, and destroying self-esteem only takes one incident. When a woman of color lacks self-worth and doesn't feel like she belongs to a place, then the only way that she feels she can occupy a space is if she is nice. As a woman, if we share our perspectives, we are considered to be aggressive or catty. Or if we are introspective, we are considered to be submissive or passive.

To counter this, we need to push the boundaries. We need to say, "I'm entitled to be here and the one slice of pie that they offer me is not enough. I can have the pie, I can have the dough to make the pie, I can have the ingredients to make my own pie."

We need to remind ourselves not to personalize the win or the loss. Remember that if you ask, there is nothing to lose. We won this Asian Pacific Islander grant for Brooklyn College. I put a lot of work into it. But so did my collaborator. At the end of the day, it's not just our ideas. They are from our colleagues, our students, and people who have done research on and off campus nationwide, globally.

Women often put our values into the work. We think that if we care, we can't make money too. But if I hire a babysitter to take care of my kid, I should pay her. Same with us. We provide a service and should get paid. We lack social capital and don't know that we should ask or negotiate salary. When we ask, we only ask for $10,000 when there is a $50,000 pay gap. Pay transparency is important so that it is more equitable for women and people of color.

WHAT WOMEN OF COLOR CAN DO

One woman I coach told me when we first met that she had struggled for years trying to get promoted. She said, "I've done everything I was told to do. I'm organized and hardworking. This is what worked when I was at school, and I got straight A's!"

We've heard the adage, "What got you here won't get you there." She and I discussed how these same behaviors in school could hold us back in our careers. For women of color to succeed, we need to release limiting beliefs, be more assertive, and advocate for ourselves. She and I worked together to release her belief that it was her manager's job to guide her career and promote her accomplishments. Instead, she learned to share her accomplishments in a way that felt authentic to her—by talking about her team and how proud she was of their results. She also learned that she needed to directly ask for what she wanted—a promotion and raise. A year later, she got both!

Here are steps to help us ask for what we want—whether it's in our existing organization or in a new organization.

STEP 1. SPOT OPPORTUNITIES TO NEGOTIATE AND STRETCH.

FOR ASKS IN OUR EXISTING ORGANIZATION OR AT A NEW JOB:

MAKE NEGOTIATION OUR DEFAULT MODE. Negotiation applies whether we are starting a new job or asking for a raise, promotion, additional resources, or more time off. We need to specifically ask for it. Don't rule out the possibility that our organization and boss are able to get us what we want. Managers don't know, unless we tell them, about our desire to move into a more senior role, be considered for an early promotion, or pursue a specific career path. Asking for what we want shows self-confidence and is also a win for the organization. The more invested in our job we are, the more likely we are to do better work and stay.

EMBRACE STRETCH ROLES. Women feel that they need to meet every requirement of a job before they apply, while men will apply even if they have only a third of the requirements. But the best opportunities are the ones where we have 60 percent of the skills. We might not even need 60 percent. According to a 2018 TalentWorks study, we're just as likely to get an interview by meeting at least 50 percent of the job requirements as meeting 90 percent of them; for women, once we meet 40 percent of job requirements, interview chances are about the same if we met a higher percentage of job requirements. The rest we can learn on the job. If the position requires 10 years of experience and we have seven, consider applying anyway. If we're not sure—maybe we feel we don't have the skills or are not qualified, raise our hand. Women don't get promoted because they don't even put themselves in the running. While there's a chance we will be rejected, not raising our hand means a 100 percent chance of not getting the opportunity.

FOR ASKS IN OUR EXISTING ORGANIZATION:

DON'T WAIT TO ASK. Claire Wasserman, author of *Ladies Get Paid: The Ultimate Guide to Breaking Barriers, Owning Your Worth, and Taking Command of Your Career*, says that she sees women waiting for the right moment. But waiting is probably the biggest pitfall she sees. Ask now because "no" isn't a one and done. It's an ongoing conversation.

STEP 2. GET OUR MINDSET READY.

FOR ASKS IN OUR EXISTING ORGANIZATION OR AT A NEW JOB:

BE AWARE OF OUR THOUGHTS. If negotiation feels uncomfortable, maybe even scary, we're not alone. For me, my "You're not good enough" demon raises its ugly head and says, "You're going to get rejected. It's much safer not to try." Or "You're greedy! Be happy with what you've got."

Instead of paying attention to the demon, pay attention to mindsets that serve us. Be positive that this could be a win-win for both sides. Do not assume that our request will be met with a "no." We've got to know our worth and ask for what we deserve.

LEVERAGE OUR EXISTING SKILLS. If we are worried about not being a good negotiator or that men are better at negotiating than women, know that women have skills that can help us to negotiate better than men. How? Recognize the skills we already have, such as relationship building and finding common ground. Use these existing skills to our advantage for negotiation.

STEP 3. RESEARCH.

FOR ASKS IN OUR EXISTING ORGANIZATION OR AT A NEW JOB:

SHARE WITH FRIENDS. In addition to conducting market research using reputable sources online for salary information, speak with friends too. Stop talking about money in vague terms. While it may feel like a "stop and do not pass go" topic, sharing this information is a way to help each other. We'll uncover whether our friends are being underpaid, and then we can role play together to encourage each other to advocate for ourselves for a raise.

FIGURE OUT WHAT WE WANT BEYOND MONEY. Now that we have our market research, figure out what we want. This goes beyond salary. While it's tempting to focus on just salary, that leaves a lot of other options off the table. Caroline Ceniza-Levine advises, "Think of ten things you want—maybe a specific title, the ability to do freelance work outside the company, the flexibility to work from home, stock options, training, more vacation, a one-time bonus, an assistant, a later start date, or an office. Prioritize these and come up with different combinations that would work for you. For example, I am willing to take a lower salary if I am able to work from home 3 days per week and get a better title."

Consider asking for funds for professional development. When we look at men and White women, they spend thousands of dollars on a career coach, C-Suite networking group, and retreats. Why? Because these are ways to speed-track our career. Talk to any senior leader, and I bet that many of them have an executive coach. So why not you?

REFLECT ON WHAT THE ORGANIZATION WANTS. Linda Babcock, coauthor of *Ask for It: How Women Can Use the Power of Negotiation to Get What They Really Want*, emphasizes that it's just as important to consider what the organization wants. If we are a current employee, the company is likely highly motivated to do what they need to do to keep us. Finding a new person takes time and costs, on average, about two months and $4,000.

FOR ASKS AT A NEW JOB:

KNOW OUR FLOOR AND STRENGTHEN OUR BATNA: If we are considering a job, be clear about the minimum salary, title, and conditions we would need. In addition, strengthen our BATNA (Best Alternative to a Negotiated Agreement). It's a fancy word that many MBAs learn in business school that means our walkaway point. The key to negotiating is to strengthen our safety, our alternative if we don't get what we want from this negotiation. So if we already have an offer on the table from Company 1, we can negotiate with Company 2 knowing that we already have a fallback.

GET CLEAR ON WHAT ACTIONS TO TAKE. If we are looking to make a move in our current organization, instead of making assumptions, ask decision makers directly about what we can do to set us up for success. For example, if we want a promotion, we could ask our boss, "Since I've been performing well in this job for the past years, what actions can I take to set myself up for promotion?" Our goal is to get specific actions to prepare for advancement and also buy-in. Ensure that our action steps will lead to what we want. Ask our manager, "If I pursue this stretch assignment, can you kindly share—what are the chances that I'll be promoted?" This also helps to get commitment from our boss.

KNOW WHY THE ROLE DESERVES MORE MONEY OR A NEW TITLE. If we are seeking more money or a new title at our current organization, be prepared to justify why. Look at the job or promotion and why it calls for a higher pay or title. Does it have a new project that is critical for the company or more responsibility? Conduct market research to learn what others with similar jobs get paid, the salary range, and how much experience we have compared to others in similar positions. Look at the job posting, ask HR, and also get introduced to people who have similar positions through our network. Talk to people who have made the transition we want to make—how did they do it, and what tips can they share?

STEP 4. CREATE A WIN-WIN.

FOR ASKS IN OUR EXISTING ORGANIZATION:

CRAFT A WIN-WIN STORY. Develop a story about how this is good for us and the company. Understand our contributions, skills, strengths, and years of experience. How do we personally help the team and organization do better? What are our past achievements and track record that provide evidence for this job, raise, or promotion?

For example, "I'm eager to take on this new project with higher level responsibilities, but I'd like to discuss my compensation so that it's aligned to market value. My current title and salary no longer reflect the work I'm doing. The market research I've done with similar positions shows that the work is more of a senior level job. What do you think?"

FOR ASKS IN OUR EXISTING ORGANIZATION OR AT A NEW JOB:

GET AROUND THE DOUBLE BIND OF NEGOTIATING. How do we get around the double bind where people don't like when women ask for what they want? First, share why negotiating makes sense; for example, it's part of the skill set they are hiring. In her book *Lean In: Women, Work, and the Will to Lead*, Sheryl Sandberg, former COO of Facebook, describes how she successfully negotiated her salary. She told Facebook, "Of course you realize that you're hiring me to run your deal team, so you want me to be a good negotiator."

We also want to show that we care about organizational relationships and are on the same team. Sandberg emphasized this when she said to Facebook, "This is the only time you and I will ever be on opposite sides of the table." Research shows that this strategy of going for what you want personally while showing you care about the organization works. Yes, it is not fair that women have to work so hard to negotiate and get what we deserve, but the goal here is to share practices that can help us get what we want.

STEP 5. PRACTICE AND EXECUTE WITH CONFIDENCE.

FOR ASKS IN OUR EXISTING ORGANIZATION OR AT A NEW JOB:

PRACTICE. Practice the conversation with friends who can give us feedback so that when we have our conversation we feel ready.

EMBRACE SILENCE. During the negotiation, embrace silence when necessary. After our request and their response, count to six to collect our thoughts before speaking again.

FOR ASKS IN OUR EXISTING ORGANIZATION:

HAVE PRE-CONVERSATIONS TO SET UP THE NEGOTIATION. If we are currently employed with a company, pre-conversations are helpful before we make our ask. This includes being explicit about what we want (more responsibility, a promotion, an opportunity to speak publicly, etc.). We can't assume that they know what we want for our career or expect them to plan our future promotion if we haven't explicitly told them that we want more. They may take our silence as being satisfied with the status quo. As women, it's not easy to be so direct and advocate for ourselves, but we've got to speak up to get what we want.

This also includes having a performance discussion where we have prepared our key accomplishments for the past year, especially where we have directly affected the business (e.g., increasing revenue or saving costs). We can then naturally shift the discussion to advocate for what we want (a promotion, salary increase).

OPEN WITH OUR COMMITMENT. Open the conversation with our investment in the organization and how we want to continue to grow and contribute with the organization. But to continue to work at our highest level, we will need to get paid so that it reflects the work we're doing.

STEP 6. IF WE DON'T SUCCEED, TRY AGAIN.

FOR ASKS IN OUR EXISTING ORGANIZATION:

EMBRACE FEEDBACK. If we make a request for a promotion and are told no, we still gain feedback. Get specific action steps so that we know what we need to do to set ourselves up for promotion or the next opportunity.

CLARIFY WHAT GAPS YOU NEED TO FILL. Get clear about what projects, senior leadership visibility, results, and targets we need to hit to be promoted. Be explicit and ask for their guidance, "To help me get promoted next year, I'm hearing from you that I need strategic projects and to be more visible to senior leaders. Can you help me identify projects that I can take on?"

STEP 7. IF NEEDED, CONSIDER AN EXIT.

FOR ASKS IN OUR EXISTING ORGANIZATION:

ASSESS FIT. If we are at an existing organization, consider whether the organization is the right fit. How do we know when it is time to leave?

In his book *When*, Daniel Pink says that if we answer two or more of these with a no, it could be time to go:

- Do we want to be in this job on our next work anniversary? Anniversaries are reflection points; if the job is not the right fit, employees tend to leave.

- Is our current job challenging? Does it give us autonomy so that we, not someone else, are able to decide how we get the work done? If not, maybe get out.
- Does our boss support us, take responsibility instead of blaming others, show humor instead of a raging temper, and not micromanage? If not, consider a move.
- Are we outside the three- to five-year salary bump window? One of the best ways to boost our pay is to switch organizations, specifically three to five years after you've started. If we're beyond this window, it might be a good time to leave.
- Does our daily work align with our long-term goals? Research says that we're happier if this is true. If these don't align, it could be time to head out.

In addition, consider these following questions:

- Are we staying out of love or obligation?
- Do we feel undervalued and underappreciated by our company despite efforts to make the job more fulfilling?
- Are we able to thrive in the organization's culture? Are we values aligned? Are we able to dress, behave, and lead in a way that maintains our self-respect?
- Do we see people like ourselves in leadership or just in support roles?
- Is the work culture toxic and resistant to change?
- Do we feel that our progress or potential within the company is limited?
- Are we not being recognized for our value and contributions through promotions or highly visible projects?
- Are we not tapped for opportunities, both inside and outside the company, such as representing the company at public forums, recruiting events, or joining special projects teams?

CONSIDER THE COSTS. It might be tempting to hold on for loyalty's sake. We might feel we've already put in so many years and don't want to start over. But consider the cost of staying, the time we are losing toward our dream, the skills we are not building, and the raise we are losing out on. Consider whether we have been there longer than others in the job.

If we are in a toxic environment, there are real costs to our mental health, performance, and commitment. If we decide to stay, we must protect and distance ourselves from toxic people. Avoid mirroring the toxic behavior. Release stress, find ways to relax, and take time to heal.

There is no shame in quitting a job. It takes courage to stand up for ourselves. If we do end up changing jobs, look for a role, team, and culture that fits with our values, goals, skills, and talents. It's not just good for us, it's good for the world.

BOOK BONUSES

Explore the Book Bonuses for this chapter:

- List of books for further reading
- Podcasts with full interviews of women leaders spotlighted in this chapter

MYTH SIX

Networking is an exhausting and fake way to make connections

I was getting fantastic performance reviews, going over and beyond, and working hard, but I wouldn't get the raise, promotion, or recognition. I noticed this happened over and over again. I didn't know why. More hours? Something else? I finally asked for help from a mentor.

My mentor told me, "You need to get on the right project and know the right people. They need to know about all the value you are contributing to the organization so that someone with influence can speak up for you for the promotion. You need to get on strategic projects that are cross-functional and are important to the company. You need to build relationships with high-status people in the company or people who are connected to the top leaders in the company and who are willing to advocate for you. You need to make time to build relationships."

I thanked him for his advice but groaned inwardly. I hated networking and the superficial conversations. Plus asking for help seemed weak. Furthermore, I was a new mom. Where would I find the time?

Before I threw in the towel on networking, I reflected on times in my career when I had mentors and sponsors. The first one in my career was Colonel Schiefer, who I met when I was a student at Stanford. He invited me to do an internship on his team in San Antonio, Texas. I thought, "Why would I spend my summer working for this guy in Texas?" Then he made an enticing offer, "The Air Force will pay for everything. Just come down, and check us out. Worst-case scenario, if you don't want to join our team after graduation, we have the Air Force Personnel Headquarters here. You can tell them wherever you want to go in the world that has an American Air Force Base, and if they have an opening, you can go." I thought, "That changes things. Worst case, I'll ask to go to Hawaii."

When I showed up in San Antonio, I met Colonel Schiefer and was surprised to find someone who was soft-spoken and informal, sharing stories about his girlfriend and how much he adored her, "She's smarter than me and faster than me." (She had a PhD and was a marathon runner.)

That summer I learned about computer programming, personnel policy, and how barbecue was a key part of Texan culture. But the biggest lesson I learned was how leadership matters. People loved working for Colonel Schiefer, so much that they told me, "I don't care what job I'd have, as long as I worked for Colonel Schiefer. I would mop floors for him."

Instead of taking an assignment in Hawaii, I decided to start my Air Force career in San Antonio working for Colonel Schiefer. Although I didn't know it at the time, he would be my first sponsor. He was the first person to ask me, "What is your dream job?" When I told him that I wanted to work in Asia in international relations, he brought me to the attention of senior leaders with this introduction, "If you know of any roles in Asia for Analiza, please consider her. She's smart and will do a top-notch job, just as she's done on my team." When a role opened up, he was willing to release me to a role in Guam focused on China, Taiwan, and the Philippines—even though it meant having an empty seat on his team. Through this new role, I had the opportunity to do a one-month language immersion in Taiwan and then later a three-month language immersion in China. I also got to work with some of the most senior military officers from countries all over Asia on top-secret projects.

Colonel Schiefer continued to be a part of my life, writing me recommendations for business school and giving me advice about my career. I got to know him as a person, as well, and learned about his son and later his grandson, and his love of Native American pottery and hiking deep into the backcountry in Utah. I even invited him to my wedding, and during my honeymoon, my husband and I visited him at his home in Arkansas.

Mentors and sponsors like Colonel Schiefer gave me many opportunities in my career. They introduced me to their personal network, opened doors to roles I did not have access to, and put their reputations on the line to advocate for me.

This realization convinced me. I needed to learn how to network—and was committed to do it authentically as myself.

THE MYTH

We're so busy with projects and taking care of our families that the idea of networking seems like more work on top of our already towering workload. We don't need a job right now, so why waste time with networking when it's not clear what we would gain. Plus, it feels icky and gross. There are few mentors or sponsors who look like us. It's exhausting to have to wear a mask to have fake conversations with people who are not "our people."

WHICH OF THESE EXPERIENCES RESONATE WITH YOU?

☐ You do not have a list of mentors and sponsors who you deliberately reach out to and spend time with on a regular basis.

☐ You are not part of a networking group.

☐ You would rather have your teeth cleaned than attend a networking event.

☐ You don't have a clear strategy about how to strengthen your network, where to network, and who to network with.

☐ You don't regularly keep in touch with your network or add value to your network.

☐ You do not regularly and proactively seek help from your network.

THE REALITY

We can get a performance review that says we "walk on water and talk to God on Tuesdays." But no matter how strong our work results, a promotion is not guaranteed. Companies are limited by the number of leadership roles and salary budgets, so not everyone with stellar performance will get promoted.

If it feels foreign to network, we are not alone. The American identity relies on self-reliance. Yet no one succeeds on their own; success is collective. When we network, we are building a professional family where we all help each other be successful. We share information, opportunities, feedback, and support.

WHY NETWORKING MAY NOT SEEM NATURAL

Why do men often excel more in networking compared to women? It starts in childhood: girls are taught to nurture relationships where we help each other, while boys are raised to view relationships as transactional and are less likely to feel they are using each other. As adults, these tendencies persist. Women often focus on building supportive relationships within their peer group (same job or same level), while men use networks strategically and interact with other men in higher positions. Women underestimate the importance of networking, viewing it as a distraction from family, whereas men see it as a crucial part of their job. Men also engage in shared activities like golf, providing unique networking opportunities that women might not have. Additionally, women hesitate to ask for connections without being able to reciprocate, while men expect their networks to support them, seeing relationships as opportunities rather than taking advantage of anyone.

These differences can hinder women from developing the broad and strategic networks needed for career advancement. Inside organizations, women miss chances to socialize our ideas, gain champions, stretch our skills, or get promoted. Outside organizations, we miss opportunities for new roles. People aren't hired because they work hard. People get hired because the decision maker has gotten to know the person, feels confident that they'll do a good job and fit into the organization's culture, and trusts and likes them.

THE IMPORTANCE OF MENTORS
AND SPONSORS

When building our network, we want to align ourselves with the right people, including mentors and sponsors, which are not the same thing. Mentors tend to be one to two levels above us. They develop and support us and have confidential discussions on issues we are facing. They don't tend to actively propel our career vision. This is the role of sponsors. Sponsors are ideally two levels above us and go out of their way to advocate for our promotion. They understand how our role fits into the organization, champion visibility, and introduce us to high-level contacts. Research shows that those with sponsors are 23 percent more likely to be promoted than those without sponsors.

With this in mind, we can see why it's concerning that women are over-mentored and under-sponsored relative to men, with men 45 percent more likely to have a sponsor than women across industry sectors. Silvia Ann Hewlett, author of *Forget a Mentor, Find a Sponsor*, found that, "Women on average have three times as many mentors as men—but men have twice as many sponsors." Being sponsored matters not just with promotions but across all dimensions of career advancement. Sponsors like Colonel Schiefer open doors, give feedback, and advocate for and promote women of color in ways where mentoring falls short. Sponsored women are more likely to ask for a raise (38 percent sponsored vs 30 percent unsponsored) and advance in their careers (68 percent of sponsored women vs 57 percent of unsponsored women report satisfactory pace in promotions). The bottom line is that women need both mentors and sponsors, especially sponsors, to advance our careers.

Finding mentors and sponsors can be challenging, especially for women of color. Research from Catalyst reveals that women of color often lack access to networks where influential colleagues gather. These networks are essential for meeting potential mentors or sponsors, gaining entry to high-visibility projects, and learning about new roles.

Unfortunately, many of these networks resemble "old boys clubs" primarily consisting of White leaders. Typically, newcomers to these circles are White males who share similar life experiences. This dynamic places women of color at a significant disadvantage. We have few senior leaders of our race or gender, and those who do look like us often lack common ground with the White male leaders in these circles. Consequently, women of color struggle to build relationships with senior leaders who hold decision-making power.

STORIES FROM WOMEN OF COLOR

Before we groan at the idea of networking, know that networking does not have to feel gross and take so much time. We can network and get mentors and still be ourselves— and do it efficiently as part of our job. Here, women of color share how they were able to network and rise in their careers without taking extra time or putting on a facade.

KANGE KANEENE
Black, VP, SAP.io Foundries North and Latin America.

Kange knows what it is like to be the "one and only" or "one among a few." At age 12, she was the only girl on a tackle football team. Later, she was one of the few computer science majors at University of Michigan and one of the few women of color at New York University where she got her MBA. Kange counters the myth that networking has to be superficial. She shares how networking by focusing on relationships helped her transition to her dream role. In 2021, Kange became one of the few female leaders of color to run a corporate startup accelerator.

In business school, they talked about networking. Meet all the people you can. I realized early on that there's a wrong and right way to network. There's networking where you find someone who you look up to and say, "Let's get coffee every month." In some cases, it's not organic, and you don't have the chemistry. Especially with people who are busy, it's hard to create something positive. But what I realized, at least in a work setting, is I try to network by getting to know people by actually doing the work.

For example, if my boss asks me, "What kind of projects do you want to work on?," I try my best to align myself with projects that are cross-functional—in my case, in other teams such as marketing or finance. People from different teams and senior levels are seeing the work that I can do and the contributions that I can make. That way, when I want to move around in the organization, I have people that can say, "Not only do I like her, but I've actually seen her in that meeting, and she killed it."

That is what is called intentional networking. It's still organic, but they have more to talk about than just personality, especially when you're from a non-credible demographic. They need to have actual facts about the quality of your work.

When you network, it's important to protect yourself. You've got to balance being vulnerable and honest with keeping your eyes open and being aware. I think I've always been naïve. When I feel like I have a relationship with someone, I believe that they have my best interests at heart. But there have been times in the work setting where I've had my back stabbed by people I consider my work friends. When I look back, I should have known that was going to happen.

You need to understand that people have different motivations for being where they are. As you go up in the organization, it's of course more competitive. So that brings out different things in people. I was right that people didn't want me to win. Try to understand how people are motivated. If I'm really good friends with someone's boss who's not my boss, how is that going to be a threat to the other person? How can I bring them into the conversations I'm having or try to preempt things? Understand what you think the person needs to move up and what role you play in that equation. Are you in the way? Are you going to be an advocate, or do they see you as a threat?

The only way I know how to navigate in personal and professional life is to create and maintain relationships. Sometimes I'm engaging with someone who I know for a fact has never had a conversation with a Black person before. So there are a lot of things to bring to the table. I'm representing billions of people. I'm also representing whatever you think I am. In that case, I try to say, "What's at least one thing I can try to connect on? Their kids, music, a type of food, their favorite cocktail?" I use it as a way to connect to them so that they are able to say, "I like her as a person."

I think when people like you, then things are easier. It's harder to consider me your enemy if you actually think that I'm a fun person to be around. If I can create these small advocates along the way, maybe one day they'll all be talking and I won't be there, and one of them will advocate for me.

Vanessa's parents moved from Puerto Rico to New York where they met, got married, and settled in Connecticut. Vanessa attended a public school, then a Catholic public school, and later received a scholarship to attend an elite private school. She did not understand why everyone did not have the opportunity to get a quality education like hers. Fueled by her determination to address this inequity, Vanessa became a teacher and later a leader in public education. Vanessa addresses the myth that networking is not critical. She shares the importance of finding mentors in order to rise in your career.

As a Latina woman at work, I didn't always feel like I could be in the room where big decisions were made. That was a space for White men. If it was going to be opened up, it was a space for White women.

This was a myth for me because especially in the work I do serving predominantly communities of color, we have to be at the table speaking on behalf of our communities, our own experiences in education, and the relevance of our personal experience in the work that we do.

I was very fortunate to have some female and male mentors who pushed me and said, "You have the experience. You have a voice that is powerful. You should be finding ways to lead, and we will support you to get into the room and be a decision maker."

But that was very hard. I faced a lot of moments of doubting myself. I had imposter syndrome for a long time. I would think, "I got lucky that I'm in the room." I hear a lot of people say that, especially women of color. It's not luck. It's hard work. We work hard. Give yourself the credit.

Mentors have been very important for helping me rise in my career. But finding them has been more organic than deliberate or intentional. My first mentor was a Black man in college, a teacher. He's the one who introduced me to Teach for America. He said, "You have a passion for justice." I said, "Yes, I'm going to be a lawyer." He responded, "No, you're going to be a teacher." I thought that was a crazy idea. But the more we talked about it, and I shared with him my own personal school experience, he convinced me that teaching was a place where I could have real impact and real change in the lives of young people.

What goes across all the mentors I've had is values alignment. We connect on something deeper than what's on the surface. For me, this is how I lean in. I consider myself a values leader, someone who cares deeply about creating space, opportunity, and access for young people. My mentors have been White men, Black men, White women, women of color. The through line is that our values align and that the work we do is more than just checking a box or getting a paycheck.

MELISHA "MEL" JACKMAN

Black, Executive Director of Brooklyn Kindergarten Society

Mel busts the myth that networking is painful. She shares how she went from hating networking to being a social butterfly.

My former Executive Director gave me some great advice, "You need to grow your social capital. You need to stop playing small.

You need to lean in, share, and talk to people about the awesome things that you're doing. You need to build your network." He then followed this up with a question, "So how did you get here?" I didn't have to think twice, "Hard work."

For every single job that I've gotten, I've shown up blank without a referral, without a reference, without anything. I didn't even have a LinkedIn. But what I have been able to do is genuinely connect with people I interact with. My resume and experience have been how I've gotten to where I've gotten.

He told me, "But if you network with people, you will go to the next level."

I took his advice, started speaking up more, and started to network and interface with other folks in the field. That's how Brooklyn Kindergarten Society came to fruition. Now I'm a networking, socializing butterfly. That has propelled so much of the work and gotten more people inspired. We've done great things diversifying revenue. Networking goes a long, long way. But I'm also authentically connecting with people because I am genuinely invested in learning about the person and building a relationship.

Mel shares her tips about how to network at an event.

STEP 1. Develop a positive attitude toward networking.

Become aware of how you feel about networking and get to the root—Do you like it or not? If you do not like to do it, then understand what beliefs you have about networking. For example, if the belief is that networking is a waste of time or that you might get rejected or you need to be fake, then it's not surprising that you would not like networking.

What new thoughts could you try on to get you to embrace networking? For example, a new thought could be that networking *is a good way to meet people in my field who are doing interesting work, and I'm going to find people I have an authentic connection with. Or networking is critical to success; today, most jobs are filled by referrals. Find a belief that will help you feel confident and be genuinely interested in networking.*

STEP 2. *Practice your elevator pitch.*

STEP 3. *Before you go to an event, have an intention and do your research. Find out who's potentially going to be there, and how you may be able to engage with them. You may have similar interests or be in a similar industry. If the person is public, do your research because you want to have an organic way to start a conversation.*

Know why you want to meet the people that you're meeting. It can't just be to pass out your business card. No one's following up with you if you just do that. Your needs have to be very clear. Why do you want to know folks in this circle? How would you add value to them and vice versa? It has to be a two-way relationship. Your added value has to be very clear in your mind so you can exude that.

STEP 4. *Follow up with anyone you interact with through an email. Try to get a connection afterwards. Be clear about what you are going to talk about. Are you pitching something or are you genuinely invested in their organization? Are you looking for a job?*

MARCELLE FOWLER
Black, Chief Coaching Officer, C-Suite Coach

Marcelle proves that the myth of networking as optional is false. She shares why building a broad network is important and how to do it authentically.

It's important to be authentic and figure out what will work for you. Spend the time to build relationships. It's not going out and partying at the office party or after hours. I was a single mom raising two small boys. It's just taking those opportunities just a few minutes before the meeting starts. A few minutes at the beginning of the day, sometimes lunch, sometimes coffee, connecting with people on an individual level.

I used to call people on the ride in, or if you are on a train, you can text people, just to say, "Hey, thinking about you, and hope everything's going well." You can also use your time on social media. If you have time for TikTok, then you have time to send a message on LinkedIn celebrating someone's accomplishment. There are probably spots in your day where you can do a habit stack [where you identify a current habit you already do each day and then stack your new behavior on top]. While you are on social media, you can also network.

You might want to reach out to someone new but think, "I don't want to bother them." To get over your fear and imposter anxiety, just do it. You'll never know until you try. There have been times when I've tried to connect with people, and they blew me off. But there are other times when I've tried to connect with people, and they welcomed it, and said, "Hey, sure, welcome to my network. Happy to have you. Let me know if you need anything."

Avoid self-selecting to opt out. Your network needs to be broad. Not everyone needs to look like you. Find shared experiences. We're so diverse as individuals in terms of our upbringing and our family situation. Chances are that there are things that are alike for us with other people that we don't even realize because we're just looking at the surface.

One example that actually set me on the path to being a coach is when I was in a role where I was supporting communications for *the Chief Financial Officer of a certain business line. I was also working with the HR team doing some leadership development programming but as their communications person. When an HR role opened up, I wanted to apply. Typically, women don't apply for roles unless they have all the specific criteria. I knew I had some transferable skills, but I didn't have all the criteria. I was willing to apply even without meeting all the criteria, which is more what men do. I applied, and lo and behold, my relationship with the CFO was what put me above over other candidates because he was the CFO for this business line.*

ISABEL CHING

Chinese American, Executive Director,
Hamilton-Madison House

Isabel's parents left China to escape its economic and political problems and settled in South America, where she was born. Later, they moved to Brooklyn, New York, where Isabel faced discrimination and prejudice for being Asian American. She was wrongly placed in an English as a Second Language (ESL) class even though her English was fluent. Despite these difficulties, Isabel never gave up on her Asian American identity. She became the leader of an organization that celebrates and promotes her culture. She also learned how to network and present herself in a genuine and authentic way. Isabel shows that networking does not have to be fake or superficial.

I'm working on my executive presence, and it's not easy. People will have assumptions about who I am. I'm a woman, so I can't make those kinds of decisions, or I'm Asian, so I won't understand what they're doing.

I have a consultant to help me with presenting and networking, but I don't take all of their advice. I listen with a grain of salt and modify it to who I am. That's always been true in my life. Everything tends to be made for a Caucasian culture. So I tweak it for myself and do what is aligned with me. This means being accepting of who I am. When I present and network, sometimes I'm giggly, I joke around, and I move my hands a lot. But that's who I am.

There's this anxiety, feeling like I have to be prepped, always ready to say something interesting, something unique, something that will grab the attention of people. But why do we put that pressure on ourselves? I think it's because we feel we need to be different and fascinating. We feel we need to prove ourselves. I'm not the smartest person. I'm not the most eloquent speaker. But I can show up as me.

I think being who you are is most important. There's only so much you can control. Don't beat yourself up so hard. You can't control what people think about you. If they're not interested, move on. Think to yourself, "Okay, this time, not this person. But next time, maybe another person will have a different perspective." Keep networking and you'll find people who will understand you, get where you're coming from, and give you a chance.

WHAT WOMEN OF COLOR CAN DO

Here's how to network authentically and efficiently.

STEP 1. Get in the right mindset.

Instead of approaching it as a purely transactional chore, think of networking as a way to build a community of shared support. For women of color, being part of a community can bring a sense of belonging. The more we invest in our network, the more authentic the relationships we can build. We can support others and receive support ourselves. When anyone in our community needs help finding a new job, navigating workplace culture, or is celebrating a milestone, we can be there to support each other. How do we think the old White boys network works? It's all about helping each other.

Rather than shrinking from our uniqueness to fit in or trying to impress someone, focus on genuine connection and interest. Networking is about getting to know many people but also about building an authentic, close inner circle. Not only are close relationships personally meaningful, research found that women who form a tight female group (two to three other women) that can share gender-specific career advice are nearly three times more likely to get a better job than women who don't have that support system. A tight-knit female group can provide critical information. If they are within our company, they can help us understand office politics to accomplish initiatives. If they are outside our company, they can share jobs that might not be on our radar and help us assess whether a company truly cares about DEI.

STEP 2. Create our dream team of 10 people who can help us rise in our career.

To help us network efficiently, deliberately focus on a smaller group instead of casting a wide net. Our dream team will be a mix of 10 people inside and outside of our organization including mentors, sponsors, peers, men, and women from different races and different industries with different expertise. We are looking for different people who can give us feedback, provide emotional support, or champion us and our work.

Within our organization, build our network beyond our manager and colleagues. Foster connections horizontally and vertically within our organization, including clients and senior leaders a few levels above our immediate manager. These connections help us understand workplace norms, navigate organizational dynamics, and gain insights into opportunities and the broader landscape. For me, some of my mentors also served as sponsors. They had clout in the organization to vouch for me for high-visibility projects and promotion and give me access to contacts and opportunities that set me up with upward mobility.

Outside of our organization, build our network by identifying our career goals and who can help support our growth. Most people tend to limit their network to coworkers and people in the same industry. But if there is a downturn in our company or field, we'll have a limited network from which to get support. For example, if we want to shift from operations to finance, seek out a mentor with finance experience. If we want to move up in the management ranks and know that strategy is one of our areas of growth, find a senior leader with strong strategic skills. We can find these people by joining an industry organization or check LinkedIn to identify and get introduced to people for an informational interview.

To diversify our network effectively and authentically, consider two key approaches: "sticking together" by connecting with people of the same race or gender and "blending in" by forming networks with senior leaders, often White males. A Catalyst survey found that "blending in" provides access to those in power, while "sticking together" offers support in handling workplace stress, a strategy adopted notably by Black women. Latinas combine both strategies, forming networks with both White individuals and females. Asian American women often follow a "blending in" approach.

While it would be nice to solely stick together with other women of color, the reality is that there aren't many of us at higher levels. In Sylvia Ann Hewlett, Melinda Marshall, and Laura Sherbin's *The Sponsor Effect 2.0*, they found that most leaders lean toward a classic command and control style. Build relationships with individuals who might not share our background or leadership style but have qualities we admire or shared common ground. We can build authentic connections while also gaining access to power and influence to open doors for us.

STEP 3. Build a mentor relationship.

After we have identified a possible mentor (who can also be a sponsor), approach them. Don't start with, "Want to be my mentor?" They are likely busy, and we want to build an authentic relationship. We can send an email sharing what we admire about them and asking if it's possible to connect.

For example, for one of my mentors, I sent this initial email:

I saw that you and I both attended Stanford University. It's exciting to meet someone who also got their MBA and is in New York working in education reform. I'd love to learn about your career path and the work you are doing now to start a school. I'm hoping to transition to work similar to this and would appreciate learning from you. Would it be possible to connect virtually or in-person—whatever is easiest for you?

1. Set up a meeting time and get to know each other. We'll want to ask them about their career path, goals, and advice they could offer us. Be prepared to share our personal and professional background, and goals.
2. Authentically connect on something we care about. Stop thinking about networking as just about work

but about a way to meet someone interesting and perhaps a new friend. If we stop dividing our work self from our true self, networking becomes more natural and fun.

3. This is not about schmoozing but creating meaningful connections and an informal ecosystem of go-to people for advice, help and mentorship—as a receiver and a giver. As we get to know them, find ways to help them. This could be personal by offering travel tips for a destination they are going to or professional by sharing market insights they might not already know.

4. Make sure to send a thank you note after the initial conversation sharing what we learned. We can also add, "Would it be okay if I followed up in a month to share an update?" Then when we follow up sharing actions we took based on our conversation, we can also ask for a follow-up meeting.

5. After three meetings, we'll have a sense of whether there is a good fit. Ideally, we have an authentic personal connection where we both look forward to spending time together. We are also able to be vulnerable with our fears, and they are empathetic and encouraging. We can either ask them directly if they would consider being our mentor, or indirectly in a thank you note, we can thank them for being a mentor.

6. Continue to develop the relationship and express gratitude for their time and support.

STEP 4. Ask for and offer help.

Networking is a two-way street of asking for and offering support. When we meet with others, focus less on "How can you help me?" and more on "How can I help you?

If asking for help makes us feel queasy because we think people will perceive us as weak, know that we are building a network of people to support us. This is about building our social capital, defined as "the relationships people have with each other, and the desire they have to do things for and with others within their social networks. People tend to do things to help and encourage those in their same social network, creating a cycle of mutually beneficial reciprocity."

Asking for help also builds relationships. The Benjamin Franklin effect is a bias that causes people to like someone more after they do that person a favor. In the *Autobiography of Benjamin Franklin*, Franklin shared an example where he asked one of his adversaries for a favor, and later they ended up being lifelong friends.

STEP 5. Embed networking into our daily schedule.

View networking not as an add-on but as an essential part of our job. No matter how busy we are, get out there and network. It's possible to network efficiently.

In Keith Ferrazzi's book *Never Eat Alone*, he provides strategies to foster meaningful relationships to achieve our goals and help others achieve theirs. One of these tactics is to stop eating lunch by ourselves and instead use that time to connect with others. Set a monthly goal to virtually or personally meet someone new, whether within our organization, on a different team, a senior leader, or an external contact. When networking, ask, "Is there someone else you would recommend I connect with?" This helps expand our network and facilitate the next connection.

In addition, take advantage of affinity, professional, and networking groups. These could be internal or external to the organization or our industry, related to race, gender, profession, or networking in general. We can also join a mastermind, a networking group that meets regularly. Networking groups are helpful for meeting others and giving or getting support, whether or not we want to be exposed to another industry or are actively looking for a job. Affinity groups provide an opportunity to have a unified voice to approach senior leaders with concerns or suggestions and often also offer leadership training and mentoring programs.

Attend networking events at work and also after work. While women of color often opt out of happy hours, showing up signals that we care about our relationships with our team. It gives people a chance to know us. We also learn about office politics and who we should trust or avoid.

Take advantage of online connections by creating a LinkedIn profile and joining relevant online groups. Get to know people as people, find shared values and things in common, and develop authentic connections. Congratulate people on their accomplishments. Find ways to help the person like sharing interesting articles, so that the relationship does not feel like it is just one way and so that it feels authentic. This online professional family is important too.

STEP 6. Find deliberate ways to stay in touch.

Building good relationships takes continual work, so be deliberate. Find a method to track contacts (e.g., LinkedIn and Excel) and stay in contact (email, holiday cards, phone calls, or texts). For example, once a quarter, connect with our dream team in our top 10. Share an update on life and ask about what is going on in their lives. Or share an article or opportunity which might be helpful or interesting to them.

One of my clients came to me feeling demotivated from her job search. She had worked with a couple of recruiters and only had one interview. We discussed reaching out to her network, but she shared that she had not been deliberate about staying in touch with people. She was also an introvert and hated small talk. Networking never felt urgent with all of the fires she needed to deal with at work. We put together a plan of reconnecting with her network and building new connections. It took several months of rebuilding her network before we saw it begin to pay off with potential job leads. Based on this experience, she vowed to be more deliberate about networking and staying in touch going forward.

STEP 7. Mentor and sponsor others.

As we build our network with mentors and sponsors, we also want to mentor and sponsor others, especially other women of color. We can take advantage of mentoring opportunities at work, with a nonprofit, or through an affinity group like our university. When we see a junior woman of color, introduce ourselves and build an authentic relationship where we can support, help them identify their strengths, give feedback, and encourage them. When one of us rises, we all rise.

A friend of mine, a Black female senior leader at a technology company, is an excellent example of a mentor and sponsor We were attending a fundraising gala for a nonprofit, and she introduced me to a young Black woman who had graduated from her alma mater, "Analiza, if you wouldn't mind, I'd like you to talk with my mentee about your work with education technology. She's passionate about this field. Perhaps you can introduce her to people in your network who are doing innovative work there."

I made introductions for her mentee, which led her to a unique opportunity working closely with a senior leader on an up-and-coming technology. I later saw my friend and her mentee at another event where my friend continued to introduce her mentee to her network. My friend told me, "Being a mentor is something I take seriously. Technology is a pretty lonely place for women of color, and I wish I had senior people look out for me and open doors for me. So that's what I hope to do for my mentees."

BOOK BONUSES

Explore the Book Bonuses for this chapter:

- Step-by-step guide to building a network worksheet
- List of books for further reading
- Podcasts with full interviews of women leaders spotlighted in this chapter

MYTH SEVEN

Women need to act like men to lead

As a new CEO, I was unsure how to lead. The leaders I had seen during my career were mostly White men, with a range of leadership styles. There was Joe Vanoni, the Cadet Commander of my Air Force Reserve Officers' Training Corps, who would yell at me that my uniform was never ironed enough and that my shoes didn't shine. There was Colonel Schiefer, my brilliant, quiet, and humble first boss, who would constantly celebrate his team and let us 22-year-olds present directly to the most senior leaders in the Air Force. There was Captain Scott Conner, who gathered our six-person team to meet me on a Sunday at 5AM at the airport when I arrived in Guam for the first time so that I could have a warm welcome.

There was General Richard "Tex" Brown III who was a fighter pilot and later the head of the Air Force Personnel Center when I met him. He and I took a small Air Force plane from San Antonio to Washington, DC. As we boarded the plane and the staff snapped to attention with a salute, General Brown laughed, "Hey y'all! Can I fly this one?" Then General Brown got into the cockpit and flew us to the Pentagon. The next day, I arrived at our intimate meeting with the Secretary of the Air Force to find that General Brown had not yet arrived. In the military, we have a saying, "To be early is to be on time. To be on time is to be late." A couple minutes later, General Brown arrived, and made a joke, "You know me, Sir, I'm on Texan time." The room laughed, and we began our presentation.

There was Captain Jon Webb who was tall and lanky and modeled leadership, efficiency, and care at work and at home. We once attended a pool party with his 10 kids, and I saw him tell his eldest child, "It's time to go." Within minutes, that eldest child had cascaded that message down to what seemed like the next eldest, who then cascaded it to the next in line. Each was helping the younger, when finally the youngest child in diapers was being helped by two of the next youngest children. They went from being sopping wet in bathing suits to changed and ready to go—in 15 minutes. It's probably not a surprise that under Captain Webb's leadership, our team had clear systems to get the work done and take care of each other.

There was Chris Smiros, my boss during my internship at Colgate-Palmolive, who was a master at building relationships and navigating organizational politics. He took time to help me practice for my final presentation and told me who on the leadership team I should ensure liked me. With his help, I was able to get one of the coveted full-time offers after my MBA.

There was Jeff Ginsburg, CEO of East Harlem Tutorial Program, who landed a spot on Crain's 40 under 40. A graduate of the Harvard Kennedy School, Jeff is an academic who loves to dig into research. He was humble and thoughtful and gathered lots of data before making decisions.

With these models and others in mind, I reflected on the type of leader I wanted to be. Should I lean on my military or corporate or nonprofit models? Since I was a woman, I wanted to counter the stereotype of being soft and instead be seen as tough, polished, and no-nonsense. But I worried that this approach did not match my natural leadership style.

I decided to ask a mentor who was a woman of color and had a decade of CEO experience, "How should I lead?" Her advice was short, "You can only lead as you."

THE MYTH

Quick. Think of a general in the military.

Think of a priest.

Think of a president of a country.

Think of a CEO of a company.

What do they look like?

If you're like most people, you pictured White men. If you did think of a woman, it was likely a White woman.

We are raised to believe that there is only one way to lead, mostly modeled after a White cisgender male. But there are many other effective ways to lead that lean on our authentic strengths as women of color.

WHICH OF THESE EXPERIENCES RESONATE WITH YOU?

- ☐ You became a leader in your organization, and you questioned whether you should change your leadership style.
- ☐ You felt pressure to adopt a White male leadership style in order to climb up the career ladder.
- ☐ You have questioned vulnerability in leadership—is it a strength or a weakness?

> ☐ You have had an experience interviewing candidates with a male interviewer. Despite being the senior interviewer, the candidate focused on the male interviewer, assuming he was in charge, not you.

THE REALITY

Have you ever been told directly or indirectly, "You don't look like a leader?"

Stereotypes about what a leader looks like (namely White male) prevent women of color from leadership roles. Despite this stereotype, women of color are a leadership force to be reckoned with. Women of color have been leading in business, government, and nonprofit industries throughout the world. They have run billion-dollar companies and countries. Examples include Kamala Harris, Wilma Pearl Mankiller, Indira Gandhi, Michelle Obama, Geisha Williams, Oprah Winfrey, and Condoleezza Rice. While women of color have always been leaders, the issue is that there have been too few of them and not enough role models for women of color to envision they too, can lead.

The lack of role models who look like us has helped bring about a myth that there is one way (namely the White male way) to lead. We used to think that leadership meant only masculine traits such as being ambitious, decisive, and relying on power from formal authority to lead. But a Pew Research Center report has shown that women scored higher than men on characteristics that make a great leader, such as honesty, intelligence, organization, and compassion. Instead of the myth that women need to lead like White men, we should choose a leadership style that embraces our unique qualities and adapts our leadership to the situation and the individuals being led. There is no one-size-fits-all approach.

Despite not meeting the stereotype that women can be good leaders, research shows that women make fantastic leaders; we have leadership traits that matter most and can thrive in top seats. A study by Northwestern University professor Dr. Alice Eagly found that women make better leaders than men because women tend to be more transformational leaders. Transformational leaders seek to develop the skills of their team, listen more effectively, and foster strong relationships. They turn an employee's self-interest into one that will benefit the organization too. Women leaders tend to motivate their team through positive, reward-based incentives, while men use less effective and more threat-based incentives. Dr. Eagly's study also found that women tend to be more outside-the-box leaders than men.

Women possess skills highly sought after in leaders. We are naturally intuitive and inclusive listeners rather than talkers, collaborators rather than competitors. Women rely on relationships instead of force to influence. We are adept at sharing power and information, actively seeking input from others, fostering a sense of recognition, motivation, and belonging within the organization.

In her book *Dare to Lead Like a Girl*, leadership consultant Dalia Feldheim shares how feminine leadership traits such as empathy, intuition, passion, purpose, self-care, work-life balance, and gratitude can build success, respect, and a healthier work environment. Her research found that women tended to foster relationships, get to know people as humans, were vulnerable, and created psychological safety by admitting mistakes and seeing failures as opportunities for growth.

Feldheim was a marketing director on the 2014 global Always ad campaign #LikeAGirl, one of Forbes' 10 most influential campaigns of the decade. In the ad, a young girl reinterprets "run like a girl" to mean "run as fast as you can," challenging the old insult boys threw at other boys. The campaign aims for girls and women to be proud and reclaim what it means to do things as themselves, rather than imitating men.

STORIES FROM WOMEN OF COLOR

Women leaders of color share how leading authentically led them to personal and organizational success.

LETICIA OSSA DAZA

Latina, Founding Partner and Chair of Latin America Practice, Willkie Farr & Gallagher

Born and raised in Colombia, Leticia knew from an early age that she wanted to be a lawyer. Her parents were both lawyers and supported her dreams, and Leticia's choice to move to France after receiving a scholarship for college in France. After graduating, Leticia found herself in New York as a lawyer, surrounded by mostly white males and not sure how to show up. Leticia shares how she got clear on her authentic leadership style and how that helped her get recognized and rise at her organization.

When I started at Willkie, one of the things that I did was to look at our business and ask myself, "How can I differentiate myself?

What do I bring to the table that the business is not doing?" Knowing I do things differently, I wanted to compete on a different level. I thought about my leadership style and the unique contributions that I could make because of my experience and cultural background. It became clear that I wanted to be authentic and open about my challenges. I also wanted to share my pro bono work. This is all part of career building. It's about knowing and sharing who you are and who you want to be and leveraging your uniqueness to build the business.

One example is with our Chair, Tom Cerabino, who has been a great mentor and friend. I remember when I started the practice as a senior associate. I told him, "I have this idea to create a Latin American practice, and this is what I need to start it." He was fully supportive, even if he didn't know me well back then. It was the first time we talked, and it was the first time we talked about this project. You need to believe that you have an idea that deserves support. This is how you get people to believe in it, too.

As I've grown in my career, I've become more confident and learned to trust myself. This means learning to show up more authentically. For example, lawyers often wear black, blue, or gray. Well, I love yellow, red and bright colors. So, I wear yellow or a dress, instead of a black suit. I have also learned to be more myself, like dancing at holiday parties because I love to dance. Because part of my culture is that we love to dance or talk with our hands. It's about being inspired by those who chose to live authentically before me and thrive, like when we see Gloria Estefan open the Kennedy Center Awards with the famous song "Conga."

We see more of the Latinx community showing up and going back to our roots and being praised. This is how we can be more confident. We see that what makes us authentic is part of our brand.

As one of the few Black students at her school, Erica's mantras were, "Never let them see you sweat," "Be perfect," "Work twice or three or four times as hard," and "Never ask for help." So when she was a Stanford student working several jobs to pay for school herself and got an overdue credit card bill, she moved out of the dorm quietly over winter break and left Stanford. Without a degree, Erica struggled to find a job in her field. She ended up working at a temp agency, where she wowed leaders with her work ethic, was offered multiple jobs, and later took on multiple leadership roles before returning to finish her degree. Erica questions the myth that we need to act like men to lead successfully. She shares that the key to her leadership has been leading authentically as herself.

My mom raised us and trained us to be comfortable in every space, to be able to, for lack of a better word, assimilate. I think I've excelled at that. I feel very comfortable being the One, the Only, the youngest or whatever. That's probably a good thing.

I started working at the age of 15 because I enjoyed the challenge and I wanted spending money. But by the time I was 18, it wasn't optional. I needed to pay for college. Working so much was a blessing and a curse. I didn't enjoy my undergrad experience as much as I could have because I was under constant financial pressure and always thinking about my responsibilities. But the blessing from it was that I had a great resume. I've worked in public relations, advertising, and high tech. Now I'm in the Public Affairs and government space. When I look back on my career, it's been about handling adversity, dealing with ever changing priorities and moving the needle for an organization in spite of setbacks and complexity. Those are all lessons I learned in life.

What helped me feel ready to take on a role [as CEO] was being in rooms with people I really admired and realizing over time that they weren't perfect or all knowing. They were human beings with insecurities and blind spots and knowledge gaps. I had put them on this pedestal of perfection and wanted to emulate them. When you start to see them in the real light, you realize they're not infallible. I learned that the person at the top isn't always the smartest person in the room. In fact, I would go so far as to say that the smartest person in the room isn't always a good leader. That's helped me with my own imposter syndrome—wondering whether I even belong here. Knowing that people I've idolized are no different than any of us – they put their pants on one leg at a time just like we do, and they're not always as competent as we think they are. They have the same questions, the same anxiety, and sometimes make the wrong decision. Great leadership isn't about perfection, it's about authenticity and empathy.

I do think that in the past we were taught to emulate some leaders who weren't that great. They just happened to be men in charge. Now I think very differently about it. I say to women, "Don't try to be just like a man. Being a woman is a superpower in and of itself. We're different and that's a good thing. Lean into that distinction. All of the things that make you different and interesting and unique are what will make your organization stand out. This is part of the diffusion of innovation and how women bring a different energy to an organization or a industry. We can solve problems and bring solutions based on our uniquely female perspectives and insights. Don't try to be some other person. There are certain aspects of a leaders' personality or skillset that certainly you can emulate, but don't try to become a clone of someone else. And certainly don't ever mask your true self.

Mala believed in the American Dream—that with hard work, anyone can do well in life. When Mala realized the American Dream was a myth, she dedicated her career to education. She had not planned on being the top leader, but the unanticipated departure of Aspire Public School's CEO led her to becoming the interim, then official CEO in 2019. When Mala became CEO, she was haunted by imposter syndrome. Mala counters the myth that we need to replicate the male leaders before us. She shares that the secret to thriving and sustaining as a CEO has been leading as herself.

I have not gone through my career thinking about what the next thing would be. Part of that is the unexpected passing of my parents which encouraged me to focus on what matters right now. If I was learning, being pushed, and contributing, I was content.

While I wasn't thinking about my career next steps, I was fortunate that there were other people who were thinking about that for me. For example, when I moved into a role at Aspire overseeing operations and strategy, I had a manager who was an awesome, strong woman. I had a much bigger team, and it was the first experience where I felt like a leader. My manager expected me to show up with a plan and a perspective and share it. She was there to give me feedback. I felt a sense of ownership and leadership that she not only expected from me but actually believed I could deliver.

My initial instinct was to think, "Now I have to own all this stuff, be accountable, and do a good job because people are expecting me to do it." But I learned that what people are hoping is that you will build a team around you, trust that they can do the work, and invest in them. Being CEO is similar—it's about how I'm setting up others to be successful.

When I took on this role, I faced a lot of imposter syndrome. Thank goodness for my two coaches. One of them, a White male former CEO, said he too, faced imposter syndrome. I fell out of my seat. I never thought those words would come out of his mouth.

The most comforting, reassuring, and empowering advice I got when I moved into this role was from my other coach at the National Equity Project, Lisa Lasky. I was going down this spiral of imposter feelings and uncertainty. She said, "You can only do this as you." It was such a simple statement but so powerful.

As women of color, it can be so easy to think, "Well, he did it that way, or people loved it that way." But I'm not the person who has those kinds of ideas or has that type of energy. There's this constant comparison and beating myself up because I'm not this larger than life, over the moon charismatic leader. I build my trust in small moments. I like small groups, deep relationships. It gave me permission to not have to change how I move through the world because I was suddenly in this very different, much more visible role.

I would advise anyone who's stepping into a leadership role that feels under a microscope, ultimately, if you're not doing this as you, it will be too hard. If you feel like it's a place where you can't be who you really are and lead as who you really are, then I would question whether it's the right role in the right organization. Of all the things that make these roles unsustainable, that is impossible.

So I found ways to lead that were authentic to me, for example recording myself on my living room couch talking about George Floyd's murder and why we talk about Black Lives Matter to all of our students, including elementary school students. I posted this video on our organization's social media. It was probably the thing *that got the most appreciation from our community—saying that out loud and moving quickly rather than a big strategic plan for how we were going to respond. My default is I don't want to do it until it is perfectly scripted and planned out. This went against my natural way of operating. It really stuck with me because I thought, "Wow, that was a fairly easy thing for me to do, to say what I believed and what we believe as an org. That wasn't hard." It made me think, "What are those messages that need to be said and how meaningful can it be coming from someone who is the face of the organization?"*

I've learned to lead as myself and also to stretch. As a young girl, and then as a woman in a working environment, I always played this role of peacemaker to avoid conflict at all costs and make people laugh and happy. I had to learn that harmony is probably just masking. People are not actually voicing their perspectives, their opinions, and their thoughts. If it seems simple, you're probably missing a lot of complexity. As a leader, it's having the courage to be disliked and sit in discomfort and sit in disagreement.

I have also had to learn that being critical is not being negative. Critical thinking, pushback, and questions are opportunities to strengthen my perspective, think differently, or share different information. Every time I walk into those spaces, I know that there's going to be some pushback, and I try to see the value in it. I think it's easy to say as a CEO, I am the only one who has this lens to see all the things. But the same is true for every role at Aspire. I am not living the experience of our teachers who are day in and day out in the classroom. I keep a note on my desk that says, "Please all and you will please none." Because I think that can't be the objective. It's not going to serve kids in the way that we're here to do.

I've also learned to balance my natural tendencies with what is needed to lead. For example, I like hearing people's perspectives, but at what point do I tell myself, "You've done the listening, it's time to make a call and be transparent about what it is and why."

As I reflect on being the first woman of color CEO at Aspire, I know that my identity has an impact on how people interact with me. There have been moments where I am interacting with teammates where I have felt that sometimes there's a lack of formality in terms of how people see me in this role versus how they saw Don Shalvey, a charismatic, White former leader. I found myself thinking, "Wow, I never saw anyone show up that way. Would you have said it that way to my male predecessor or CEO?"

Leadership is so personal. It can be so easy to psych yourself out and think, "Everybody's got this, and I'm the odd one out." Getting to meet more people in roles like this, I realized that the majority of people in the CEO role sort of stumbled into it one way or another, which is true for me too. There is something very empowering about realizing that very few people, regardless of how they come across, actually feel like they know what moves to make next.

NICHOL NG

Chinese, CEO of X-Inc Private Limited

Nichol debunks the myth that we should model our leadership on men. She shares that one of the keys to her success has been leading as herself—at work, home, and life. She has learned to be vulnerable and share her struggles, ask for help, and let go of the need to control others.

I suffered from an eating disorder from a very young age since I was five, because I was a much bigger girl than my peers. My relatives used to say, every Chinese New Year, things like, "You seem to have put on weight," or "You're stealing your brother's food." I've learned never to say that to anyone because I suffered from bulimia and anorexia for 20 years since I was 11. I was abusing laxatives, slimming pills, trying to starve myself to death. The longest duration without food was five days. This left me with not being able to get pregnant easily.

There was a stigma back then about eating disorders. There wasn't a support group system in Singapore, so I started the support group for eating disorders. I became the poster girl in the media to talk about it because they didn't feel this was an Asian problem. They always felt that it was a Western problem. When I spoke about it, I said, "It's not about the figure, it's not about the size, it's not about the weight. It's a form of addiction. We use food as a form of addiction to control our lives."

In addition to my eating disorder, I also faced problems with our family's business. In 1997 during the Asian currency crisis, we were bankrupt. I was there when the banks came to seize the house. I was 19 years old. We were given 30 minutes to pack. Everything else was the bank's.

These experiences prepared me to be the leader I am today. I had the privilege of continuing my grandfather's business. I told myself that I did not want my mom to go through another bankruptcy. That includes our employees. My longest serving employee has been with us for 46 years, and I wasn't even born when she started with us. When the pandemic started, I told everybody that we would survive. I also vowed that I would give back to society. So in 2007, I acquired the family business and cleaned up the debts.

I drew inspiration from my grandfather and our values statement, that we put thought into everything that we do. Thought comes from a Chinese word, which is made up of two Chinese characters. The top one means field, and the bottom word means heart. So you grow whatever's in your heart.

For the last 10 years, we've adopted technology, digitized invoicing, and shared with the industry to help the ecosystem improve. This has been great for not just our business but everyone else's.

I've been vulnerable to share my struggles—with bulimia and bankruptcy. I want people to know what I've gone through. I share my stories as a form of encouragement to help people going through tough times, that they will see better days.

ARVA RICE

Black, CEO of New York Urban League

Arva's parents were sharecroppers in Arkansas and dreamed of a better life for their family. Arva and her siblings all went to college, with Arva attending Northwestern University. A professor asked Arva, "How did you get into Northwestern?" Fighting off tears, Arva used this experience to motivate her, graduating with honors. Arva took her mother's advice to "Leave the door open for the next person" and dedicated her life to service. Arva counters the myth that women need to lead like men. She shares how she has learned to "dance" in her leadership, staying authentic to herself in a White dominant culture.

How do I stay true to myself while working in a predominantly White environment in an organization that was designed to work with African Americans to help move us to equity? One of the things that I find challenging is that even in spaces with all Black people, there are times where the standard is still very much White.

For example, I had just recently become the CEO of the Urban League. I was in a program called Greater New York, which matches nonprofit leaders and for-profit leaders in mentoring relationships. I was very anxious to be paired with a CEO of a Fortune 500 company. Everybody got their matches, and I still didn't have a match. They told me, "We couldn't find a CEO for you to be matched with. Would you be okay with having a Black woman who is a consultant?" I said, "No, I want a CEO. Do you want to match me with a White guy? That's fine."

Famous last words. So they matched me with a White male head of a company. He told me some things that didn't sit so well with me. He talked about how passion is sometimes perceived by White males, and I needed to follow my passion with statistics, the goal, that sort of thing, so that I would be better received.

Did I want to hear that? Absolutely not. Do I think it's right? Absolutely not. But it gave me another piece in my toolkit. For me to get the grant in order to move my organization forward, I need to reach people so that I can develop the partnership. I don't love it. But I have that knowledge. So I can choose to step into that. Or I can choose to step out of it. Or I can choose to do a dance because I'm actually better suited to make a presentation to multiple audiences because I can speak in different ways. So that was something I have learned about having to be in a White majority culture.

The other thing that I would encourage people to do is affirmations. I wrote an affirmation in the beginning of 2020, and it's one that I still carry with me. It starts with Arva Rice, I'm God's daughter. So if I'm God's daughter, how am I going to be in the world? How am I going to express myself in the world? Then it goes on to say all these other affirmations about things that at the time when I wrote them, were very aspirational. Over the course of the last two years, some of these things that were in this affirmation are very much true for me.

Some people read their affirmations in the mirror every morning or read theirs from their journal at the end of the day. For me, I pray.

When I am in my moments of self-doubt, I reflect, "Where were you one year, five years ago, 10 years ago? Look at your accomplishments." Zora Neale Hurston says, "The years that have questions and the years that have answers." So you may not have a straight line to success. But even during challenges, remember your darkest of days and that you got through them.

One of the things that I say to the young professionals at the New York Urban League is that if there is a single person that they admire, I guarantee that person has cried themselves to sleep at night. Because you just don't get to that level without struggle.

DIANA COURNOYER

Member of the Oglala Sioux Tribe, CEO of National Indian Education Association

As a child, Diana describes herself as "very shy, very introverted, borderline fearful of the world." Her childhood dream was to help animals, not people. But once she took a college class in Native American studies, she realized the injustice her own people had suffered and decided to commit her life to supporting Native students. Diana dispels the myth that to be successful in leadership, we need to model after extroverts. She shares how she is able to lead authentically as an introvert.

Growing up as an introvert, I did not have the confidence to stand up in front of an audience in elementary, middle, and high school. I did not even have the confidence to stand up in front of my very own family.

But as I got older and became a leader in my field, my grandmother told me, "There should be no fear in you standing up in front of

people because you're the expert." Whatever you're standing up and talking about, you must research and become a knowledge keeper.

So I apply this knowledge in everything I do, including going to Capitol Hill. I make sure that any words that come out of my mouth are purposeful, impactful, and that anyone who's going to listen to this will walk away and start thinking, "How can I change the way I approach the work?"

As women of color, we must be careful about what we say and how we say it, or we will lose our audience. We're already starting pretty far back in the starting line as women and minorities.

As an introvert, I focus on my passion to educate. So I love to have conversations with people. When I speak, I tell stories. I love to tell stories, especially stories filled with knowledge that leave people questioning their own behavior. That's blending my introverted space of discomfort speaking in front of people with what I need to get across. So I put my fear of speaking in front of people aside. I've left people in tears. I've made people laugh. All I want to do is leave an impact.

SONIA PÉREZ
Puerto Rican, COO and Former Interim CEO, UnidosUS

Sonia was the youngest of eight siblings, growing up in the projects in Brooklyn, New York. Despite limited access to quality schools, Sonia was accepted into an elite public high school and later Brown University. But her father did not understand why Sonia wanted to leave their community to attend Brown. He did not speak to Sonia for the entire summer. What did Sonia do? She stayed true to her commitment to education and opportunity. She also stayed true to her family. She knew she would return. The day before Sonia left for Brown, her father reconciled with her, "You will always have a home here."

Sonia shares how this experience helped shape her life choices. She shares how throughout her three-decade career at UnidosUS, the nation's largest Hispanic civil rights and advocacy organization, including her stint as interim CEO, she has stayed true to her authentic self and leadership. Sonia discredits the myth that we need to lead as someone other than ourselves.

In this recent interim CEO period, I had to do a press event with Representative Joaquin Castro. People were uncertain about how I was going to do at this event because I hadn't done something like this in a really long time. It was the first week in this CEO role. I thought to myself, "I'm not in Washington, DC anymore. People don't know who I am because I've been behind the scenes."

We were talking about the lack of representation of Latinos in the media. I was there at our press conference thirty years ago when we did that first report. I thought about drawing on that experience. I also channeled my father and how he used to talk about how we are not seen, how there's not enough Latinos in TV shows.

After my remarks, I heard from many that they found my words powerful and that I did a good job. But in that moment, I had to reflect. Even though my style is not to get out there, I was still authentic and able to decide how I'm going to say it and to separate how it's received—that was beyond my control.

WHAT WOMEN OF COLOR CAN DO

Women of color can lead authentically by knowing ourselves and our strengths and finding a leadership style that is most authentic to us.

PRACTICE 1. LEAD FROM PURPOSE.

Research shows that people become leaders by seeing and internalizing themselves as a leader and having a sense of purpose. Women who were able to acknowledge their ambition to be a leader were motivated to develop their skills and raise their hands for experiences that were new, difficult, and beyond their job description. They also found others who affirmed them as a leader.

PRACTICE 2. DEVELOP STRATEGY SKILLS.

WORK ON ORGANIZATIONAL PRIORITIES.

Women of color are often limited in our career because we are seen as not "strategic," which means that we are seen as not able to create a larger impact. This view is compounded if we are seen as a technical or functional expert who doesn't have a broad perspective of the business. To address this issue and counter this stereotype, we can intentionally build our skills in strategy and even develop a reputation as a strategic thought leader in our company.

Deliberately seek opportunities to take on strategic projects, which will allow us to get to know our organization and work with senior leaders. Rather than focusing on just the work given to us, take initiative and demonstrate our willingness to learn and do stretch projects with a broader impact. Volunteer for roles that give us a broad perspective of the business, especially aspects that drive the business (such as sales, marketing, and product development). This will help us learn how priorities are determined, decisions are made, and how to navigate challenging situations. The women of color I interviewed started with small projects that grew over time.

Work on organizational problems that may be outside of what our job entails. Many of us have been taught to be rule followers, to solve problems that are given to us, and to check boxes to get an A. We do everything we're supposed to do without being asked. But to rise in organizations and have more impact, we need a new way to forge our own path and identify and solve organizational problems.

As we learn about the organization's priorities, reach out to people working on these projects to see if there are opportunities to raise our hand and either lead or support. Meet with our manager, our team, the customers we serve, and other leaders in the organization. Listen for problems and connect these problems with our experiences and ideas from conferences or current trends and innovations. We are looking for problems where we can have the largest impact, saving resources, resulting in more money, or enhancing the overall impact for the organization. Consider solutions and gather input so that we can start persuading leaders about our ideas. This will show leaders that we are proactive and think outside of our lane. According to research collected by Target Training International, the single most important trait serial entrepreneurs possess is the ability to persuade.

For example, one client I coached got feedback that she needed to be more "strategic" and more "visible." She admitted that she was focused on doing the technical aspects of her work (specifically marketing). To be more strategic, we brainstormed a key organizational project that was not directly related to her day-to-day work. She identified a fundraising project that was an organizational strategic priority. Even though she did not know anyone personally who was involved in the project, we created a relationship map and identified a colleague who was connected to the leader of the fundraising team. My client approached this colleague to share her interest. The colleague introduced her to the fundraising team leader, who then invited her to be one of the leaders on the project. My client would update her team on the fundraising project and share how this connected with the team and the larger organization's direction. At her next performance review, her manager highlighted her impact as a strategic leader.

BUILD BIG-PICTURE SKILLS. Along with taking on strategic projects, deliberately build big-picture skills. Don't stay focused on the details. Instead, take a big-picture view of potential opportunities and threats for our organization. Watch how senior leaders share their vision for the organization and create a vision for the project and team's future. When we lead projects and make decisions, communicate how these play into the big picture.

For example, create a vision and strategic plan for our team by reflecting on the following questions:

- How does our team contribute to the company's mission and vision?
- What are our ideas for where this team will be in 30, 60, 90, 180 days and one and five years from now?
- What would success look like, and how would we measure it?

- What additional resources would the team need?
- How can the team be more effective?
- Even if you aren't leading the team, what would our plan of action look like for the first 180 days if you were leading the team?

Share this vision and strategic plan on how to grow the team and contribute to the organization with our manager and leadership. Be respectful that our manager may feel like their toes are being stepped on, so offer these ideas as opportunities for all of us to have more impact. Offer to lead one of these projects to build and showcase our strategic and leadership skills.

PRACTICE 3. BEWARE OF "INVISIBLE WORK."

As we raise our hand for strategic projects, be selective in taking on extra roles to avoid falling into the trap of professional herding. Professional herding is where a man and a woman who start out in the same position get herded into different directions, with women getting herded into service roles and busywork that involve a lot of work but little recognition. Women, especially women of color, are often burdened with unpaid, unrecognized, and non-promotable "invisible work" like unofficial diversity advising, support roles for teaching and teamwork, holiday party planning, and menial duties such as note-taking or coffee-making.

Knowing what we want can help us avoid this. Dr. Alice Eagly, coauthor of *Through the Labyrinth: The Truth About How Women Become Leaders*, says that because we want approval and respect from others, it can be tempting to do what others want us to do rather than what we want. Assess tasks based on their strategic importance, alignment with organizational goals, potential for recognition and advancement, and networking opportunities. Consider the impact on our current work and what we will have the time to do.

Here are statements that could be helpful when responding to your manager:

- To take on this project, what would I need to give up from my other priorities?
- If I lead this project, how will it be measured for my end-of-year performance review?
- I can take on this role, but for the next cycle, I'd like to sit on the organizational level committee.
- Unfortunately, I'm not able to take this on. My plate is full and I want to make sure I'm doing quality work. How about I recommend someone else?
- How about we create a team rotation system. I can take the role for the next 3 months, and then we can switch off?

Then stop talking, and allow them to solve their problem. Many women tend to shoulder not just their own responsibilities but also those of others, believing, "If not me, then who?" For managers, resist the urge to complete tasks for our team because they lack time or it's faster to do it ourselves. Embrace these moments as invaluable teaching opportunities; investing in their learning now will pay dividends in the long term.

Remember, promotions are based on accomplishing tasks, not merely doing them. Balance completing tasks with strategic career building to advance professionally.

PRACTICE 4. BALANCE COLLABORATION WITH DECISIVENESS.

Women tend to be masterful at working together, getting everyone's input and agreement. But the flipside of being collaborative might make us seem unsure or weak because we hesitate to make tough decisions or act quickly without consulting everyone. To balance this, sometimes it's good to involve the group in decisions, but don't make it a habit. Decide on our own when necessary, even if it means delivering tough news. Making independent decisions shows our authority, and people will respect us for it.

Women, as collaborative leaders, tend to share responsibilities too much, letting committees decide. But this can make others think we can't decide or that we aren't comfortable with having formal authority. To show our leadership, have a clear vision, a strong opinion, and let our team work independently toward it. Resist the temptation to delegate too much or rely on committees for decisions; maintaining our firm stance reinforces our leadership presence.

One woman I coached wanted to improve her decision-making skills. Her 360 indicated team members doubted her ability to make tough choices. In our discussion, she revealed, "When I have a hard decision to make, I almost always ask my team what they think I should do. This gives me great ideas, and I usually end up doing one of them." While this approach built trust and showed she valued their input, she saw how this default leadership style—especially when she used it for both big and small decisions—could be interpreted as her inability or unwillingness to take a tough stance herself. This "polling" approach, typical among women, sought early approval but slowed decisions.

Reflecting together, she adapted her strategy. Urgent, low-impact decisions were made independently with input from one or two key leaders. High-impact choices that allowed more time and needed more information included input from more senior leaders. She evolved, acting swiftly and independently, balancing team input with decisive action.

PRACTICE 5. SEEK FEEDBACK, A COACH, AND PROFESSIONAL DEVELOPMENT.

Research shows women receive feedback based on personalities, not skills, limiting senior role opportunities. Natalie Johnson, cofounder of Paradigm, a DEI consulting firm, notes, "Not only are women getting criticized based on their personality traits, which could impact their opportunities, they are missing out on feedback that is more actionable." Feedback tends to be vague and not connected to objectives or business outcomes because managers worry they will be perceived as racist or sexist.

To counter this tendency, proactively ask for feedback from our boss, mentors, and teammates. Make this a consistent part of our after-action report when projects are completed. Even though getting criticism is not easy, view this as an opportunity to accelerate our development.

Given most people struggle with feedback, being able to ask for and receive it can greatly impress others. Just a straightforward ask such as, "I value your opinion and would like your honest feedback on my leadership. Can we have 15 minutes?" Use a 2x2 feedback method: highlight two strengths and two areas to improve. This proactive approach demonstrates our commitment to growth and leaves a strong impression.

Beyond feedback, connect with a coach experienced in guiding women of color in leadership. Get referrals from professional networks or diversity-focused groups. Ensure our coach empowers women of color, offering personalized advice for challenges related to race, gender, and intersectionality. Seek a coach who creates a safe environment, offering practical strategies for overcoming obstacles in predominantly White and male-dominated spaces. Look for a coach who fosters self-confidence, resilience, and effective self-advocacy.

Additionally, consider participating in leadership programs or mentorship initiatives specifically designed for women of color. These programs often provide valuable insights, support, and encouragement tailored to the unique journeys of women of color in leadership roles. By investing in ourselves, we can gain the necessary mindset, tools, and community to rise in our career.

PRACTICE 6. SPEAK UP.

In leadership roles, especially as a CEO or in similar positions, effective communication is paramount. We represent not only ourselves but also our organization when addressing the board, clients, and the media. Even if we haven't reached the CEO level yet, the ability to articulate our responsibilities and embody our organization's values is crucial for success. Developing our executive presence involves refining our public speaking skills.

I used to fear speaking at meetings, let alone in front of a room. However, a mentor once shared, "People who know how to speak get listened to. People will think they are smarter than they are." He encouraged me to join

Toastmasters, an organization dedicated to enhancing public speaking confidence. Thanks to this guidance, I learned to speak with confidence, leading to more opportunities to present and connect with senior leaders. Though I still get butterflies, they now fly in formation.

As we climb the corporate ladder, mastering public speaking becomes integral to our role. We must excel in delivering prepared speeches, engaging in spontaneous discussions, and confidently asserting our viewpoints. I've been in meetings where individuals, mostly White males, interject and interrupt. If I hadn't spoken up, I wouldn't have had the chance to share my perspective. I used to meticulously plan my words, waiting for the perfect moment, only to realize I had missed my chance. With practice, I've discovered that being assertive and proactive ensures our insights are heard, particularly in fast-paced environments where others are quick to voice their opinions. Seize these opportunities to express our thoughts openly and powerfully, reinforcing our position as a capable and influential leader.

PRACTICE 7. LEAN INTO AUTHENTICITY.

I must address how authenticity has been discouraged by the "old boys club," forcing women of color to choose between assimilating to fit in or disrupting the status quo. We often find ourselves code-switching to navigate various spaces. A Catalyst survey revealed that 79 percent of women of color felt the need to alter their demeanor or appearance to fit in at work.

Ideally, we could be our true selves without judgment, but biases persist, influencing how people perceive our behavior and appearance, impacting our careers. However, this doesn't mean compromising our values or suppressing our identity. A client of mine, upon becoming a CEO, wondered, "How do I need to change so that I can be a good leader?" We emphasized anchoring her leadership in her unique qualities, like empathy, humor, compassion, and passion. Embracing her authentic self, she shared personal and funny stories, allowing others to know her better. She also incorporated her Latin culture at work through food and traditions, encouraging others to do the same.

As women of color, don't be afraid to be ourselves and lead as ourselves. Embrace our values, heritage, and strengths. Act from a place rooted in our identity and intentions. Recognize that our uniqueness is our strength; it defines our distinct brand. Sharing our perspective and culture enriches the workplace, bringing diverse insights, family values, traditions, and knowledge to others.

BOOK BONUSES

Explore the Book Bonuses for this chapter:

- List of books for further reading
- Podcasts with full interviews of women leaders spotlighted in this chapter

MYTH EIGHT

We can have it all

Wake up at 5:15am.
Head out the door by 6am.
Work.
Get home at 8pm.
Eat a quick dinner.
Work until 11pm.
Repeat.

This was my schedule for four years while I was starting and leading a school. Until I got pregnant with my first child.

As excited as I was, I was also stressed. I worried, "How could I manage my job while being a new mom?" There were few models I could look to. Most of the teachers and leaders who worked at our schools were young without kids. None of the senior leaders offered advice or support.

It was two months before the baby was due. I still had no solution. Luckily, the decision was handed to me. My husband's company asked our family to move to India for a temporary assignment for 6 months.

I didn't need to figure out work-life balance. We were moving to India! The move to India was a relief because I could leave my job graciously without needing to sort out my personal situation.

I grew up hearing, "Shoot for the moon! Dream big! Anything is possible! You can be whatever you set your mind to!"

I wanted a life with the perfect job and the perfect family. I wanted to be the best mother, leader, partner, and friend. I wanted it all.

THE MYTH

We can have it all. We can have work-life balance. It just takes discipline and commitment.

> ### WHICH OF THESE EXPERIENCES RESONATE WITH YOU?
>
> ☐ No matter how hard you work, how efficient you are, how many books you read, and how many podcasts you listen to, you can't seem to have it all.
> ☐ You feel that you are falling short. Your work, family, and personal life are not where you want it to be.
> ☐ You feel caught in an endless and exhausting cycle of projects or demands.
> ☐ You feel angry at people who ask you for favors, even reasonable ones.
> ☐ You struggle to say no even when you want to.
> ☐ You feel burned out or have lost your motivation.

THE REALITY

Never get so busy making a living that you forget to make a life.
— Dolly Parton

The reality is that the myth of "having it all" is bunk. If we look at where the phrase "having it all" started, it came from

Helen Gurley Brown, editor in chief of Cosmopolitan magazine. In 1982, she wrote *Having It All: Love, Success, Sex, Money, Even If You're Starting With Nothing*. Seen as one of the most successful women in publishing, Gurley Brown aimed for women to want more, to not have to choose between career, family, and self-care. In her 462-page book, only six pages mention children. She admits that she never had children herself and struggles to integrate children into her "having it all" program.

The problem with the idea of "having it all" is that it assumes that all women want the same thing—to be a mother and have a successful career. But "having it all" can mean different things to different people, so let's let each decide what life we want. The other problem with "having it all" is that we develop unrealistic expectations. We think that if we don't have it all, then our life isn't perfect. This leads us to cram in non-essentials such as staying up past midnight to bake a cake for our kid's school's fundraiser, insisting that we need to personally grocery shop instead of outsourcing, and checking our email constantly even when unnecessary. All of this leaves us stuck on a never-ending hamster wheel.

It's not true that achieving the Good Life means juggling everything flawlessly—a flawless job, partner, kids, social life, and body, all effortlessly managed. There are varying levels of good, better, and best. Not everything has to be perfect or the best. We don't need to have every item on the list to find happiness.

If we've fallen prey to the "having it all" delusion, we're not alone. Back in 2012, Anne-Marie Slaughter wrote an article for *The Atlantic* titled "Why Women Still Can't Have It All." In her piece, she aimed to dispel the myth that a woman can effortlessly balance a high-powered career and a flawless family life if she's dedicated enough. She argued that this myth unfairly holds women accountable, deflecting blame from dysfunctional systems consuming women's time and pushing away female talent.

Slaughter herself had bought into the "having it all" myth. On the surface, her life seemed perfect— a significant role in the State Department and a mother of two sons. However, in reality, she was miserable. She made the decision to leave her job and be home with her children. According to her, the issue isn't about women's commitment, ambition, partner support, or time management. The problem lies in the very concept of "having it all," which places women in a situation where they cannot possibly win.

Many of us have been inspired by feminist leaders like Angela Davis, Gloria Steinem, and Ruth Bader Ginsberg, who carried the torch for female equality. While we advocate for equality, we also need to accept that we cannot have it all. We have limitations. Time is finite. Life is uncertain and unpredictable. Control is an illusion. Instead of trying to "have it all" and make everything perfect, we need to prioritize what really matters, do what makes us happy, and release what matters less. Then in six months, we can reevaluate our focus.

THE PROBLEM WITH WORK-LIFE BALANCE

"Work-life balance" is the idea of balancing professional and personal life and assumes that they are not in conflict.

But they are in conflict. This balance often leads to perfectionism and a constant feeling of inadequacy, especially in a capitalist culture that values relentless hustle. Women of color especially are left feeling undervalued, empty, and not enough. Never feeling enough on the inside leads us to feel that whatever we have on the outside is not enough. We then end up chasing enoughness that seems to have no end. We have no time for self-care or rest.

David Whyte, in his book *The Three Marriages: Reimagining Work, Self, and Relationship*, argues that the traditional understanding of work-life balance is overly simplistic. Instead, he advocates for integration, where happiness and wholeness are integrated across all parts of our lives. Stew Friedman, a professor at the Wharton School of the University of Pennsylvania and author of *Leading the Life You Want: Skills for Integrating Work and Life*, agrees. He emphasizes integrating mind, body, and spirit to allow for "four-way wins" to contribute meaningfully to work, home, community, and individual well-being.

In this pursuit of integration, self-care is essential, contrary to the myth that constant sacrifice is noble. When we deprioritize rest, skip meals, spend long days at the computer, sacrifice family and friends, and ignore our well-being and mental health, we are less able to support others. By prioritizing our well-being, we expand our capacity to lead and create inclusive environments where everyone, regardless of differences, is acknowledged, heard, and appreciated. As the saying goes, we can't pour from an empty cup—by nurturing ourselves, we enhance our ability to nurture others and foster spaces of genuine value and respect for all.

These women share their personal journeys toward integrating work, home, community, and well-being to align with their values and priorities.

THALY GERMAIN
Haitian, CEO and Founder, Onward and Managing Director of Transformation and Culture, Berlin Rosen

Thaly developed independence early in life. She got a bachelor's degree from Bryn Mawr College, a master's in administration from Fordham University, and another master's in education from Trinity University, then held various senior education positions, including school principal. Thaly's perspective on leadership transformed after a significant personal experience challenged the notion of work-life separation. Through launching Onward, she crafted workplaces reflecting her values, benefiting not only herself but also her team.

I've had the opportunity to work in various settings, and I've learned that prioritizing personal well-being and maintaining open communication is crucial for a successful team. I once experienced a situation where I had to choose between work and my personal life, which made me reassess my priorities. As a result, I believe in creating a shared leadership model where team members are empowered to lead their own work and make critical decisions, irrespective of their "position."

On our team, we believe in open conversations and creating a culture that values the well-being of each team member. For example, we've eliminated the traditional approach to evaluations.

Instead, we trust our team members to take responsibility for their work and manage their time. We also provide one another feedback directly and consistently. This approach is based on respect, rigor, and trust.

Furthermore, we have embraced a non-hierarchical structure where seniority does not dictate decision-making or work leadership. Team members lead their respective areas, regardless of their level or title. This can be uncomfortable for some, but it allows us to foster an environment where people can be creative, share ideas, and be their authentic selves while contributing at their fullest potential.

We also understand the importance of self-care and intentionally create moments for rest and rejuvenation. During team meetings, we incorporate short activities like chair yoga, quick workouts, or joyful moments to allow us all to recharge and connect on a human level. Additionally, we are actively exploring opportunities for long-term sabbaticals in collaboration with a partner who focuses on embodied restoration and rest. These intentional breaks help us address the challenges and traumas of our work, enabling us to better support and show up for our team.

Our team embraces individuality and we provide opportunities for personal growth and exploration. Our research and development shop, Onward, offers an avenue for creativity, thoughtful reflection, and diversification of skills. We believe that each team member possesses unique talents and perspectives, and we encourage them to explore and leverage those talents.

Ultimately, our focus is on building a team culture that prioritizes well-being, open communication, and shared leadership. We recognize that by showing up as our authentic selves and supporting one another, we can create a productive work environment.

Erica defines what it means to have her all, instead of a generic "having it all."

What does it mean to have it all? You have to define "all." My all is going to be different from yours. For me, having it all today is so different from what it was three years ago.

Six months into the pandemic, I drove my kid to and from school every day. As the schools were opening back up, I said to my son, "We're probably about to have the mandate lifted. I'm going to start traveling for work again. So let me know what you like about what we've been doing and what you don't like." He said, "I really like that you pick me up every day and drop me off every day. I really want to keep that."

For me, having it all means that I arrange the time and the space to be able to pick him up and drop him off because he said that matters to him. So now I will not take a business trip during the week that I have him. I will not take a meeting over that time. I will make sure that my work schedule accommodates him. I will make sure that I have the flexibility to be his mom. To me, that's what having it all is, in addition to the professional goals and all the things I want to do.

You can have your all. But you have to know what your boundaries are. You have to know what your goals are. You have to know what your all is and know that it's not going to look like somebody else's. Someone once told me to think about it in the context of your tombstone. What do you want on your tombstone? You can't put a whole laundry list on there because it's not all important. What are the five to ten words that you want there? That's how you prioritize your life. You shouldn't compromise on those key values that are going to matter to you when you etch them in stone.

Be able to find those boundaries in those life goals, try to live in that truth, don't cross lines that are going to make you feel like you have given up a part of yourself. I think a lot of people especially now are seeing how important it is sometimes to just walk away and not feel bad about that.

I rewrite my tombstone regularly. I want "great mom" there for sure. I want my kid to really like me. I want to be somebody that's memorable. There's another saying, "People might not remember what you said, but they will remember how you made them feel." I want to make people feel a certain way. That's what I aspire to, to be a person who makes other people feel like they are important, valued, and special. That's what I would want to bring to the community, my profession, to my kid, to my partner, to my family, to my friends.

Guerschmide's commitment to equity in education stemmed from her upbringing. She experienced firsthand how children of color were not given equal access to great schools. Guerschmide channeled her anger and became a classroom teacher, then later a student recruitment leader, charter school authorizer, charter school Executive Director, senior leader at the National Charter Schools Association, and CEO and Founder of GSA Consulting. Guerschmide shares her discovery that to rise and thrive at the top, she needed to find a rhythm of rest.

It is a myth that rest and work are constantly at odds with each other, that there's this tense relationship between work and rest. What I've learned is that it's really about finding the right balance between work and rest that lets you maintain your career without burning out.

In our 20s and our early 30s, we were nose to the grindstone working oftentimes at the expense of our families and definitely at the expense of ourselves. In some cases, we were having nervous breakdowns. Then I realized I didn't have to do that. I used to approach a presentation by working 15 to 18 hours to make sure that it was perfect. After the presentation, I would collapse and spend the weekend sleeping to recover. Now, my approach is to figure out the specific work blocks I want to work on it and the specific times I will engage in deep rest ahead of it too. You need to have the capacity to deal with things going wrong. If you're tired, you're not able to meet the moment when something happens. To rise to the top, it's not just about the journey to get there. It's also about how to stay there, which means reflecting on how you work, while also resting deeply.

As an Executive Director, I was purposeful about modeling for my team what healthy rest and work looks like. Even as a school leader for a turnaround school, you can get meaningful work done and also have time for yourself and family. It is about being clear about your boundaries. Find a culture that actually does value rest.

JESSICA SANTANA
Afro Latinx, Puerto Rican, Co-Founder and CEO of
America on Tech

Jessica discredits the myth that success means sacrificing self-care. She points to self-care as part of the social justice movement. As women leaders of color, we model the need to prioritize and normalize self-care.

My favorite quote by Audre Lorde is: "Caring for myself is not self-indulgence, it is self-preservation, and that is an act of political warfare." When I don't make an investment in myself, I see it as an act of betrayal to the movement. I also see it as an investment in myself with a guarantee of return. As a result of me getting a return, I can pour back into my community in a way that if I wasn't investing in myself, I wouldn't be giving from my overflow. I would be giving from a very empty cup.

For example, Sundays are Jessica appreciation days. I'm in nature, I'm with my dog, we're by the water, we're going hiking, or we're just taking a nice walk and grabbing some Starbucks. It also might look like getting my nails done and maybe a massage. Sundays are days where you are not going to catch me between the hours of 11am and 8pm because I realized that I do my best personal work in silence. I've also made sure that I prioritize taking my vacation. I was recently on vacation and for 12 days, I didn't look at my email.

Another thing I'm doing for myself is normalizing luxury for Black and brown girls. That means if there's a week where I don't want to do laundry, I'm calling the laundry person. If there's a week where I don't want to sweep the floor and mop the floor, then I'm going to order a TaskRabbit. I realized that those small financial investments can make a world of difference for your mental health.

In normalizing luxury, we also looked at getting an executive assistant. I talk to nonprofit leaders who are so afraid to put money toward helping themselves, and I tell them that I was there. I know what it looks like when you're trying to schedule meetings, talk to a board, talk to a funder, clear your email, and you have no help. My co-founder was not my executive assistant. He himself was also leading projects. We had each other. We didn't have anyone to support us. It was about normalizing that I also deserved help at work. This work doesn't just fall on me to figure it out alone. This is something that I've come to grips with in the last two or three years.

Five years ago, I'd have said, "Self-care, what do you mean? I'm out here grinding." But now I realized—why grind when life is short, and we've seen so much destruction and so much death and so much grief around us? These last two or three years, I've told myself, "The work required for me to get to the next level starts with me." I'm working on my own internal traumas, healing my inner child, spending time with people who I love, and prioritizing my health and self-care.

STEPHANIE MORIMOTO

Chinese American and Japanese American, Owner and CEO of Asutra

Growing up, Stephanie's grandparents were her inspiration. They modeled tenacity and positivity. Her grandmother moved from Indonesia to the US amidst civil unrest. Her grandfather was imprisoned in the US as part of Japanese internment during World War II. Filled by a deep conviction to create positive change, Stephanie found herself working 18-hour days and burning out. She made a big pivot, prioritized self-care, and bought a small natural remedies business called Asutra (where Venus Williams is a co-owner and Chief Brand Officer). Stephanie challenges the myth that self-care is selfish. She shares how self-care saved her life.

I had these incredible role models in my grandparents and parents working extremely hard, working lots of hours. I grew up with the idea that hard work and trying your best were the most important things, that productivity meant you were worthy.

After graduating from college, I went into a development role at a national nonprofit that focused on the education realm. It was a culture that reinforced those ideas that it was all about how hard you worked, how many hours you were there. The mission of helping kids is so critical that if you weren't giving it 120 percent, if you weren't working crazy hours over the weekend, then you weren't doing enough for the mission.

It reinforced that aspect of my upbringing that if you weren't getting all A's, doing your absolute best, and working your absolute hardest, it wasn't good enough. I wasn't even 30, and I was working 18-hour days, traveling across the country. I was on this crazy hamster wheel helping to grow an organization by leaps and bounds. But come the weekend, I would literally collapse on the sofa. I was so tired, I couldn't even change and get in bed.

I realized this is no way to live. I have no joy in this. If I don't sleep, if I don't eat well, if I don't exercise, if I'm not taking care of my mind, my spirit, or my body, I'm not going to make it too far. So all of those things hit me at once.

I had a dear friend who said to me, "Everyone deserves to be happy." It took me a while to really hear him. But now that is my mantra and what I share with other people. He really made me realize I didn't have to do this, this level of productivity, this level of working hard. I didn't need to do it to prove that I was worthy.

I quit that job and was fortunate to be able to give myself a year off of work. I promised myself that I was going to take that year to really reset and figure out who I wanted to be in the world, and what my purpose was. That was the turning point that led me to realize just being is enough. There's more in this world for all of us if we're willing to welcome that joy and be present in the moment.

Here's my recommendation for someone in a similar struggle:

- *Practice self-awareness – Get a good therapist to understand your patterns, often tied to what we learned in childhood.*
- *Embrace that we are enough – We don't need to be productive to prove our worth.*
- *Take time to reflect – I took time to reflect and get clear on who I wanted to be. I also used Julia Cameron's The Artist's Way to journal and find a way I could be creative and give back to the community.*
- *Prioritize yourself – To take care of our world, we need to be in community and take care of each other. To take care of each other, that means we need to have a reservoir of energy, which means taking care of ourselves. Everyone deserves to be happy.*

JUDIE SAUNDERS
African American, Partner, ASK LLP

Growing up in Alabama with a father who was a professor of African American studies at Howard University, Judie valued education and justice deeply. She became an attorney, supporting clients who had experienced sexual abuse, and co-authored the book *A War on My Body* with Gloria Allred and Paxton Smith. When Judie became a mother, she faced a pivotal decision about how to balance work and family. She chose to prioritize her family while still working. This led to an internal conflict where Judie questioned her identity. Judie's story highlights the myth that "having it all" must be solely rooted in work. She realized that she was not her work; she encompassed much more than that.

Understanding who I really was took a lot of work. It was a lot of frustration, separating myself from these different identities. The learning was accelerated when I was trying to balance career and parenting. There is no greater teacher that will accelerate you in divorcing yourself from identity. Becoming a parent, being married, and being a litigator in New York City who was building a career—that brought a lot of tension.

It came to the point where I broke that identity to be this particular person you dreamed of being, twirling around New York City, living in this glass box with floor to ceiling windows, and going to fancy parties. My two boys, literally and figuratively, took me by the face with their little sticky hands and said, "Look at me." By looking at them, I saw myself and was able to say, "The only way you're going to really achieve any type of personal and professional success is if you stop being so inflexible about who you are." I learned to be more fluid, to lose the identity based on the expectations I had of myself and what society expected of me. I let go of what I thought I was going to achieve in certain time periods. I told myself, "It's not going to happen. And guess what? That's okay."

Growing up in Hawaii as a "hapa" (half White and half Asian), Aarika felt confused about her racial identity and never felt like she quite belonged. She was eager to leave the island and after college focused on early literacy and closing the opportunity gap for students. Aarika struggled with integrating work and motherhood with two young boys. Aarika counters the myth that work must come first to be successful. She shares how she learned to set boundaries and prioritize her family and self-care.

When I started at Reading Partners as an Executive Director, I was pregnant. I had to go on maternity leave a few months after I started this big role. I was grateful that they were accommodating. When I came back to work, I felt like I owed it to them to work really hard. I've always had this sense of loyalty.

But over time, I was spending more time working and less time with my family. We had vacancies that took a long time to fill so I was taking on a lot of those responsibilities. You go into nonprofit, and people tell you, "You're going to wear a lot of hats." I was wearing a lot of hats, but I was wearing three people's hats. Most nights, we would put the kids to bed, and then I would work for several hours for multiple consecutive nights in a row.

One night, my husband sat me down and closed my laptop. He said, "You can't keep doing this. This is not sustainable. Do you want your kids to look back on this time, and say, 'Mom was always working'? You don't want that." That was the wake-up call that I needed. I realized that my loyalty has led me to really poor boundaries. I probably should have said no a number of times.

It was about loyalty and also about empathy. The empathy side of me was trying to protect my team from being overloaded. It was also about the culture of the organization. Ultimately, the blame comes down to me. I could have been the one to put my foot down and say no. I had a hard time figuring out how I was going to dig myself out. Once you've set those expectations, it's hard to pivot.

Coincidentally, an opportunity came across my desk to be the Executive Director for Kristi Yamaguchi's nonprofit organization. It came at the right time in my life. People talk about the stars aligning. This was one of those moments for me. Kristi's organization, Always Dream, is focused on literacy, which is something that I was already doing. They were doing work in the Bay Area, which is where I live, and also Hawaii, which is where I was born and will always call home. This opportunity aligned so well to my own story. I decided to apply and got the role.

Going into the Executive Director position at Always Dream, I had that talk with my husband in the back of my mind. I started with, "How do I set more boundaries around my time so that I'm not on email all the time and dropping everything for work? How do I work smarter and prioritize my time?"

I became intentional about blocking off my calendar for work time to do the strategic work, instead of doing it after hours. I also blocked off family time. I was deliberate about communication—for example, was a meeting needed or could this be a quick phone call or email?

The key for me was realizing that my loyalty to my organization led me to compromise my family, and I needed stronger boundaries to live the life I want as a mom and leader, consistent with my values.

MELISSA KWAN

Chinese Canadian, Co-Founder and CEO, eWebinar

Growing up in Hong Kong, Melissa was raised with the belief that the ultimate goal is financial success. Her parents hoped she would pursue a career as a professional, like an accountant, doctor, or lawyer, but Melissa chose entrepreneurship. She faced challenges with her startup and had to borrow money from her parents to pay credit card debt. Despite setbacks, Melissa was relentless and successfully built three companies without the support of venture capital.

In 2017, Melissa made the decision to leave New York City and travel the world while working on her second startup. Melissa debunks the myth that to achieve it all, one must sacrifice and postpone happiness. She firmly believes that happiness should form the foundation of a career and offers advice on how to enjoy life in the present while pursuing professional success.

My path to being a digital nomad began in 2017. We left New York to travel full time. We were paying astronomical rent in New York and also traveling. One day, I asked, "For $3,500 a month that we're paying for this room in New York, what can that get us somewhere else?" I've always worked remotely, before it was cool, because we couldn't afford an office.

I was looking at Airbnbs in Chile, Argentina, Vietnam—amazing places that we could get for half the price. These New Age storage units had come up, and you could put your stuff into boxes, store them in New York, and then return and repack by retrieving them through an app. Traveling the world became really easy. So we left New York to give it a try. We ended up doing it for three years.

It was probably some of the best days of my life. We ended up finding Amsterdam, one of the best cities in the world with a high standard of living, people who want to have fun, clean water, clean air, and affordability if you don't make money locally. In 2019, when I sold my company, we bought an apartment in Amsterdam to be our home base.

Don't forget to live your life and have fun. I'm a huge advocate for life/work balance now. We don't need to work more. We need to work creatively. This is why I created eWebinar. Our mission is to give people their time back. Instead of doing live webinars, they can automate it with a video, combined with live chat, and pre-programmed interactions. I think you should automate as much as you can so you can live the life you want with complete freedom.

There's this idea that you need to work more, be more efficient, work longer hours. If you leave work on New Year's Eve, then you're lazy. We are supposed to be machines for other people. If working all the time is what you want and what makes you happy, then you should absolutely do that. But there are so few things at work that can't wait for tomorrow. If you remove those artificial deadlines, you open up the possibility that you can spend more time with friends and family and with yourself.

KRISTE DRAGON
Mixed Race (Filipina and White), CEO of the Pahara Institute

Growing up in a racially ambiguous family in Georgia and later Alabama, Kriste sought a place where she could truly belong. She moved away from her family to focus on her career in education. She faced challenges in recent years;

her mother died of COVID, and her father is battling cancer. Kriste gained a broader perspective on life, which led her to clarify her priorities, align her life with her values and purpose, and make more deliberate decisions about where to live.

My dad is very sick. He has late stage cancer, and we had no idea until four months ago. He was presenting perfectly healthy, and then his bones started breaking. It was a sign of how long he's probably had the cancer because it already hollowed out his bones.

I don't think I realized when I moved so far away in my early 20s from Atlanta to Los Angeles that I would be gone so long. In my heart, I thought I would go back. I ended up having my first child literally nine months after I landed in Los Angeles. While there's a beautiful career story, I didn't stop and ask as my kids and my career got more inundated in Los Angeles, "What are the potential transition points to go back to Atlanta?" I never consciously really decided to stay; I just never decided to go back.

So what I missed is thinking through what it would mean to live this far from my parents through the upbringing of my three children, through all the highs and lows of life, marriage, parenting, and especially at the end of their lives, which for my mom was very fast. I go back as often as I can, but I don't see my dad nearly as much as I would like, given what I know is probably not as long a future together as we had hoped.

I wouldn't go as far as to say it's a regret because I don't think you can pick out one thing and change and have everything else be the same. I deeply believe that the puzzle is what it is. But I do really love conscious decision-making, intentional discernment. I didn't have that frame of mind before, partially because of my age and partially because I didn't talk to people about it.

I didn't do what I would do now at work. I didn't talk to five people who had done this before and ask, "What are the pros and cons?" That is what I am coaching my daughter who is out of college and my son who's a little bit younger. I'm saying to her, "There are no bad decisions in a perfect world. But there are trade-offs and choices. So just be conscious when you're making them. You're signing up for what you can live with." I'm watching her, as early as 23, start to think about how close she wants to be to her family because she knows what it feels like to have been really far away. She's still very close to my dad and was very close to my mom.

If I knew then what I know now, I would have made the priority list with my mother, sat down with my parents and said, "Look, I'm going to live in Los Angeles. That's where my career is." That's where I felt at the time I belonged. We could have said, "What does that mean? How much time do we want to spend together?" We could have made different financial choices and prioritized differently for long periods of time together. We could have been in partnership around how we thought about real estate. Maybe it even would have pushed them to think about the potential of relocating out here, which we never really talked about.

I'm trying to do something different with my kids. I say, "Look, the world suggests that we should all save, retire in our own separate places, maybe in the same city, but still separately, be very independent of one another. I think there's another way for us to think about it. What would it look like for us to think about ourselves as a unit, knowing there will be people added to the unit?" I assume my kids will have life partners. What would it look like to make a plan around what we prioritize? We might prioritize being within driving distance, so that we're not doing this on our own, and I'm not getting old on my own, they're not raising kids on their own. What does it look like to have a more communal sense of all of it, so that we are setting up the life we want?

Maybe it'll look like we all buy one big house together, which is probably my dream. My mom's family is still in the Philippines, and they are all still living together. They're literally in one house or on one huge piece of property, and they're sharing literally a birth-to-death life. So it's not surprising to me when I really think about it that I would yearn for that a little bit. What are we going to build for ourselves that keeps us together and supports each other in the back half of our life the way we have in the front half of our life, knowing that we may develop mobility issues. They're all still questions for me, questions that just weren't there ten years ago.

WHAT WOMEN OF COLOR CAN DO

How can we define our all and live our values? How can we take action now instead of delaying gratification?

Here are steps we can take:

PRACTICE 1. PUT OURSELVES FIRST.

REFLECT ON OUR BELIEFS ABOUT REST. Do we believe that taking "me time" is selfish? Or do we view rest as a right? How much rest, leisure, family, and friend time do we get each day? What gets in the way? Think about the quality of our sleep in an age where Netflix CEO Reed Hastings has said that sleep is Netflix's number one competitor, "And we're winning!"

VIEW REST AND SELF-CARE AS A RIGHT. We deserve to put ourselves first. We don't need to prove our worth by being martyrs of sacrifice and obligation. We need time to heal and rejuvenate so that we are able to lead in a way that is sustainable for all of us.

PRIORITIZE SELF-CARE FOR SOCIAL CHANGE. Audre Lorde, a Black lesbian poet, and activist, said, "Self-care is a political act." In a capitalist culture not designed for women of color, it's our responsibility to reclaim our wellness, health, and rest. Capitalism values tireless productivity and devalues rest, implying that we must earn it. Overworking hampers our ability to lead and problem-solve effectively. Strive for a work pace that enables thriving. Prioritizing our well-being allows us to present our best self, open to possibilities and capable of generating innovative ideas that benefit us all collectively.

PRACTICE 2. CREATE OUR DEFINITION OF SUCCESS.

CLAIM OUR DEFINITION OF SUCCESS. Explore and claim our own definition of success and what it means to "have your all." How best can we start to live an authentic life that is completely and uniquely our own? How can we bring this alive today?

Ask ourselves these questions (these prompts are also included in the Book Bonuses):

- Who am I? What are my values?
- What do I want? What matters to me?
- What legacy do I want to leave in and outside of my work? What do I want to be remembered for?
- Where and with whom have I felt the most alive?
- What have I enjoyed most in my career so far?
- What career move would I make it I couldn't fail?
- Who am I trying to impress? Am I trying to prove myself to my family, parents, friends, or boss? If so, what am I losing by trying to prove myself to them?

- What would I do if I did what I wanted?
- What do I want this next phase of life to look like?
- What do I need to let go of to embrace what's next?
- Evaluating my choices through the lens of myself as a happily retired woman, what choices am I happy to have made?

Some of my clients want to become senior leaders; others want to start their own nonprofits or businesses. Others want to focus on family and building community. One woman wanted to live abroad with her husband and two young children for a year or maybe even three.

Identify our own priorities. Our lives—not just careers—will not give us the fulfillment we want unless we define what it means for us. The more we can align our time and energy to our values and what we care about, the more we will live lives that are meaningful.

PRACTICE 3. CHOOSE A STRATEGY TO BRING OUR ALL TO LIFE.

WOMEN'S PATHS TO "HAVING IT ALL"

A study asked 40 women from four occupations and a wide range of class and race backgrounds the question, "Can I have it all?" While their responses showed that there are no standard or easy formulas for how women manage trade-offs, three strategies emerged.

STRATEGY 1. ANSWER: "No, I can't have it all, but I can have what is most important."

ACTION: Prioritize the endeavors most important and let go of the rest. Each woman was willing to forgo something she cared about, such as children or a higher income, for what she considered essential.

WHAT WORKED AND WHAT DIDN'T: This approach worked well when choices were clear, enduring passions. This approach also worked because they were comfortable saying "no" to their non-essentials. But some felt the sacrifice was too much, like one woman who left an abusive marriage and chose career and an adventurous life. When she turned 40, she realized she wanted children and shifted her focus from a carefree lifestyle to family. After unsuccessful fertility treatments, she accepted that she would need to adopt.

STRATEGY 2. ANSWER: "Yes, I can have it all, but not all at once."

ACTION: Sequence life elements, focusing on one or two endeavors at a time. One woman devoted herself to her career and finances, then shifted to family, becoming a mother at 38.

WHAT WORKED AND WHAT DIDN'T: With this strategy, women felt they were able to invest fully in one or two areas. However, similar to the first strategy, downsides included feeling that an endeavor was delayed too long. One woman lost her chance for a second child due to fertility issues.

STRATEGY 3. ANSWER: "Yes, I can have it all, and all at once."

ACTION: Pursue all endeavors without postponing or conceding. Delegate tasks by seeking help from work, family, or friends, for example by hiring help or partnering with a spouse who played a range of roles from co-equal to primary caretaker in the home.

 This approach allowed for a full-spectrum life, but many felt overwhelmed. For instance, one woman struggled to balance being a good mother and maintaining an exciting career. Half eventually shifted to Strategy 1, prioritizing and cutting back. They reduced loads, for example by finding remote work or a job closer to home, shifting to more manageable work, and shedding non-essential commitments.

As we can see, "having it all" meant different things to different women, guiding their strategies. Life stage, resources, and community support also influenced their decisions. Each approach has advantages and risks. Many women switched strategies when they found flaws in their initial approach.

Consider for us what it means to "have our all." Are there specific endeavors that we are most passionate about that we want to focus on, and are we able to let go or limit the rest? Are there specific priorities now that we want to focus on and then turn our attention to other priorities later? Do we want to have it all (for example, career, wealth, family, relationships, spirituality, lifestyle) without any compromise and right now? What resources (for example financial, community, partner) do we have available?

There is no definitive, right answer. The key is to make a conscious and meaningful choice and not fall prey to traditional male systems where the wife takes on all the childcare and household responsibilities.

PRACTICE 4. FIND WAYS TO INTEGRATE WORK AND LIFE.

Instead of compartmentalizing life, consider embracing the interconnection of all aspects: work, home, family, community, personal well-being, and health. Work-life integration fosters synergy across these areas, improving personal lives and enhancing work performance. We can integrate work and life through the following strategies:

UNDERSTAND OUR WORK-LIFE INTEGRATION. Recognize that work-life integration varies for each person. Define our priorities, such as more time for family, friends, self-care, or creative projects. Create an ideal weekly schedule that reflects our priorities. Identify our most productive times and focus on work tasks during these periods. Schedule time for rest, family, and community engagement.

AIM FOR FLEXIBILITY. Strive for a flexible schedule that allows seamless integration of work and personal tasks. Remote work or flexible hours provide opportunities for integration. For instance, we can exercise or attend virtual therapy during the day, take phone meetings while walking, or handle emails from home. Adjust our schedule to accommodate family and personal needs.

EXPERIMENT AND ADAPT. Work-life integration evolves through experiments. When personal or work circumstances change, try new approaches to balance work and personal goals effectively.

PRACTICE 5. SIMPLIFY.

STEP BACK. Assess our commitments and activities. Identify what truly matters to us and let go of the rest.

Simplify our life by asking:

- What can be eliminated?
- What can be delegated?
- Is every project or errand on our plate necessary?
- Does our child need excessive extracurricular activities?

APPLY THE 80/20 RULE. Instead of aiming for perfection in everything, discern what requires top quality and what can be good enough. Relieve stress by allowing certain aspects to be satisfactory rather than flawless. When we stop trying to do it all at 100 percent, we can have our all.

ESTABLISH BOUNDARIES. Challenge society's obsession with constant productivity. Define our work hours and stay true to them. Avoid responding to emails during off-hours to maintain a healthy work-life balance. When we respond to emails in the early and late hours, we are training our team and leadership that we are available during those times. Remember Parkinson's Law, "Work expands to fill the time available."

LEARN TO SAY NO. Politely decline requests that don't align with our priorities. Offer alternatives or suggest revisiting later when we have more availability.

SET PERSONAL LIMITS. Limit excessive social media, news, and email consumption. Ensure our time reflects our priorities, not others'.

SEEK SUPPORT. As women, we are socialized to think we have to do it all on our own, and we can't ask for help. But there is equal power to giving and receiving. Don't hesitate to ask for help, both at work and home.

Delegate tasks, and ensure an equitable division of household responsibilities with our partner. Even with a full workload, women often take on the brunt of family and household work, including managing the family's emotions. Research shows that in full-time working couples with a child, women do twice the housework and three times the childcare compared to men. Create a shared understanding with our partner where they contribute not only by executing tasks but also by planning and organizing them. This is a team effort.

CULTIVATE JOY AND ENERGY. Identify daily practices that restore our energy and bring us joy. We're not talking about once a year vacations or even once a week yoga classes. What are daily practices that build our energy and feed our soul? These can be simple activities like exercise, walks, or taking a moment to celebrate something we accomplished that day.

There's no one formula for doing it right. Our approach is unique to us. It's our choice.

PRACTICE 6. CREATE THE WORKPLACES WE WANT.

As we reflect and make changes in our life, consider how we can extend this to our team, organization, and community. Let's create a workplace and society where all of us can contribute, grow, and thrive.

Deepa Purushothaman, a former Deloitte executive and Deloitte's first Indian-American woman partner, urges women of color to redefine power in our own ways, "As we become the growing majority of the educated workforce, we have an opportunity to be the change the world needs right now. We can come together and push against a system that was not constructed with our voices and truths in mind." She advocates for a power that is distinct from the White male heteronormative standard, "Power needs to be coupled with safety, and the leaders we gravitate toward should make us feel less guarded." As women of color, we can create change by banding together as a collective and creating a "power for good" that is about championing equity.

BOOK BONUSES

Explore the Book Bonuses for this chapter:

- Work-life integration worksheet
- List of books for further reading
- Articles
- Podcasts with full interviews of women leaders spotlighted in this chapter

MYTH NINE

There is one path to success

I'm at a typical Filipino party. Half a dozen "aunties" give me hugs and then immediately launch into their first favorite question, "Have you eaten yet?" As they pile my plate full of *bangus* (fish), *lechon* (roasted pork), and *pancit* (noodles), they ask their second favorite question, "So what do you want to be when you grow up?"

The first time they asked me this question, I was five. I was balancing my plate piled high with food and didn't know how to respond. My dad was in the US Navy. My mom was a nurse. My dad was gone most of the time, so his job didn't sound appealing. So I picked my mom's. "Um, nurse?" I saw my aunties frown. One of my aunts clucked and patted me on the shoulder, "How about doctor? They work with nurses."

So my dream of becoming a doctor began. I didn't know much about being a doctor. But I did know that every time I was at a Filipino party, and they would ask me about my future job, I would say, "Doctor." Then all of my aunties would beam, "Yes! She is definitely part of our family!"

Fast forward to high school. Each student was required to meet with their guidance counselor, so I met mine for the first time when I was a junior. Ms. Williams had me sit down in front of her desk stacked high with papers. I moved slightly to the left so that I could see her better. Ms. Williams gestured to the candy dish of Hershey's Kisses tucked between piles of paper, "Help yourself." She then proceeded to shuffle through some manila folders, "Tell me your name again?...

Oh, that's complicated. Can you spell it?" She found my folder and spent a minute rifling through whatever was in there. "Okay, your grades are good. I imagine you are here to talk about possible careers. What do you enjoy doing?"

At that point, I hadn't really thought much about what I enjoyed. I worked hard at whatever was given to me. I thought for a moment about the different activities I participated in—sports, community service, church, and music. What did they have in common? "Uh, I guess I like helping people?" She clucked and gave a knowing nod, "Yes, yes, of course you do. But what specifically do you like to do to help people?" She saw that I was having trouble and gave me suggestions, "Maybe you like teaching or writing or doing experiments or organizing?" Those all sounded interesting, but the one that got my attention the most was organizing. I really liked helping people make ideas happen, and organizing plans was fun. Relieved, I told her, "I think organizing?" She clapped her hands, "Oh good. I know of a perfect career for you. A secretary! You can help your boss and other leaders get their work done. You'll be great at it!" She made a quick note in my manila folder, closed it, and put it at the top of a stack. "Now off you go. You don't want to be late for class."

A few years later in college, I found myself exploring different majors. I was deep into Chemistry and questioned whether I wanted to spend four years on pre-medical courses. The summer after my freshman year, I found out that my Filipina neighbor had just graduated from college, and she was getting ready for medical school. Her family was hosting a graduation party for her, and I was excited about the Filipino food and getting her advice. At the party, I gave her a hug and launched into my questions, "Are you excited to be a doctor? What was your experience like in college? What do you wish you knew earlier?" She frowned and checked around us for who was listening. She bent her head toward me and lowered her voice, "Actually, I'm not sure why I want to be a doctor. I spent four years suffering in labs. And now I have so many more years of preparation ahead of me. I wish I had stopped and thought about other careers earlier. I would love to be a teacher, maybe even a professor."

I was grateful to get her advice. Back at Stanford's campus, I happened to meet a student also from my hometown of San Diego who told me that he was majoring in industrial engineering. I discovered that industrial engineering was about organizing systems—of people, processes, and products—bringing ideas to life to make the world a better place. There were many career paths, including being a consultant, project manager, entrepreneur, or nonprofit or for-profit leader. So it was no to being a doctor, and yes to not having a clear path!

THE MYTH

"Follow your dreams! You can be anything you want to be!" Many of us hear this from family, teachers, and society. But behind this, we also hear that the choices for careers are much narrower than meets the eye. If we want to be successful in life, there is one perfect job and career—namely, being a doctor, lawyer, or engineer. Not only that, but there is one clear and direct career path to success.

Can you relate? Whether or not we followed through with getting a Good Job, we probably heard someone tell us about what a Good Job is. What we likely didn't hear was—would it lead to fulfillment?

THE REALITY

For many of our parents, education and a professional career were the paths to upward mobility, status, and success. When I think of my father and mother, both were able to come to America because of a US shortage of military and health care workers after the passage of the Immigration Act of 1965. So it makes sense why my family would encourage a career as a doctor.

While there's nothing wrong with being a doctor, lawyer, or engineer, it's important to look inside ourselves. Many of us have not been deliberate about what we want in our lives. Our parents and teachers told us what to do, and we did what was expected of us. We said yes to opportunities because we believed it would "look good," prove we are worthy, or not disappoint others.

Instead, we can create our own career path, and consider what will bring us fulfillment. We need our own definition of career success which considers our strengths, values, and purpose so that we can not only perform well but have high job satisfaction too.

We also need to know that our career path is likely not going to be one straight route but non-linear. We need to shed the scripted school path of courses given to us. When we were students, we followed a set course: Algebra 1, Algebra 2, Precalculus, Calculus, etc. But career paths are not so spelled out and come with many forks in the road. Deciding which fork to take means understanding ourselves and our desires. It may mean putting aside the career goal that we set (or someone else set for us) when we were a child. It means paying attention to ourselves as we grow.

Most people's careers today have twists and turns, including the path to becoming CEO. We can't rely on organizations mapping out our careers for us. We need to own our advancement by staying connected and open to how we feel and remaining flexible with our career path.

What does that mean? Rather than picking one of the Good Jobs off of the list and then molding ourselves to fit that job, it's more impactful for us to know ourselves and from there, find the job that best fits. What's the key to doing this? Find what we desire, what lights us up. Desire is a powerful compass and will lead us to a path of greater impact, which is a win-win for us and our workplaces.

Why focus on desire and fit? Gallup, which measures employee engagement, says that employees are much happier, more productive, and more effective with customers, patients, and teammates if they are in the right job fit. Employers also benefit from having workers who want to be there instead of workers who are going against their natural abilities and burning out quickly.

PERMA

Positive psychology founder Dr. Martin Seligman created the acronym PERMA to highlight the five building blocks of well-being and happiness:

- Positive emotions – feeling good
- Engagement – being completely absorbed in activities
- Relationships – being authentically connected to others and having a sense of community
- Meaning – purposeful existence
- Achievement – a sense of accomplishment and success

Seligman's formula doesn't prescribe what a good life is for everyone. Different things make different people happy. The key is for people to know what they need across all five realms.

The PERMA model encourages us to make informed choices that are aligned so that we can live a more fulfilling life. We need to consider all dimensions of our life and figure out our values and vision. Only then can we create a life of well-being and happiness.

This means knowing ourselves—our purpose, strengths, weaknesses, and values.

UNIQUE NEEDS OF WOMEN OF COLOR

To effectively pursue our career goals, women of color must consider our unique needs, distinct from those of men and White women. A 2013 study examining 860 US managerial women compared the career aspirations of White, Black, Asian, and Latina women, revealing both similarities and crucial differences. Across all groups, three key aspects shaped their career goals: 1) finding meaning in work and making a positive impact, 2) achieving work-life balance, and 3) attaining conventional success in terms of status, leadership, and income.

Meaningful work emerged as the most significant factor influencing career goals for women in the study. For women of color, this aligns with a deeply rooted "ethic of giving back," especially prevalent among immigrant children. However, Asian women stood out, prioritizing conventional success, likely due to cultural hierarchies where status hinges on titles and employer prestige. Additionally, Asian collectivist cultures emphasize harmony and meeting others' needs before one's own, shaping Asian American career choices through family involvement and acculturation rather than personal interests.

Beyond the overarching goal of meaningful work, differences surfaced among the groups' second and third priorities. For women of color, achieving work-life balance took precedence as the second most important goal. This emphasis may stem from the greater divide women of color experience between their personal and work lives compared to White women. While White women often transition between homogenous personal and work environments, women of color frequently navigate from their ethnic personal lives to predominantly White work settings, with limited overlap. Moreover, women of color frequently play active roles as community and church leaders and caretakers, making flexibility crucial. Unfortunately, many organizations lack policies accommodating responsibilities beyond child or elder parent care.

The study highlighted that ethnic and religious communities often serve as sanctuaries for Black women from hostile workplaces. Latinas also prioritized achieving balance, reflecting their collectivist family culture, where community welfare, traditional female roles, and family priorities, such as marriage and motherhood, take precedence over career advancements that may disrupt home responsibilities.

As we can see, a universal one-size-fit-all approach won't cut it. Women of color need to acknowledge the unique factors that shape our career aspirations. Our identity impacts our career and personal goals, and it's important to resist conforming to mainstream career goals and instead embrace our unique, individual aspirations.

UNIQUE NEEDS OF FIRST GENERATION COLLEGE STUDENTS

As women of color, we may find resonance with a study involving first-generation low-income college students of color where 82 percent were female. The study sheds light on how meaningful career choices can be made while honoring diverse backgrounds. In a unique one-credit college course that encouraged self-expression through photos and self-reflection, key themes emerged.

The first theme explored the balance between internal motivations like joy and community impact, and external pressures to fulfill family expectations, make their families proud, and achieve financial stability. These students delicately balanced personal passion with societal expectations, especially in fields like medicine, law, or engineering, which are often pursued for stability and social status.

The second theme highlighted struggles tied to their identities as people of color, immigrants, and women. These students faced challenges in preserving their cultural heritage while adapting to American society. They valued their parents' sacrifices while envisioning a different future, one that was upwardly mobile but also could challenge stereotypes and act as agents of change within their communities. Many considered careers in medicine, teaching, or service-oriented fields, aiming to make a positive impact on their families, local communities, and even the broader world. Some female students of color hoped to break traditional gender norms by entering male-dominated fields, showing their determination to challenge stereotypes and inspire others.

A significant revelation was their ability to embrace uncertainty, a trait stemming from diverse experiences like refugee camps and witnessing their parents' struggles with low-wage jobs. Despite societal pressures, these students welcomed ambiguity as part of their journey, navigating challenges effectively.

This study helps women of color because it shows the importance of providing space for self-knowledge through self-expression like photographs and narratives. We can document our strengths, draw from our lived experiences, and envision future possibilities. Personally, I faced similar struggles explaining to my parents my interest in nonprofit work and the practicality of earning a living. Balancing self-prioritization with familial expectations can be guilt-inducing, but finding that equilibrium can lead to invaluable support and trust from our family.

STORIES FROM WOMEN OF COLOR

There are many rewarding careers out there beyond the standard doctor, engineer, and lawyer. Here are stories of women of color and how they learned to find those careers through being open to non-linear career paths, using visualization, and taking risks.

LIZZIE CHOI
Korean American, Chief Strategy Officer, Envision Education

On her journey to accept and trust herself, Lizzie debunks the myth that society defines success. Instead, she shows that success, rather than coming externally, needs to be defined internally. Lizzie shares how she learned to choose courage over comfort, allowing her to be true to herself and find the right role and environment where she could thrive.

Growing up, I didn't get pressure from my parents. I felt so determined to push the envelope. If I did something with one project in third grade, I wanted the next project to be something that no one else had done before.

My parents saw that drive and would talk to me, "You need to say no to more things. Please rest more."

I had this idea that at some point after putting all this work in and making enough contributions, I would arrive. But I was getting tired. I was in college. I hadn't even started working yet. But it didn't matter. I still got back on that hamster wheel. The truth was that I was so motivated at that point by other people evaluating me that I could sense that I would feel crushed if I didn't get a good grade in college. I pushed myself that by the time of my junior year, I decided not to look at my grades. I felt like one letter would change the way I felt for a week about myself.

I went to all of my professors and I asked them, "This is an experiment that I'm doing. I would really like you not to share the grade with me but to give me feedback."

They did it, and it was very interesting to be in relationship with feedback without a grade. It was fun to learn. It was fun to focus on mastery. But I also knew at the end of the day, I would have loved to have seen the grade.

So after college, I became a teacher. I got promoted, eventually becoming one of the top people besides the CEO at Summit Public Schools. I was going to be 30, and I remember thinking, "This is going to be my best decade yet." But I just felt sadness. I knew that I needed to make some hard choices. I needed to step away from something that felt very meaningful and people who I loved dearly. I needed to figure out how to be grounded, find my compass, and to be firm in who I am.

I took a couple months off. I also started therapy. I got a coach working on designing my life. I also met my lifelong partner, my husband. I decided I wanted to experiment and built three or four different 10- to 15-year visions of what life could be that were really *different. All of my consulting work were little experiments of what those lives could look like. So I let myself sort of be in that space of ambiguity for a couple years before I decided to join [an organization] full-time.*

The process of figuring out my compass was hard. It comes with self-acceptance. I needed to be honest that I am someone who cares about what other people think. I needed to have the courage to own it. I think the other part is also practicing speaking my truth, practicing saying things that are me but are not well thought out, maybe contradictory to what I said yesterday. But they're authentic to where I am today. And that is the best gift that I can give the world.

LUVLEEN SIDHU
Indian American, Founder and CEO of BM Technologies

Harvard undergrad. The Wharton School at the University of Pennsylvania MBA. Investment banker. Consultant. Luvleen counters the myth that success comes from checking all the success boxes. She shares how she decided to stop checking more boxes and instead take the leap to follow her passion. This led her to start BM Technologies and become the youngest woman to take a company public.

I feel lucky to have a strong father figure. My dad always would say to me, "If it's humanly possible, you can do it." He built so much confidence in me growing up.

The myths that I had were all self-inflicted. My biggest enemy was myself. I had perfectionism, a desire to please, and my own sense of achievement and doubt. I think women are more prone to doubting and putting limitations on ourselves. I've realized that we're so much more powerful than we think we are.

How did I get to where I am today? It was a combination of different experiences. My father was a banker. I guess dinner table discussion kicked in, though I never imagined I would become a banker. But I worked at several banks, investigating different business models in digital banking. I went to business school at Wharton where I got the entrepreneurial bug. I worked in consulting for my summer and loved it. I helped a large financial institution launch their own digital bank and then graduated from school.

It was at that time where I had a decision—either I could be a consultant and spend every Monday and Thursday on a plane. Or I could explore my idea of a new way to do banking. People hated banks in 2008. I thought that this moment was unique, and technology was catching up to do banking in a different way that wasn't branch-based.

I asked myself, "If not now, then when? How much are you going to keep doing what you think you're supposed to do versus what you have an itch to do?" I had done enough of what protects me if something goes wrong. There comes a certain point where you've done enough, and it's not exciting. There was a moment when that excitement came, and I took the leap with the idea of digital banking, which has now become BM Technologies, a publicly traded company on the New York Stock Exchange.

LIZETTE DUBACHER

Mexican American, Senior Business Advisor, Compass Point Consulting

Lizette graduated from Harvard Business School and climbed the corporate ladder. She also fell in love, and she and her husband had two daughters. Lizette found herself choosing between her own career aspirations and her husband's and decided to take a few years off to focus on her kids. Lizette dispels the myth that there is one path to success. She shares her process to find a meaningful career that puts family as number one.

I spent six months working with a career coach. She asked, "What do you want?" I would always respond, "Well, I think I should do this." She would then say, "No, no, no, no, this is about what you want to do. What makes you happy? What gives you a reward? What type of people do you want to work with? Do you want to work alone? Do you want to work on a team? Picture yourself. What is the best setting for you? What type of questions or tasks do you want to be doing? What type of conversation do you want?"

I reflected on her questions and also put together an Excel matrix. I asked myself, "What are the things I value?" Then I weighed them. Which one is more important? Do I care about money, title, commuting, the people who I am working with? Do I care about flexibility? I took ten or so criteria and then the types of jobs that I could do, and I ended up with five or six different jobs. Then I applied each criteria to each job and weighed them. I showed it to my husband and other thought partners who knew me well to make sure I was prioritizing things correctly.

Figure 3: Lizette's job matrix. (This matrix is also available in the Book Bonuses.)

	High priority	Medium priority					Low priority			
	Fexibility and Autonomy	Work with/for interesting people	Challenging Work	Have experience needed	Career Impact / CV Builder	Pay	Need to Look for Clients	Community Impact	OVERALL	Comments
	6, 3, 0	4, 2, 0	4, 2, 0	4, 2, 0	4, 2, 0	4, 2, 0	2, 1, 0	2, 1, 0	30	
Boutique consulting	4	4	4	4	4	4	4	4	27	· Local, medium sized business consulting
Corporate job	4	4	4	4	4	4	4	4	20	· Hard to find a job after a resume gap
Pro Bono Consultant	4	4	4	4	4	4	4	4	20	· Working on a team with interesting people (not alone) · Projects might be not too challenging but they add value to the client
Independent Consultant — Large Business	4	4	4	4	4	4	4	4	20	· Work alone, client might be interesting · Don't have top-tier consulting experience · Need to build client portfolio · Need to look for clients, marketplaces help
Independent Consultant — Small Business	4	4	4	4	4	4	4	4	19	· Work alone · Need to build company and portfolio · Might get bored, projects not too challenging, but adding value · Conflict of interest?
Insurtech Job	4	4	4	4	4	4	4	4	16	· Not very interested in going back to insurance · No start-up experience, maybe I am too old to work on that culture
Non-Profit, Full-Time, Paid Role	4	4	4	4	4	4	4	4	15	· No non-profit experience (yet)

I also spent time networking and met some wonderful people. It's important not to try to find a solution on your own. You have to have conversations with other women, women like you, people who know you well, and people you have worked with. It's really amazing how it takes a village. If you have taken the time and you are honest with yourself, you can find what you want.

My top priorities were flexibility and autonomy. I wanted to see my girls' soccer game or walk or do yoga. I wanted to work with good people where I could have a relationship and common interests. I also wanted to find a job that used my strength of strategic planning. I had also spent time helping small business owners with their business on a pro bono basis, and I really enjoyed that. I wanted to have a job that had these values and where I could use my strengths and help people.

So I found a job at a small boutique consulting company, which is focused on helping family-owned businesses. It's very similar to what I have been doing pro bono but on a bigger scale. The companies are in the community. I can work from home unless I have to see clients, but they all live in Pennsylvania. I can't believe that I really found what I really wanted.

STEPHANIE CHEN BANJO
Chinese American, Leadership Coach, Have Your All Career

By the time Stephanie was 30, she had gotten married, had two kids, lived in six different countries, and gotten promoted in her corporate career. Yet she felt empty. Stephanie had a painful identity breakdown, which led her to reevaluate who she was and what was important to her. Stephanie shows that the myth of using solely our heads to make career decisions is not true. She shares how her emotions, trusting her gut, and using a visualization process led her to a career and life of her dreams.

I got together with a friend, and we spent an entire afternoon on this exercise.

STEP 1. *Set up.*

We put up paper across a wall horizontally, one wall for each of us. Then we set aside 45 minutes on a timer and played some music. We identified the top categories that would spell out our vision: career, family, friends, mental health, physical health, finances. We put each of these categories in the center and put a little circle around it.

STEP 2. *Get clarity.*

We asked, What is the thing you most want in each category if you knew you could have it? If this could drop in your lap today, what's the thing you truly want? Then every 15 minutes, we would share with each other.

STEP 3. *Bring your vision to the present.*

It's not enough to create vision boards and set goals. You need to keep it alive and nurture it every single day. Sometimes we want to create these step-by-step plans, but this prevents us from seeing all the opportunities to bring that to life in the present.

Ask yourself:

- *If you already achieved this vision, how would you approach your mornings?*
- *If you were already the type of person who achieved this goal, how would you approach this situation? What are the three actions you would take today?*
- *Each morning, ask, "What are the three things that I'll do to get myself closer to this?"*
- *At the end of the day, ask, "What are the three things that I did? Is it closer or is it further away? What does my vision need from me today?"*
- *Ask, "How will achieving the goal make me feel?" Then ask,*

"How can I create all of that today? How can I learn how to be content and fulfilled today?" Use what we think we will get in the future and try to find it in your today.

STEP 4. Create an accountability plan.

To stay accountable, my friend and I set a meeting for a year after to check-in.

STEP 5. Enjoy the journey.

Sometimes we think it's all about the goal and the destination, but loving the journey is as important. Through this, you are channeling the person you are in that future state and bringing that to the present. This helps us stay present, while also focusing on what you want in the future.

The beauty is the becoming, not just the destination. It's becoming the person who knows how to build a five-million-dollar business. You can lose the business, but your mental muscles, your know-how can never be taken away from you. Learn how to be kind to yourself in the present. Think, "When I get to my goal, that will be great. And today, I am enough."

In December 2019, I did this exercise. I wrote down that I was a leadership coach working with people who are in seats of power like politicians and lawyers and who are making decisions that impact people all around the world. Six months later, my husband introduced me to a contact who was the head of Diversity, Equity, and Inclusion of a large DC law firm. We hit it off, and I worked with them on a women's initiative to empower emerging leaders to build their career paths. It was a confirmation that when you put something out there in the world, you bring it to life and call opportunities to you.

HANSEUL KANG

Korean American, Executive Director of The Broad
Center at Yale School of Management

Born in South Korea, Hanseul moved to the US at 7 months old. She was set to start at Georgetown University but discovered that she was undocumented and thus no longer qualified for financial aid. But she didn't let this stop her. Hanseul reached out for help, and her teachers and a pro bono lawyer helped her family become naturalized citizens. Hanseul questions the myth that career paths need to be perfectly planned out. She shares how being open to different possibilities led her to take on top roles to serve kids like her.

One lesson I've learned is that if you're feeling frustrated or stuck, you don't need to think that your path is already determined for you. Opportunities may still come along, and they may come from a really unexpected place.

I had a junior role at Teach for America that I loved. I decided to leave that job to go to law school. After graduation, I decided to go back to public education. I found a job that checked all the boxes of what I wanted: managing a team, learning about instructional leadership, and being in DC. Yet, I was miserable. It was technically a higher-level role, but I felt more constrained and less trusted and had much less responsibility. I was really questioning where I would go from here and how to look for the next role.

That was when Kevin Hoffman reached out to me. Kevin had moved to Nashville, Tennessee's Department of Education to become the Commissioner. Kevin had been my manager's manager in my first role at Teach For America. We had worked directly together on a couple of projects that I worked really hard on and had done a good job. Kevin thinks about talent in a way that is different from a lot of other people. He looks at someone who others might consider very junior and sees that they are ready for a big jump. He was looking for a Chief of Staff, and he asked me to take on that role.

I think my path could have gone in a very different route had Kevin not become Commissioner and needed a Chief of Staff right at that moment. Had I not been struggling in the job that I held at the time, I'm not sure I otherwise would have been willing to move to Nashville where I didn't know anyone. I didn't know much about what a state education agency did or what a Chief of Staff did. But I was excited about what Kevin was putting forward and wanted to be a part of his team. I figured I could work hard and learn. It took being willing to take that chance.

Over time, I've noticed this pattern in myself and others. Sometimes the things we look for in jobs are not actually things that end up mattering. I think the people matter a lot, especially your direct manager. That was not one of those things I factored in when I looked for that job out of law school.

Another thing that actually matters a lot is whether you are someone who really wants to step into a role that's well-defined, has clear measures of success, and where you know exactly what you're aiming for. Or do you want to step into a messy and ambiguous situation and figure out your own definition of success? One is not better than the other, but the answer guides at what point you want to come into an enterprise.

I remember saying to Kevin when we talked about the Chief of Staff opportunity, "Could I wait and come in the spring after the school year is mostly over?" He said, "We'd love to have you at any point, but we're building out our team right now. If you were to come in then, your role will probably be at least one layer deeper into the org chart than what we're trying to fill right now." I ended up making the decision to jump earlier and come in at that Chief of Staff level. That was the right move for me.

ANDREA FOGGY-PAXTON

Black, Entrepreneur in Residence, Education Leaders of Color

Andrea's story proves that the myth that career paths need to be pre-calculated is false. She shares how she landed top roles by being open to career pivots aligned with her North Star and seeking out sponsors and mentors.

My mother was a significant influence in my life. She always had at least two jobs and at one point had her own business. My parents divorced when I was fairly young. Growing up, it was just me and my mom. My first job was babysitting some neighbors' children to pay for piano lessons, since my mom couldn't afford the lessons. Then I worked fast food and volunteered at the same time at the mayor's office. Then my senior year after volunteering for a year, they offered me an internship. I went from making $4.25 at McDonald's to $8 an hour.

After college, I ran a youth employment program in Los Angeles. I wondered, "Why is education not giving students what they need? Why aren't they prepared for college and career?" Then I reflected on my own opportunity. While I was in a diverse school, my classes weren't diverse. Oftentimes, I was the only Black student in these gifted and talented courses. I knew there was inequity.

I remember standing at the fax machine pregnant with my first son. I thought, "My child is going to have everything that they could

possibly need to be successful in life. They have two parents who have degrees. We have resources and a network." I asked myself, "How am I going to make sure education is accessible for all students so they get what they need to be prepared for life?" I had this conversation at the fax machine, and I decided. I'm not going back to this job. I need to pivot right now.

I applied to grad school and did National Urban Fellows, which allowed me to work for the Annie Casey Foundation with a school board member from Baltimore City Public Schools. Diane Bell McCoy became a mentor, a longtime friend, and boss. I was at a Freedom school [an educational summer and after school program for low-income children], as a site coordinator. This is when Bill introduced me to Howard Fuller. [Howard Fuller is a civil rights activist, education reform advocate, and a co-founder of the Malcolm X Liberation University.]

I shared my vision for education with Howard and his wife, and they encouraged me to start a school. I was excited! But then my body responded Red Alert, Red Alert, and I listened. I knew that starting a school would mean throwing my whole self into it. I was already working weekends and 12-hour days.

I think it's important to listen to your body. Your body tells you before your mind tells you what the answer is. Really pay attention to how you're responding to different situations. Because I listened to my body, I decided not to start a school. Instead, I pivoted and worked for Jim Shelton as a Program Officer at the Gates Foundation. I never expected to be doing this.

The surprises kept coming. When my son was three, we found out that he was on the spectrum for autism. At that time, I didn't know what that meant, and I panicked. But over time, I learned that it's possible that people can still navigate life, regardless of the diagnosis. But the earlier the diagnosis and support, the better. It *gave me clarity on my personal goals and to be a present mom. It also gave me clarity on my professional goals, to focus on how to make our educational system equitable. There are so many kids who don't get the diagnosis, don't get the support they need to be set up for school, and fall further and further behind.*

CHANDRA ROXANNE

Black Indian or Afro-Indian, Former Managing Director of Astia Edge Fund and Founder, Alice B. Woodland Legacy Fund

Chandra's story shows that the myth of following one path to success is not true. Beginning her career in nonprofit, Chandra shares how she made a mid-life career pivot into venture capital by connecting to her higher purpose and ancestral calling. She shares strategies of how we can do this too.

I pivoted from a nonprofit career to venture capital. I saw early stage venture capital as a tool for incubating consciousness in capitalism by operationalizing the principles of Conscious Capitalism within startups and scaling them together. The Astia Edge and Alice B. Woodland Funds provide access to capital to Black and Latina entrepreneurs. My aim is to help these entrepreneurs understand the higher purpose of their businesses while helping to fund our collective economic liberation.

To understand your higher purpose, you can follow these steps.

STEP 1. *Know your unique position with the world or environment around you.*

The place you occupy within the larger society provides a unique perspective with which you can see opportunities to contribute

significantly and take action.   Consider the concept of the rainbow. You are distinct, yet a contributing member of the whole. If red and blue are removed, the possibility to create purple does not exist. Similarly, there's a balance of being distinct and yet knowing where you are positioned and with whom to collaborate for creating that secondary and tertiary layer of impact.

STEP 2. Look at your own culture and investigate your roots.

I'm a descendant of the continent called Africa and this place called America. Regarding America, I'm a descendant of the Piscataway Indians of the Chesapeake Bay area of Southern Maryland. I have come to realize that I am a part of a larger cultural legacy of heroic figures. Reconnecting to my cultural identity enabled me to glean from them my ancestral purpose, and integrate and reconcile within myself who the Piscataway Indians were and what happened to them, alongside my African ancestors who were enslaved in America. I can understand and see both groups as having their own cultural values, systems, and structures for organizing their societies that were disrupted in creating this Western idea and form of capitalism. There is something beyond the American concept of capitalism. This form of capitalism is not the end all and be all and—given my position as a descendant of enslaved Africans and the Piscataway Indians—its evolution requires my input.

STEP 3. Reclaim your ancestors and legacy.

Reconnecting with my cultural identity felt very much like I was reclaiming my ancestors, reclaiming and activating a legacy that I did not know that I had. When you come here, or when you are forced to have your language and culture removed, when you strip people of their cultural identity, then you're able to replace them. You're able to make them into something else or even make them into objects. Reclaiming the truth of my cultural identity repairs *this trauma and sets me free to pursue a higher purpose that can have lasting effect.*

Our distinct cultural legacies extend far beyond America, and being able to reach back and now pull that wisdom forward is necessary fuel for an ancestral purpose. If we can look back into our cultural troves, we will find connection to our higher purpose as well as the strength to accomplish it.

DR. SHAI BUTLER

Black, Founder of StratHERgies

Shai shares her personal journey of becoming a mom at 14, failing out of college, and becoming addicted to alcohol and opioids. Shai shares how she was able to take charge of her life, get her doctorate, and have a decades long career in higher education as a C-suite executive. She also started StatHERgies LLC, a leadership development consultancy that works with current and aspiring C-Suite managers. Author of *Better. Not Perfect*, Dr. Shai debunks the myth that we need to have one career path. She encourages us to embrace multiple careers in our life journey.

Because of my faith and because of my analytical side, I cannot think that there's an all knowing, all powerful creator who would give us on average 80 years of life and one thing to do. So shed the notion that you have one thing to do. Start to see purpose through the lens that it's a purpose for a season. Ask yourself, "What is my purpose in this season?" Take the weight off of yourself.

We put so much pressure on our young undergraduates. We ask them at 18 years old, "What are you going to major in? Because that's going to be the career that you're going to do for the rest of your life." Then when they graduate at 21 or 22, we tell them, "Pick your career. Because that is going to be the thing you do."

Thankfully, they've rejected all of that. Even the Gen Z millennials. They are bouncing jobs every two, four years.

I'm not promoting job hopping. But what I am saying is to embrace the idea that I can have this career, and then maybe five years later, I can have another career, and then maybe five years later, I can have another career. Purpose is more than a career. When we think about vocation, calling, and mission, and connect them to our profession, it's good to know that there can be seasons.

WHAT WOMEN OF COLOR CAN DO

If I didn't define myself for myself, I would be crunched into other people's fantasies for me and eaten alive. — Audre Lorde

Success isn't determined by external factors (our families, friends, or society) but by internal ones (how we define success and how we feel). This means knowing ourselves, paying attention to our feelings, noticing how our bodies respond when we envision different scenarios, and testing out different career opportunities to ask, "Is this opportunity right for me?"

I have come to believe that each of us has a personal calling that's as unique as a fingerprint, that the best way to succeed is to discover what you love, and then find a way to offer it to others in the form of service, working hard, and also allowing the energy of the universe to lead you. — Oprah Winfrey

How do we own our career? Where do we find happiness and fulfillment? What are our strengths, weaknesses, beliefs, fears, and core values? From my research and personally getting to know women of color who rose to top roles, I found that what they shared was not just competence but knowing themselves. They were able to lean on their strengths when facing challenges and be aware of their weaknesses when they were under pressure. They understood the difference between should and must. *Should* is about societal and family expectations, while *must* is about passion and heart. This clarity creates our compass to ensure that we, and not others, decide what direction to go.

It is not about finding the right job but about finding the right job for us. Find a job that fits into our purpose, joy, strengths, and values and have those shape our career. It's possible that the right job for us is a doctor, lawyer, engineer, but rather than picking a job and molding ourselves to it, figure out who we are and pick a job that suits us. When we live by design, we align our time and energy with our purpose and take consistent meaningful action toward our goals. Our passion, creativity, and purpose serve as fuel, and we feel less exhausted or guilty and instead move with purpose and peace toward our goals.

Get a pen and paper or feel free to bring together photos, similar to the first generation college students described above, to reflect on questions about ourselves and our career aspirations. Better yet, consider meeting with other women of color or a coach to create a safe space as we reflect and share our responses to these questions.

PRACTICE 1. DEFINE WHO WE ARE AND OUR PURPOSE.

- What is the first answer that comes to mind when we ask the questions: What is our "it"? What do we secretly long for? What are we built for?

- What is it we were born to embody—to be, do, say, stand for, and contribute to the world?
- What is one thing we have always wanted to do with our life, for as long as we can remember, but we have sometimes been hesitant to admit? What would we do if we weren't afraid, if we knew we could not fail, and the money would definitely come?
- If we were about to die, what are the three things that people would say about us? How would they describe the difference we made?
- What do we want our legacy to be?

As Chandra Roxanne advised, we can find our purpose by connecting to our culture, history, and ancestors.

- Who were our ancestors who came before us? For me, I discovered generations of hard-working Filipinos who lived on the islands before Spain had colonized it and named the country after Spain's King Philip II.
- What is our people's legacy? We may find that part of our people's legacy is our own life story and what opportunities our ancestors opened up for us. I found that my ancestors were committed to uplifting their children and children's children so that we could have better lives.
- How does our people's legacy connect to our higher purpose? Perhaps our own story is our people's legacy. My ancestors' legacy and sacrifices have made my life and opportunities possible. Just as my people helped me, I see my higher purpose as helping others, especially marginalized groups such as women of color, to have opportunities to live meaningful and impactful lives.

- How can our higher purpose apply to our work? This higher purpose can be applied to businesses, where we can serve something bigger, not just financial gain. For me, my higher purpose has guided me throughout my career, beginning in education and now as an executive coach for women of color and diverse leaders.

As an example, my career purpose statement is: I want to help women of color rise in organizations. When I look back on my career, I hope to say that I helped diverse leaders become the change we want to see in the world.

PRACTICE 2. CLARIFY OUR CORE VALUES.

Values in our life serve as our own personal compass, guiding us toward what really matters. They are the underlying motivation for all our choices. Identifying our core values is one of the most profound realizations we can have. When we realize what is truly driving our choices, life makes a lot more sense. When our actions and our values are aligned, we are congruent and life flows effortlessly. Start by identifying our core values using the list below as inspiration.

WHICH 5 VALUES RESONATE THE MOST?

ADVENTURE	FULFILMENT	POWER
BALANCE	FUN	PROGRESS
CONFIDENCE	GENEROSITY	RESPECT
CREATIVITY	GROWTH	SECURITY
CURIOSITY	HAPPINESS	SELF-EXPRESSION
DISCIPLINE	HEALTH	SELF-RELIANCE
EASE	HOPE	SERVICE
EDUCATION	HONESTY	SPIRITUALITY
EFFICIENCY	HUMOR	STRENGTH
ENDURANCE	INDEPENDENCE	SUCCESS
EXCELLENCE	INTEGRITY	TOLERANCE
FAITH	JOY	TRUST
FAIRNESS	KINDNESS	TRUTH
FAMILY	KNOWLEDGE	UNITY
FINANCIAL SECURITY	LOVE	VULNERABILITY
FRIENDS	LIFESTYLE	WEALTH
FREEDOM	PATIENCE	WISDOM
	PEACE OF MIND	

When assessing different options, we can use these 5 values to narrow down to the option that is most values-aligned with us.

REFLECT ON OUR PERSONAL VS FAMILY VALUES

Consider our personal values in comparison to our family's values and culture. Reflect on the internal struggles we face, such as balancing our passions with our parents' desire for financial stability and respectability in our chosen profession. Many people of color grapple with the challenge of following their dreams while meeting family expectations.

Reflect on these questions:

- Does our career choice align with our parents' aspirations or ours?
- How can we express gratitude for our family's sacrifices while paving our own path?
- If we have dreams of making the world better, how can we align our dreams with a viable career?
- How do we navigate giving back while building generational wealth for our family?

The expectations placed upon immigrant children often lead to complex conversations. Immigrant families make sacrifices to ensure their children's success, yet disagreements and discomfort arise in this journey. Finding a balance between personal goals and family dreams can be a shared achievement. Despite feelings of inadequacy and self-criticism, working through these emotions is part of an ongoing journey, where accomplishments are measured not just by external achievements but by the growth and understanding gained along the way.

PRACTICE 3. STRUT OUR STRENGTHS.

Lean into ourselves! Be who we are. We are often socialized out of our strengths—to be viewed as small, palatable, and people pleasing. But no more—we must be ourselves! Strengths are what no one but we can do the way we do it. It's a unique blueprint—no one has our upbringing and life experience. Strengths are the areas in which we have the most potential and impact, where we are doing what feels natural. Sometimes we get so focused on what we are not that we don't focus on what we are. Focusing on our strengths should take priority ten times out of ten. What if we believed we have everything we need? We just need to know our strengths and leverage them.

DISCOVERING OUR STRENGTHS:

- When are we energized? When are we naturally joyous and excited?
- When do we lose track of time because we are so engaged and immersed? Positive psychologist Mihály Csíkszentmihályi described this as a flow state. Flow is when we are challenged and engaged at the perfect ratio, resulting in effortless, increased performance.
- What successes have we had and what enjoyable skill did we use to achieve them? The successes might come from work with positive feedback from our boss or they might come from personal life through healthy relationships or fun hobbies.
- What is one hidden talent that we really love but are not currently using?
- Reflect on three moments: one from our childhood, one from our young adult years, and one from the last few years, where we were at our best, in flow, and feeling a sense of purpose. What were we doing, and who were we surrounded by? What was the goal we had to achieve?
- What topics do people commonly seek our advice? What activities do people frequently invite us to participate in or express gratitude toward us for?
- Ask for feedback. Choose three people who know us well. Ask them for our top three strengths. Then ask them, "What's the essence of what I bring to any problem or opportunity?"

- Take strength-finding and personality assessments:

  - Big 5 Personality Test measures well-being (predicted by extraversion and neuroticism), spirituality (predicted by conscientiousness, openness, and agreeableness), and health (predicted by conscientiousness, neuroticism, and agreeableness).
  - Clifton Strengthsfinder helps us identify and build on our greatest strengths.
  - Kolbe helps us find our natural way we take action in four distinct Action Modes.
  - DISC helps us understand our leadership style and suggests tactics for increased effectiveness.
  - Myers-Briggs Personality Test uncovers our personality characteristics.
  - Emotional Intelligence 2.0 assesses EQ skills such as self-awareness and self-management.

PRACTICE 4. CREATE OUR ZONE OF GENIUS.

Guy Hendricks' *Big Leap, the Zone of Genius* concept brings everything together: our personal legacy or mission, our strengths, and our values.

ANSWER THESE QUESTIONS TO GET TO OUR ZONE OF GENIUS:

- What do we love to do? We love it so much that we can do it for long periods without getting tired or bored.
- What work do we do that doesn't seem like work?
- In our work, what produces the highest ratio of abundance and satisfaction to the amount of time spent?
- What is our unique ability? What can we do that others are unlikely to be able to do at this level?

PRACTICE 5. CREATE A CAREER ROADMAP.

STEP 1. Define our ultimate long-term career goals. Dream and think big!

STEP 2. Find the gaps between our desired role and our current role.

Identify the knowledge, skills, and abilities we still need to prepare us for our big goal. This could be people management, budget oversight, technical skills, stakeholder management, or public speaking. Build skills not just for our current role but the ones above us as well. For example, if we are one or two levels away from being the CEO, we're focused on organizational vision and change. If we are more junior, we are more execution and detail oriented. To become CEO, we need wide-ranging experiences that help us create value for the company. "You can't run the company until you get some broader set of experiences," said Ursula Burns, crediting her engineering degree for helping her with different roles before she became Xerox's CEO.

STEP 3. Pinpoint which skills are possible and not possible to build in our current job.

Assess the unique needs of the role we want, the skills we need to develop, and whether we are getting the breadth of experience needed in our current role.

STEP 4. Tie our long-term goal to an 18-month plan which includes making asks and building specific skills.

Guerschmide Saint-Ange, CEO and Founder of GSA Consulting and Chief Operations and Talent Officer of the National Charter Schools Association, says that the best advice she got from a mentor was to plan 18 months ahead.

After clarifying our dream job, ask, "What steps do we need to take to get there? What can we do now?"

Take action toward manifesting our vision. Share our desire for advancement with our boss and collaboratively create a plan for professional growth. Advocate for new experiences in our current job or seek a new role at our current organization or another organization. As women of color, it may feel uncomfortable to share our ambitions, that ambition is a bad word. But the right manager will applaud our ambition and support us to rise.

PRACTICE 6. CONSIDER COMPANY CULTURE.

Consider how we prioritize meaning, balance, and conventional success (status, leadership, money). Ensure that the organizational goals and culture fit our values and motivations. Otherwise, we'll feel inauthentic, conflicted and unsatisfied.

If meaning is important to us, ensure that the organization is in alignment. Many organizations continue to struggle to reinvent themselves and to acknowledge, accommodate, and benefit from diverse employees. How can women, who are in the midst of that struggle now, stay true to their own goals?

If balance is a top priority, be wary of organizational practices that prioritize 24/7 availability, extended "face time," and career-enhancing constant travel. In these environments, flexible work arrangements could result in our commitment to work being questioned.

In addition, we want a company culture that is diverse throughout all levels and inclusive so that everyone, regardless of who they are, has fair and equitable support and opportunities to learn, grow, and advance. Gather information to understand how well aligned we are with the organization's mission, goals, and values. Become aware of the organization's view on diversity, equity, and inclusion, and whether they actually do value people of color.

ANSWER THESE QUESTIONS TO ASSESS COMPANY CULTURE:

- Does the organization have accountability for their DEI goals, including recruitment, promotion, and retention for people of color?
- Does the organization have leaders of color on the senior team and on the board of directors?
- Does the organization have an open, inclusive environment or is it cliquish?
- Is the organization open to other perspectives or is it more close-minded and slow to innovate?
- How many other people of color are on our team? Interview these people to ask about their experiences and how they have been encouraged and discouraged to thrive and advance.

PRACTICE 7. BE PREPARED TO BE UNPREPARED.

Be prepared for changes to the plan. Know that a career path is often not linear. There will be jobs we apply for that will not work out. As long as we follow our Zone of Genius, have faith that we are on the right path. No matter the job we are in, we are clear on our why, our purpose, what drives us, what energizes us, and what makes us want to get out of bed in the morning. As we go through our journey, our vision and purpose are the most precious resources for rejuvenation and motivation as we face twists and turns in the road of life.

BOOK BONUSES

Explore the Book Bonuses for this chapter:

- Zone of Genius worksheet
- Lizette's job matrix template
- Resource on Martin Seligman's PERMA theory of well-being
- List of books for further reading
- Podcasts with full interviews of women leaders spotlighted in this chapter

MYTH TEN

We will get the workplaces we want through incremental change led by DEI officers

A NOTE FOR OUR ALLIES FOR EQUITY

This chapter is for all those who are not women of color but want to create change and make organizations and our society more just and fair. It is a heartfelt invitation for everyone, regardless of gender or race, to join forces in creating a more equitable workplace. This book is not merely about empowering women of color; it's about a shared commitment among all of us—men, White individuals, leaders at every level—to create genuinely inclusive and equitable workplaces. Thank you for reading this book and walking in the shoes of women of color to develop empathy. Together, we have the power to transform our professional environments into spaces where every individual, including women of color, can rise and flourish. We don't want women of color to bear the burden of changing the system and are thrilled to have you with us on this journey. Let's stand together and pave the way for a future where everyone can thrive.

RETHINKING DEI PROGRESS

I had the privilege of being part of a panel discussion with senior leaders from diverse backgrounds, all centered around the critical topic of DEI progress. In the wake of the killing of George Floyd by police in May 2020, many companies voiced support for the Black Lives Matter movement and took initial steps to demonstrate their commitment. By 2022, Russell Reynolds reported that three out of four companies had filled chief diversity officer positions. But were these organizations making genuine progress toward building workplaces that are truly diverse, equitable, and inclusive? Or was it just performative? In the face of recent backlash against DEI efforts, we confronted this challenge head-on. How do we navigate this resistance while striving for meaningful progress?

During our discussion, we delved into the distinction between superficial, check-the-box actions and profound, transformative change. While some companies drafted DEI statements, appointed Directors of DEI, and conducted one-day DEI training sessions, we recognized that these efforts, while well-intentioned, were not driving the deeper transformation needed.

What does it truly require to create equitable workplaces? Can we genuinely change existing, deeply-rooted systems? Should we consider rebuilding from the ground up so that every individual can thrive? How can allies get their organizations to try to make their workplaces more fair?

THE MYTH

Despite facing current backlash, organizations have made progress with DEI. With George Floyd's murder in 2020, organizations rolled out DEI statements and made DEI training sessions mandatory. These steps, driven by hired diversity leaders, have been sufficient and are paving the way toward the inclusive and fair workplaces we all envision.

THE REALITY

DEI work is facing pushback, leading many companies to backtrack on racial justice initiatives. The Supreme Court decision in June 2023 to overturn affirmative action in college admissions has further complicated matters, potentially making elite colleges—the pipelines to CEO positions—less diverse.

Organizations are bracing for how this will impact them. While companies have taken initial steps in the right direction, true progress demands a deep, introspective transformation. It requires more than just hiring a DEI leader and changing recruitment and HR policies. It involves looking in the mirror and reflecting on our own internalized racial superiority or inferiority. It involves recognizing power and privilege and White people releasing power. It's about dismantling systems of privilege that are embedded into all aspects of society. This shift requires more than a DEI leader; it requires all of us to actively participate.

MISCONCEPTIONS

MISCONCEPTION 1: DEI is solely the Chief DEI Officer's responsibility.

REALITY: DEI is everyone's responsibility. We all need to make sure that people of all backgrounds feel welcome and successful at work.

MISCONCEPTION 2: DEI is in our organizational statement, and that's enough.

REALITY: DEI requires genuine commitment from CEOs and leaders, setting a vision and leading by example. It requires collective dedication.

MISCONCEPTION 3: We just need to get more diverse candidates in the door, which means lowering our standards.

REALITY: DEI isn't limited to recruiting and hiring. DEI is about creating a more inclusive environment for all employees to thrive. It's not about lowering the bar. There are many top quality diverse candidates; we just need to do a better job finding and attracting great people.

MISCONCEPTION 4: Mandating DEI training sessions once a year is enough.

REALITY: DEI is more than an annual session; it's about building a culture of open and honest discussions and integrating DEI into each employee's day-to-day work experience.

MISCONCEPTION 5: Assigning DEI work to employees of color is sufficient.

REALITY: DEI isn't an additional task for specific individuals; it requires dedicated resources, including staff and budget.

MISCONCEPTION 6: DEI is a temporary focus area, allowing for incremental changes.

REALITY: DEI is a long-term focus area. It is about revolutionary ideas and models, not just tweaks to existing systems. It's about creating new systems so we can create win-win strategies for all.

STORIES FROM WOMEN OF COLOR

Women of color who are leading DEI efforts in their organizations share their on-the-ground stories and advice about what we can do to champion DEI amidst the backlash and against entrenched systems.

KRISTEN HOWARD
Black, Senior Director, Michigan Medicine

When Kristen was a kid, she couldn't stop talking—her third-grade teacher even put her in a little room at the back of the classroom to keep her quiet. But Kristen turned her gift of gab into a force for good. After becoming a lawyer, she championed equity in education and DEI. Kristen busts the myth that we can achieve the workplaces we dream of through small changes led by DEI officers alone. With her experiences in leading DEI, she sheds light on why these efforts often miss the mark.

I think the reason that DEI often fails is not that people don't care. It's that we were socialized in this capitalistic system built on the backs of one-upping the next person, literally as enslaved people. When we're trying to be anti-racist and create equity, we're pushing back on everything we were taught to desire by our society—bigger TVs, bigger cars, fancy vacations. You either want to make money on the backs of others or you want everything to be fair and equitable.

Second, the law is pushing back on DEI. At the Supreme Court level, they're fighting against affirmative action. In California and Michigan, they have constitutional amendments which bar universities and public institutions from affirmative action and considering race or gender in their admissions applications. As a result, enrollment of people of color has plummeted in those states' public universities.

In the legislature, we're at 28 states with laws against teaching critical race theory. These laws are saying, "Don't teach history that makes people uncomfortable, that makes people question our systems. You can't break our socialization cycle. You can't stop teaching young people that they need to be capitalistic and step on the backs of others to get where they need to go. We need to lift up heroes who were slaveholders as positive examples in history and not let you teach children to question how these people got their success, or feel bad for the people on whose backs people had to step on to get where they were going."

As women of color, feeling like we're not worthy, it is because we're buying into a vision of what worthy looks like that is based on this capitalistic standard. If we slow down our careers to focus on our children, who are our greatest gift and our greatest opportunity, that means we've opted out, we quit on ourselves, we're not giving enough to the capitalist machine. For me, doing this equity work instead of being a corporate lawyer, it's like I failed, because I'm not making more money than I was 10 years ago. I'm not measured by the impact on people's lives.

I am very hopeful. We need to get woke and stay woke. When I say get woke, I mean understanding the systems that prevent equity. While there is a very clear conservative political effort happening to shut down anything that is averse to a dominant cultural stance, we can come together to open those doors back up. After Roe v. Wade was overturned in Michigan, grassroots organizers got a constitutional amendment in Michigan that said, "No, women get to decide whether or not they will reproduce." In the 2022 elections, young people, ages 18 to 25, voted in the largest proportions. At the University of Michigan, students waited for three, four, or five hours to vote.

When I say stay woke, I mean staying educated and consistently pushing back. When we make progress, they're going to push back against that progress. For Brown v. Board of Education, which desegregated schools, there was a case called Milliken v. Bradley ten years later, which allowed segregation through the use of property taxes. You need to vote, look at local initiatives, think about running for office, and think about getting involved from a policy standpoint.

Find ways at your organization or in industry to make change. For example, hospitals used a calculator to determine how critical your disease was and if you were eligible for a kidney transplant. If you were Black, your disease was less critical than a White person who had all the same kidney functionality because Black people can survive with lower kidney function. Similarly, for a vaginal birth after cesarean, if you were Black, you got a point against you;

you're too lazy and won't do the work to have a vaginal birth after cesarean, so we're less likely to offer it to you. In our hospital, we removed these race-based indicators in our calculators.

At companies, you can implement DEI work that gets you better quality talent. Update hiring practices to blind-read resumes, recruit more diversity, and conduct longer trainings that decrease bias. A Harvard School of Public Health study found that it takes about 12 hours of bias training to change your mindset. Change your policies as a system. Have zero tolerance for sexual misconduct or microaggressions. This helps with the bottom line. As our younger Gen Z comes into the workforce, they have expectations of diversity principles. They care a lot about the belief systems and the organizations that they join. If our organizations don't shift our culture to meet them, then we lose money.

I believe women of color are best positioned to lead this change. We naturally look for ways to create a culture that's more welcoming to people from diverse religious and cultural backgrounds and people who are pregnant and parenting. As we become leaders, we can't do it through assimilation. We need to bring our authentic selves to change the status quo.

DEI is not a destination, it's a journey. It's like a Sisyphean task—you have to keep pushing that rock up the hill. If you let it go, it will roll back down. The more people we bring to the table, the more hands we have to push that rock forward.

LEAH GORDON

Black, Afro-Latina, Associate Dean for Inclusive
Excellence, Diversity, and Belonging and Associate
Professor of the Practice at Boston College

Meet Leah, a resilient leader who faced adversity head-on. At 19, she was a young mom on welfare, often rejected from jobs because she lacked the "right" degree. But Leah's journey took a turn when mentors recognized her talent. With their support and her determination, she not only earned an associate's degree in nursing but went on to get a bachelor's degree, a master of science degree in nursing as a Family Nurse Practitioner, and ultimately earned her Doctorate in Nursing Practice. Now, as the Associate Dean at Boston College, Leah challenges the myth that small DEI changes are enough. Drawing from her own experiences, she emphasizes the need to be proactive advocates for racial justice and transformative, systemic change. Her story inspires us to be systems changemakers in our own right.

I'm a walking, living, breathing healthcare disparity. I was a young mother who gave birth at 19. I was on welfare. My father had hypertension and died of a heart attack. My mother, an immigrant from Panama, had a stroke. I share these personal stories and my lived experience because they have the power to change minds, beliefs, and ultimately systems.

If you want the world to be more just, find a way to be your own covert agent inside systems. The system is not set up to work for people of color. But that doesn't mean we can't change it. Share your wisdom with the person next to you, beside you, who's coming up behind you. Share so that they don't have to experience the same trauma that you've experienced.

For me, DEI in nursing is absolutely imperative. It wasn't right that I had to get my doctoral degree to prove to people I was enough. But the degree also puts more weight to what I say because I have more alphabet soup behind my name which in society provides a broader stage and wider audience.

I remain focused on the fact that the profession is mostly White nurses. Our white nursing colleagues need to know how to take care of diverse populations because that can make the difference for somebody's health. We need to put health equity at the forefront and get our White nurses to rise to the occasion and prioritize DEI, just like preventing falls, just like managing pain. That's always been our Code of Ethics through our American Nursing Association, caring for everybody equally and equitably.

We now have multiple bodies that govern what we do in nursing education that are on board with DEI. For example, the National League of Nursing, which helps govern nursing education, has a DEI toolkit that we can use in academia to make sure that we're addressing this in our coursework. The American Nurses Association (ANA) is on a racial reckoning journey. At the National Black Nurses Association Conference in May 2021, the ANA talked about that racial reckoning statement and highlighted their commitment and concern. So when people doubt whether we can discuss racialized medicine, health disparities, and health equity, we can point to these governing organizations and how they are charting a path for health equity. For me, I'm in an inaugural position in a school of nursing with all of this support from the mothership organizations, and we can gain ground in the larger health landscape.

This is different from other spaces, like corporations. Their decision to hire DEI people is very tethered to what the board and higher leadership wants. If it's not in alignment, they can only go so far.

Reflecting on the George Floyd murder of 2020, it bothers me that it feels like we need another nine minutes of watching a Black body be disrespected, to lose life, to then find momentum. The momentum was when we were brought here against our will and treated as poorly as we've been and Indigenous people had their land taken.

BETTY NG

Chinese American, Founder and CEO, Inspiring Diversity

Betty faced discrimination as an Asian American from childhood into her 20+ years in the corporate world. Instead of letting it break her, she turned her pain into power and purpose. Betty founded Inspiring Diversity to help organizations, educators, and families build inclusive cultures. She refutes the myth that traditional DEI methods are enough. Betty's approach focuses on well-being, inclusion, and even pickleball, offering a unique perspective on creating real change.

If organizations continue on the diversity, equity, inclusion, and belonging (DEIB) path of the same old, same old, then we're not going to get very far. The Harvard Business Review had an article in March 2023 which showed that there is a significant disconnect between HR leaders' perceptions of DEIB progress versus what employees believe the progress was.

There's resistance, there's burnout. If a more engaging and relatable approach is not taken, we're not going to go very far. Relatability is key to all this. Storytelling is also key, with the data to support, showing the impact on real people. These honest conversations need to happen. It's not just talking about the strong business case for DEIB. We know that diversity and inclusion drive innovation, but we haven't seen progress.

That's why Inspiring Diversity is focused on well-being and also on embedding conscious inclusion into the cultural DNA. When we talk about DEIB, it can be overwhelming. But when you take a step back, you think about culture, which is the sum of the individuals. We as individuals ultimately drive everything else. How inclusive we behave ultimately drives how an organization looks with respect to diversity of representation, how it acts with respect to promoting diversity and inclusion, and ultimately how the organization feels with respect to equity and belonging. If we can get the individual behavior right so people think, act, and interact inclusively, everything else like putting policies and infrastructure in place becomes so much easier.

But if you don't address individual inclusive behavior, everything else with respect to DEIB is that much harder to achieve. I think organizations need to focus more on that and recognize it's not just about these one-off workshops. Research shows that when it comes to real, lasting behavioral change, only 20 percent of it comes from insights that one-off workshops may offer; 80 percent of it comes from how we live and breathe these behaviors in the day-to-day reinforcement learning that has to occur. That's what really needs to be focused on, and a lot of organizations aren't doing it.

Everyone is at a different point in their journey, which is one of the reasons why it's important to establish a baseline. As part of Inspiring Diversity's work, we have Think Act Interact Quotient (TAIQ) assessments for inclusive behavior. How many of us really understand what it means to be inclusive? Based on extensive research and experience, we have boiled inclusive behavior down into eight key behaviors [being open, aware, unbiased, performance/goal-oriented, curious, culturally competent, collaborative, and courageous]. We've developed an assessment that measures how people think versus act versus interact. It's really important for people to assess their own inclusive behaviors and see their areas of development and strength. After taking our online assessment, you get your personalized, individualized heat map with red, yellow, and green. It comes with recommendations based on how you answered the assessment in terms of things that you should consider doing, as well as things that you should continue to do. It's about honing in on specific behaviors. We focus on what we call conscious inclusion to promote, coach, and develop positive behavior. How can we all be more inclusive of each other?

I also integrate pickleball into the work that we do. Because when people hear pickleball, they don't think DEIB, they just think fun. But actually, there are so many lessons from pickleball that can help us play, work, and live well together. That includes lessons specific to DEIB. Pickleball is an inclusive sport. People of all backgrounds, ages, sizes, abilities can play pickleball. Pickleball is also typically played as a double sport. It's always about teamwork as opposed to an individual level sport. We tie lessons into broader lessons that apply not only on the court but also off the court. By bringing people together to play pickleball, you can embed mindfulness with respect to teamwork, collaboration, and DEIB in ways that pull people into the conversation and help them be more mindful in a very relatable way without cramming it down their throats and creating walls and resistance. It's about camaraderie, community, and mindfulness.

RHONDA BROUSSARD

Black, Founder and CEO of Beloved Community

Rhonda's passion for building a Beloved Community is rooted in her education leadership and Reverend Dr. Martin Luther King Jr.'s vision "to create a beloved community" that would "require a qualitative change in our souls as well as a quantitative change in our lives." With critical race theory and LGBTQ rights under attack, Rhonda shares practical steps to keep DEI moving forward. She dispels the myth that DEI can be handled solely by a few and encourages us to unite, finding our unique place in this vital movement.

Am I brave? Am I doing the things that I'm espousing? My son asked me when he was little, "Are you going to be an activist when you grow up?" I appreciated his generosity of thinking that I still had growing up to do. And also that I could become an activist at whatever age.

Alice Walker has a book called Hard Times Require Furious Dancing. *That is the place that grounds me from a dance perspective, that we have always created moments of joy within the hard times, right within the context in the oppression and genocides that our families have faced for centuries.*

Some people know from a young age that they want to be in public service. They want front-facing elected roles in public service. There are other folks who know they want to be in public service but in behind-the-scenes roles. I want to be the behind-the-scenes functionary who is doing the nitty-gritty work of policy change, influence, and strategy. Some people don't figure out either of those things until they are inspired by some life event that is happening.

What I think about when I'm naming this bravery, I think it's to know which of those folks you are first. This goes back to—how well do I love myself? How well do I know who I am? How am I showing up in the world? Once you can get clearer about whether you are trying to live that external-facing life or you want to be doing more of the behind-the-scenes work, then you can start to find a pathway that demystifies all of that.

I think bravery comes in being in proximity with people, organizations, and ideas that help you demystify it. This is why organizations like Run For Something or Monzón in Arizona are helpful. They explain the whole process and how it works. Here's what you do. Here's what others do. Here's how you build campaign structure and funding. Then there are organizations that once you get elected help you figure out how to navigate the role of that particular elected official, like school board partners who work with elected school board members. You don't have to do it all by yourself. You just have to figure out where you want to start.

Once you can get clear about that and what matters to you, you can manifest it. You can talk about it as prayer or talk about it as a strategy. You have to be able to envision where you're headed, communicate it to yourself, and communicate it to at least one other person out loud or in print. Then the universe will help you identify the resources that are going to help you get there. I think that's where bravery comes. It's one step at a time.

From the Thich Nhat Hanh perspective, the larger your beloved community, the more you can accomplish in the world. I think about all the different roles that people have to play. There are the roles for the agitators. There are roles for organizers. There are roles for folks who are more on the policy side. There are roles for people who are doing daily service and frontline facilitation with current power holders. There are roles for the people who do shadow work in terms of what they fund and don't fund in communities.

We've been talking in an informal space with other people of color who are either nonprofits or in funding. We've talked about how we get stuck; it's thinking that we all have to be moving toward the exact same end. The folks who are on the abolitionist side don't want to engage with folks who are about DEI because that sounds transactional, and we want something that's more radical and moving toward a liberation agenda. We talk about getting rid of capitalism, and those aren't the same things.

We need to admit that the tools that we have right now are imperfect. How can we leverage these imperfect tools toward a collective future? How can we all align on where we're headed, and the fact that we have different roles to play to get there, as opposed to if you're not moving toward this radical future in the same way, with the same perspective, then it's not worth a collaboration? What are the ways that we collaborate with folks who are doing more on-the-ground action? What are the ways that we collaborate with folks who are in the funding space or research space? What are ways that we collaborate with folks who are in elected and political strategy work? Because we all have a different role to play.

WHAT WE ALL CAN DO TO ACHIEVE EQUITY

While this book is written for women of color to overcome challenges at work, it will take everyone working together to make the workplace more fair so that women of color are able to rise and get a seat at the table. This means White women, men, and leaders at all levels making the workplace more equitable.

WHAT WHITE LEADERS OF ALL GENDERS CAN DO

PRACTICE 1. UNDERSTAND AND CHALLENGE YOUR BIAS.

Self-reflect and identify your own biases and prejudices. It may involve acknowledging uncomfortable truths about your privilege and confronting deeply ingrained stereotypes.

Acknowledge the harm biases cause, especially to women of color. While it may not be your intention, bias hurts people of color, making their journey harder than it should be. Imagine a qualified woman of color being turned down for a job because her name sounded "different" or being disregarded during meetings because her voice isn't valued or being denied a leadership opportunity because she doesn't "fit in" with the White male leaders. These unexamined prejudices add up and are disheartening and unjust. When a woman of color is consistently treated with skepticism based on unfounded assumptions, it strips away her opportunities, confidence, and ability to lead effectively. This stunts not just her individual growth but also robs organizations of diverse perspectives and innovative solutions.

Confront your biases by reflecting on your own beliefs and attitudes. Own your learning by reading books, attending DEI workshops, and watching documentaries that challenge your viewpoints. Educate yourself about racism and its historical context. Understanding the systemic nature of racism can help to dismantle deeply ingrained biases.

Build real relationships with people from different backgrounds by breaking bread and sharing stories. Authentic connections, rooted in respect, trust, and mutual understanding, break down stereotypes and promote solidarity.

Keep an eye out for moments where biases might influence your thoughts or actions and actively challenge them. In professional settings, bias could impact job interviews, performance evaluations, promotions, or project assignments. In social settings, bias could impact your choice of friends where you favor people similar to yourself and shape your opinions about strangers and who you trust.

Take responsibility when your actions cause harm. Apologize and create a plan so that you don't repeat the mistake. By being aware of and confronting biases, you can prevent more harm to people of color.

PRACTICE 2. RECOGNIZE AND ADDRESS WHITE FRAGILITY.

When you encounter discomfort or defensiveness in discussions about race, recognize these feelings as signs of White fragility. Instead of shying away from these emotions, acknowledge them openly. Understand that these reactions, although natural, can hinder meaningful conversations about racial issues.

To navigate this, educate yourself by reading books and articles, like Robin DiAngelo's *White Fragility: Why It's So Hard for White People to Talk About Racism*. Learn how to recognize and address these reactions.

Have honest conversations about race with both people of color and fellow White individuals. Instead of judging or dismissing others' perspectives, listen empathetically. Engage in open conversations with fellow White people to unpack these issues. Create a safe space for dialogue with people of color by validating the perspectives and experiences of people of color. This fosters understanding and helps bridge the gap between different perspectives.

When confronted with your own biases, see this as an opportunity to improve rather than as a personal attack. Resist the urge to deflect or dismiss. Instead, embrace these moments and feedback as a chance to learn and grow.

PRACTICE 3. BE AN UPSTANDER.

Being an upstander means standing up against injustice and discrimination, especially when others are passive or indifferent. Unlike bystanders who observe a situation without getting involved, upstanders actively intervene. Your voice is powerful and can lessen bias and discrimination, one conversation at a time.

Here are steps to take to be an upstander who challenges racist behaviors or comments, even in everyday situations:

STEP 1. Learn about different forms of bias and prejudice to be more aware when they arise.

STEP 2. If you witness someone being treated unfairly, step in and address the bias or discrimination directly. Use simple, clear language to express your concern, explain how it affects others, remind them of the importance of fairness and respect, and suggest ways to make things better.

STEP 3. Show empathy and support to those facing discrimination. Put yourself in their shoes to understand their experiences better. Offer support such as an encouraging word or a listening ear. Encourage others to join you in supporting the affected person.

PRACTICE 4. MAKE SPACE FOR WOMEN OF COLOR.

Use your influence to level the playing field. In meetings, step back and ensure every voice, especially those of women of color, is heard. Empower them to share their insights and experiences openly. Actively curb dominating voices and invite diverse perspectives to enrich discussions. When opportunities arise, be a champion—recommend a woman of color for speaking engagements or pivotal projects.

Recognize the limited high-level positions and intentionally create room for women of color to ascend. It's about acknowledging privilege and making conscious choices. A seasoned White male leader and friend shared with me, "I could've taken the CEO role elsewhere, but I chose to make space for a Latina leader. It's time to uplift diverse voices."

PRACTICE 5. BE A SPONSOR OR MENTOR.

Extend a hand to women of color as a sponsor or mentor, guiding them with your own experiences and valuable advice. Share negotiation strategies, introduce them to important contacts, and offer support in navigating challenging situations and workplace dynamics.

A good sponsor actively advocates for their mentee, creates opportunities for their visibility within the organization, and ensures they receive the recognition they deserve. By investing your time, expertise, and influence, you can empower women of color to thrive and succeed in their careers.

PRACTICE 6. FOSTER CONFIDENCE.

Boost the confidence of women of color through heartfelt encouragement and recognition. Take the time to acknowledge their skills, talents, and contributions, especially in the presence of senior leaders. Your genuine praise can work wonders, providing colleagues with the reassurance they need to believe in themselves. Additionally, offer continuous support and mentorship, sharing your experiences and wisdom to guide them along their path. By fostering a nurturing culture of positive reinforcement, you can empower women of color in your workplace to embrace their capabilities and excel with confidence.

PRACTICE 7. GIVE HONEST YET KIND FEEDBACK.

For those who manage women of color, encourage two-way feedback where both manager and direct report give feedback to each other. For example, in 2x2 feedback, the manager and direct report both share what they're good at (strengths) and where they can improve (areas for growth). It's like a friendly conversation where both talk about what's going well and what could be better, helping both grow together. For any tough feedback, connect feedback with sincerity and care, "I'm sharing this because I genuinely care about your growth and success."

PRACTICE 8. SUPPORT WOMEN OF COLOR AS WHOLE PEOPLE.

For managers, create a win-win where women of color can achieve both organizational and personal goals. Encourage them to share their personal aspirations and set boundaries that honor these priorities. Grant them autonomy to accomplish their work in ways that resonate with their unique styles. It's not just about embracing differences; it's about celebrating them. Take a step beyond inclusivity: personally invite women of color to office gatherings and even your home, ensuring they're woven into the fabric of the workplace community. Create an environment where women of color feel welcomed and supported.

PRACTICE 9. ADVOCATE FOR CHANGE.

Champion inclusive policies. Advocate for flexible remote work, unbiased recruitment and promotion, zero tolerance for harassment, and return-to-work policies for mothers. Provide opportunities for people lower in the company to share their ideas, for example, through open office hours, surveys, or listening tours where you connect with smaller groups to hear their thoughts.

PRACTICE 10. SUPPORT MISSION-ALIGNED ORGANIZATIONS.

Lastly, actively engage in anti-racist work. This involves supporting organizations and initiatives that promote racial equality and dismantle barriers for women and people of color. For example, Sharhonda Bossier and Aimée Eubanks Davis have founded organizations such as Education Leaders of Color (EdLoC) and Braven, respectively, championing social justice and empowering underrepresented individuals. EdLoC supports leaders of color in education to thrive as leaders in the larger social justice movement. Braven helps underrepresented college students develop the skills, confidence, experiences, and networks to get strong first jobs after graduation.

WHAT WHITE WOMEN CAN DO

"Each time a woman stands up for herself, she stands up for all women." — Maya Angelou

PRACTICE 1: CREATE COMMUNITIES OF SUPPORT.

I've witnessed instances where instead of standing together against an unjust system, women have seen each other as rivals, undermining and sabotaging one another. The term "queen bee syndrome," was coined in 1973 to describe how some female leaders in male-dominated environments keep female "worker bees" down. That said, it's important to note that "queen bee syndrome" ignores the role that men play and oversimplifies women's relationships.

Let's stand together, supporting rather than competing with one another. By sharing our successes and earnings openly, we equip fellow women with career navigation and negotiation tools. We can see the impact of women being in top roles. In a study of America's top 1,500 companies in 2015, researchers found that when a woman became CEO, other women were more likely to advance to senior roles. As we rise, we can help others rise.

PRACTICE 2. SHARE YOUR STORY.

Use your platform to share stories of empowerment about your leadership journey, mistakes, and lessons learned. Through platforms like my podcast, *Women of Color Rise*, we've witnessed incredible courage and vulnerability, inspiring others to rise.

PRACTICE 3. EMPOWER THE NEXT GENERATION.

Model for our daughters. Equip our daughters to recognize and combat racism and sexism, sharing our own stories.

Foster their self-worth, confidence, and resilience. Encourage self-love, perseverance, and the courage to overcome challenges, empowering them to lead so that they can slay the monster of discrimination for themselves and others.

WHAT WHITE MALES CAN DO

Being a White male gives you a unique opportunity to dismantle racial biases and create a more inclusive society.

PRACTICE 1. BE AN ALLY.

An ally is not a member of an underrepresented group but has privilege and power—often White, cisgendered men—and can support less represented groups. Men are more likely to be taken seriously by other men when they advocate for women. How can you be an ally? Publicly declare yourself to be an ally who stands in solidarity with women of color to your leadership team and direct reports. Build trust with women of color by offering mentorship, sponsorship, or access to your network, including your "old boys club."

PRACTICE 2. LEAD BY EXAMPLE.

Lead with kindness, respect, and inclusivity. Encourage open discussions about biases and discrimination, creating a safe space for dialogue. As a White male leader, your actions set the tone for those around you. Speak up when microaggressions occur, and take responsibility when your actions have caused hurt. By being an upstander for fairness and equality, you inspire others to become upstanders too. Call out misogyny and racism in White-male-only conversations. Engage in conversations about biases with other males and encourage them to become allies. This not only helps you but also encourages others to confront their prejudices, fostering a workplace where everyone is treated with dignity and respect.

PRACTICE 3. ADVOCATE FOR CHANGE.

Use your privilege to amplify the voices of people of color and the changes needed to support a more just world. Advocate for diversity and inclusion within your workplace, community, and social circles. Challenge discriminatory practices and support initiatives working toward racial equality. By being a vocal ally, you can help challenge systemic racism and encourage others to join you.

WHAT ORGANIZATIONS CAN DO

Organizations can take bolder steps to support women of color. It can't be up to individual women of color to facilitate change. A 2020 McKinsey report showed how diversity at the leadership level remains slow due to a lack of "systematic approach" and lack of "bold steps to strengthen inclusion."

In this section, we share a roadmap of how organizations can go beyond airy goals to making meaningful progress on DEI. We need to move from incremental, ad hoc "feel-good" steps, to fundamental changes. We need to come to terms with our unconscious bias and help women of color who have been overlooked because they are not part of the "good old boys network." This isn't just about being "not racist" but being "anti-racist," actively opposing racism and discrimination in all its forms and actively promoting equality, justice, and fairness for all races. It means creating a diverse workplace of belonging and inclusion where each person matters and thrives.

PRIORITIZE DIVERSITY, EQUITY, AND INCLUSION

PRACTICE 1. MODEL INCLUSIVITY AT THE TOP.

Before we bring women of color into the organization, we must create an inclusive environment. This starts with a genuine commitment to DEI, led not just by a DEI head but by the CEO, board, and leadership team. The CEO must communicate the why of DEI and treat DEI as a core company value. Ensure a safe environment for diverse leaders, conduct regular culture surveys to gauge inclusion, and maintain a zero tolerance policy for discrimination and harassment.

When the most senior leaders actively support DEI, they set the standard for the rest of the organization. For instance, 3M's CEO Diversity Inclusion Council, led by senior management, works toward achieving goals such as doubling the pipeline of diverse talent globally and achieving 100 percent pay equity. According to Just Capital, in 2023, 3M ranked second in their industry for investment in their workers. 3M plans to invest $50 million over 2020 to 2025 to address racial opportunity gaps through workplace development initiatives.

PRACTICE 2. INVOLVE THE BOARD.

Boards should hold CEOs accountable for DEI progress, just as they do for financial results. Transparent metrics should be established to include racial diversity and supplier

DEI (i.e., working with businesses that are at least 51% owned and operated by an individual or group that is part of a traditionally underrepresented or underserved group). Boards can tie DEI targets to their decisions on CEO and top executives' compensation, a practice that in 2021 51 percent of companies practiced.

Boards themselves should mirror the diversity of the company's customers. For example, initiatives like the 30% Club aim to increase gender diversity at board and C-Suite levels globally. As another example, in 2018, investment management corporation BlackRock required all companies it invested in to have at least two women on the board and urged the Russell 1000 companies with fewer than that to address this issue. Within five months, the number of companies with fewer than two women on the board dropped by 14 percent.

PRACTICE 3. MEASURE AND PUBLICIZE PROGRESS.

As with other priorities, measure progress because "what gets measured gets managed." Track DEI metrics that break down data by gender and race, covering recruitment, promotions, and retention. Include metrics for mentorship, sponsorship, and professional development opportunities for diverse leaders. In addition, publicly share DEI goals and metrics with employees to enhance transparency and keep everyone informed about the company's performance against diversity goals.

PRACTICE 4. HOLD ALL LEADERS ACCOUNTABLE.

Just as the board holds the CEO responsible for DEI progress, hold all leaders responsible by integrating DEI targets into performance reviews and linking progress to advancement, compensation, and incentives. In 2020, the Wells Fargo CEO announced that Operating Committee members would be evaluated based on their progress in improving diverse representation and inclusion within their area of responsibility. In 2020, Starbucks pledged to increase the diversity of its workforce at all levels to 30 percent people of color and created a long-term incentive program to increase Black, Indigenous, and Latinx representation in manager roles in the US.

EMPOWER EACH EMPLOYEE THROUGH ONGOING TRAINING

PRACTICE 1. ENGAGE EVERY EMPLOYEE AS A DEI CHAMPION.

Regardless of their position, every employee plays a pivotal role in cultivating a DEI-rooted culture. Encourage employees to actively engage with DEI initiatives, align one of their job goals with the organization's DEI vision, and integrate this into their performance evaluation for accountability and celebration.

PRACTICE 2. PROVIDE COMPREHENSIVE TRAINING.

Require ongoing training sessions on anti-racism, unconscious bias, and DEI for all staff. These sessions should explain the importance and benefits of DEI, cultivate empathy for the challenges people of color face, and empower White people to become effective allies. Invite external speakers to provide valuable perspectives on the challenges women of color face.

PRACTICE 3. ENSURE ZERO TOLERANCE FOR MICROAGGRESSIONS.

Promote a culture of respect by clearly stating that microaggressions have no place in the workplace and then punishing employees who do it anyway. It's essential for leaders to communicate this message, emphasizing that disrespectful behavior won't be tolerated. To achieve this, companies can develop a code of conduct outlining acceptable behavior and highlighting what's unacceptable. Educate employees about microaggressions and empower them to challenge these behaviors. Many individuals aren't fully aware of the impact of microaggressions, often unintentionally causing harm. By providing high-quality bias and allyship training and senior leaders setting an example to discuss issues, companies can encourage an open environment where employees have the knowledge and skills to identify and address microaggressions effectively.

PRACTICE 4. NORMALIZE CRUCIAL CONVERSATIONS.

Normalize race conversations. Address White fragility, where a White person is uncomfortable, defensive, or dismissive when confronted by racism, and emphasize that it is unacceptable. Encourage self-awareness of privilege and bias through resources like the Harvard Implicit Association

Test. Stress White people owning their own learning and not burdening people of color with the task.

GET WOMEN OF COLOR IN THE DOOR

It's a common misconception that there's a shortage of talented diverse candidates and leaders, but that's simply not the case. There's a wealth of incredible and talented people of color out there. Let's explore some effective strategies.

PRACTICE 1. POLISH YOUR PRESENCE.

UPDATE YOUR WEBSITE. Make sure your career site proudly displays your DEI values and showcases an inclusive culture. Include photos of employees from diverse backgrounds and highlight benefits like parental leave or childcare. Clearly state that your company is anti-racist and prioritizes diversity and inclusion.

REVIEW JOB DESCRIPTIONS. Scrutinize job postings for language that might discourage diverse candidates. Avoid unnecessary requirements like "expert" or "top university" or vague requirements like "entrepreneurial nature," which can make candidates feel excluded.

ENCOURAGE WOMEN OF COLOR. Encourage women of color within your organization to represent the company in external presentations and panels. Having diverse faces as the face of your company sends a strong message: Diversity is not just valued; it's celebrated. However, it's crucial to implement this practice in genuinely diverse workplaces. In predominantly White organizations, assigning people of color the extra work of showcasing diversity can be tokenistic, unjust, and a distortion of the company's true cultural fabric.

PRACTICE 2. DIVERSIFY YOUR RECRUITMENT SOURCE.

NETWORK WITH UNDERREPRESENTED GROUPS.

Networking is at the heart of job opportunities, with a staggering 85 percent of jobs found through professional connections. If leaders are White and male, they'll refer people they know who are likely also White and male. That's how you end up with a homogenous workforce. To break free from this cycle, expand your network intentionally. Actively seek out underrepresented groups and connect with them. Encourage these communities to recommend talented individuals they've worked with, ensuring a rich pool of diverse candidates. Avoid limiting your search to prestigious or non-diverse institutions; tap into a wide array of candidate pools. By doing so, you enrich your talent pool and create an inclusive, innovative workplace.

REQUIRE TWO WOMEN OF COLOR CANDIDATES.

Make it a rule to consider at least two women of color candidates for every position. The Rooney Rule, which transformed the National Football League, requires all teams to interview minority candidates for head coaching positions. Studies show that having two diverse candidates significantly boosts their chances of selection; when a diverse candidate is by themselves, they are almost never selected for the role. In 2015, President Obama praised Amazon, Microsoft, Xerox, and others for committing to variations of the Rooney Rule for senior roles. In 2019, Humana Inc. and Alexion Pharmaceutical added the Rooney Rule in their board searches. Let's continue this legacy, giving people of color a fair shot at roles.

PRACTICE 3. ENSURE A FAIR HIRING PROCESS.

BEWARE OF BIAS. Hiring processes are fraught with bias, creating challenges for women of color. Research reveals that interviewers often fall victim to "confirmation bias" where they seek information that confirms their existing beliefs. For example, if the interviewer believes that a candidate's alma mater produces excellent marketers, the interviewer will seek out information during the interview to confirm this belief. In addition, interviewers have a "similar to me bias," a tendency to favor people similar to them (such as where they are from, where they went to school, and what hobbies or interests they have) over people who are less similar to them, despite job qualifications. Even just the name on a resume can determine whether the candidate is offered an interview: "Black-sounding" and female names were not selected as much as "White-sounding" or male names.

TACKLE BIAS HEAD-ON. Recruiters and managers are also susceptible to biases, favoring prestigious schools or companies over job relevance. Combat these biases by implementing anti-bias training for all hiring staff. Remind evaluators to slow down, be aware of bias, use evaluation tools consistently and fairly, and gather additional information before making decisions. By raising awareness about biases and their impact, employees can make more objective evaluations, ensuring a fairer hiring process.

STANDARDIZE EVALUATION TOOLS. Utilize a consistent evaluation tool for all candidates so that the evaluations are more fair.

Begin by constructing a clear evaluation scorecard with the team responsible for the hiring decision, listing essential job attributes with specific criteria and assigned assessors within the hiring team. Exclude irrelevant factors like school reputation. This proactive approach ensures a focused assessment, emphasizing skills and values over vague concepts like "fit."

All candidates should be given the same set of questions tied to vital job attributes, reducing bias and ensuring fairness. Each question should directly relate to a specific role requirement, eliminating potentially biased questions.

Implement a quantitative rating scale, such as a five-point scale, to assess candidates' responses. This structured process produces the most fair and unbiased hiring decisions.

Whenever possible, introduce real job tasks for candidates and then have the evaluation team grade these anonymously.

Allocate sufficient time for structured team discussions to prevent rushed decisions based on initial impressions.

Monitor and track hires to check for bias. Adjust the hiring process to address any inequities.

PRACTICE 4. ENSURE FAIR PAY WITH TRANSPARENCY.

When a company uses a candidate's prior salary to determine starting salary, this maintains the gender pay gap. To avoid this, create salary scales, regularly review compensation across the organization, and resolve inequities. Holding the CEO accountable for achieving pay parity reinforces the commitment. Standardized, transparent compensation systems not only prevent backdoor negotiations (which women often don't do) but also shields women from backlash when negotiating higher pay.

STRENGTHEN MANAGEMENT SUPPORT

Why are there so few women of color in senior leadership? There are "broken rungs" on the ladder of success, where women are failing to get a promotion out of their entry-level jobs at the same rate as men, according to a 2023 study. These promotion decisions are heavily impacted by their direct manager. The study found that for every 100 male employees who got their first promotion from entry-level to manager, only 87 women and only 73 women of color received a similar promotion. As a result, women of color lag behind, and the gap only grows wider as they progress through their career.

What drives the "broken rung?" Studies show that women's hiring and promotion often hinge on their past and what they have done, while men are assessed for their future and what they can become. This practice puts women in a challenging position since early in their careers, they tend to have shorter track records and similar work experiences compared to their male counterparts. Even when women receive higher performance ratings than their male counterparts, managers frequently perceive them as having lower leadership potential.

Here are practices to strengthen management support:

PRACTICE 1. ASSIGN STRONG MANAGERS TO WOMEN OF COLOR.

Having a strong manager who believes in your potential can make all the difference. Reporting to a manager who lacks the necessary skills is not only demoralizing but also hampers women of color's progress. It's a setback both for women of color and the organization. When women of color don't receive the manager support they deserve, their talents often go untapped, sometimes leading them to leave. To truly thrive, women of color should be assigned strong, skilled managers who can nurture their abilities, ensuring they flourish and contribute meaningfully.

PRACTICE 2. HOLD MANAGERS ACCOUNTABLE.

Support managers in becoming diversity champions by clearly outlining their roles and encouraging them to take positive actions. One way to do this is by including tasks like career development, diversity, equity, and inclusion, as well as employee well-being, in their job descriptions and performance reviews. Hold them accountable for specific DEI goals, such as hiring, promoting, and providing growth opportunities for women of color. It's also important to hear from employees about their managers' efforts in creating an inclusive workplace. Surprisingly, only a few companies evaluate managers based on metrics related to employee growth and satisfaction. Even though 61 percent of companies recognize DEI as a vital managerial skill, only 28 percent of managers feel their companies acknowledge DEI efforts in performance reviews.

PRACTICE 3. PROVIDE TRAINING AND REDUCE MANAGER BIAS.

Provide ongoing training for managers to incorporate into their daily management practices. Train managers to recognize their biases and how to make space for and support women of color. Reduce manager bias in performance reviews, for example, by sending a "bias reminder," reminding managers how biases can impact their assessments. Ensure that managers share their rationale behind their evaluations and promotion recommendations to stay focused on clear, measurable, objective criteria instead of gut or bias.

Set expectations that managers address discriminatory behaviors as they arise. For example, a woman of color is not getting credit for their work or is interrupted when speaking. Provide resources and scripts managers can use for challenging conversations or to assess job satisfaction. Invest in ongoing education so that managers are able to build their awareness and skills to build trusting relationships with their team.

PRACTICE 4. HELP MANAGERS SET WOMEN OF COLOR UP FOR SUCCESS.

Research reveals that women of color, particularly Black women, are often entrusted with high-risk projects that may set them up for failure. Black women take on these projects as opportunities to prove their credibility. Instead of giving women of color projects that are "glass cliffs," ensure managers give them projects where they are able to learn and shine.

INVEST IN WOMEN OF COLOR

PRACTICE 1. CREATE PROGRAMS SPECIFIC TO WOMEN OF COLOR.

When programs or policies are focused on women generally, women of color tend not to benefit. Take the women's rights movement, for example. In 1920, the US Congress ratified the 19th amendment, which ruled that women could not be denied the right to vote because of their sex. But this predominantly benefited White women. Not all women, especially women of color, gained this privilege immediately. Black women faced racial discrimination, which suppressed their votes. In Puerto Rico, literate women gained voting rights in 1929, but it took until 1935 for all women to enjoy this right. As for Asian American immigrant women, they had to wait until 1952 when the Immigration and Nationality Act allowed them to become citizens and exercise their right to vote. Progress was made, but there were still hurdles to overcome for many women.

With this in mind, companies should create policies and programs specific to both gender and race so that women of color are more likely to benefit and advance. As an example, design career development initiatives unique to the needs of women of color. It's not just about courses and conferences, it's also about personal executive coaching and healing too. Provide mental health programs and reimburse 1:1 healing practices and therapy. When women of color are able to access tailored support, they are better equipped to overcome challenges and ascend the professional ladder confidently.

PRACTICE 2. FUEL NETWORK CREATION.

Establish a company-sponsored women of color networking group that serves as both a formal and informal support system. These networks are more than just connections; they're pathways to growth, skills, confidence, and influential contacts. By funding these networks and events, you invest in building a supportive community that propels every woman of color toward success.

PRACTICE 3. FORMALIZE MENTORING AND SPONSORSHIP PROGRAMS.

Tailor mentoring and sponsorship programs to empower women of color. Mentors offer guidance, but sponsors are game-changers. Sponsors don't just advise; they open doors, advocate, and fast-track careers forward. Picture this—women of color showcasing their skills, building loyalty with the organization, earning trust, and making mentors and sponsors proud. It's a win-win, benefiting women of color, the organization, and mentors and sponsors.

Take accounting firm Ernst & Young (EY), for example. By integrating equitable sponsorship into existing programs, they fostered a culture of support. With ongoing programs such as Career Watch and the Inclusiveness Leadership Program, sponsorship became the norm where high performers were assigned influential sponsors. EY ensured accountability by reviewing data such as promotion rates, representation of women at the partner level, and engagement survey feedback. Through these efforts, EY set up a sustainable pipeline of engaged women leaders. Let's replicate this success and nurture a pipeline of empowered women leaders.

ELEVATE WOMEN OF COLOR TO LEADERSHIP

PRACTICE 1. REDEFINE LEADERSHIP.

It's time to shift away from stereotypes and redefine what leading truly means. Redefine leadership to go beyond White male stereotypical qualities like aggression and competitiveness to include qualities like empathy, creativity, fairness, and relationship building. This will alleviate the double bind and double jeopardy expectations for women of color and what it means to lead. When we embrace the richness of leadership styles, women of color can feel empowered to lead authentically, whether it's being authoritative, nurturing, or anything in between. Empowered leaders enhance your company's success.

One client I worked with described her leadership style to be a cheerleader who motivated her team, "No matter who they are or what they contribute to the team, I make sure they know we can't do our magic without them." She admitted that her style was not the norm at her financial services organization, but her strong team results and retention spoke for themselves. Her management never forced her to assimilate and continued to promote her.

PRACTICE 2. SPOT POTENTIAL EARLY.

To create a bench of potential CEO women of color, identify talent early. It's not just about degrees and skills; it's recognizing untapped potential. Often, women of color miss out because they lack access to the same opportunities as their White male peers. By focusing on potential, we help level the playing field.

PRACTICE 3. STREAMLINE PATHWAYS TO LEADERSHIP.

Build skill by entrusting women of color with highly visible, challenging stretch projects. Offer them exciting opportunities they might not be aware of. These tasks not only expand skills and leadership horizons but also foster valuable connections.

Encourage women of color to rise in leadership. Eliminate barriers such as self-nomination hurdles. Managers can recognize potential and nominate team members.

PRACTICE 4. BUILD A CEO PIPELINE.

Explicitly nurture women of color CEOs. Research shows that compared to men, women don't strive for the CEO role. A Harvard Business Review study with 57 female CEOs found that they had not considered the CEO role until another person recommended they consider it. Female CEOs tend to get top positions because companies (specifically White male leaders) deliberately developed them. This was the case with Xerox's Anne Mulcahy, IBM's Ginni Rometty, and GM's Mary Barra.

PRACTICE 5. CEOS SHOULD MENTOR.

CEOs play a pivotal role in nurturing diverse talent. They should personally mentor individuals within their teams, expanding the pool of future leaders. For women of color, demystify the path to the top, making the CEO role accessible and attainable. Share the appeal of the position—the chance to make a real impact, shape culture, and enjoy flexible work dynamics, as highlighted in a Korn Ferry study. Let's champion diversity from the helm, fostering a new generation of diverse leaders.

RETAIN WOMEN OF COLOR

PRACTICE 1. CREATE AN INCLUSIVE CULTURE.

Imagine a workplace where authenticity is not just welcomed but celebrated. Often, workplace cultures reflect the dominant group, leaving those from underrepresented backgrounds feeling alienated.

To bridge this gap, reevaluate the events celebrated at work, ensuring they resonate with all employees. To promote inclusivity, foster open dialogue and value everyone's input. Encourage a sense of belonging by promoting open-mindedness, empathy, and compassion among employees.

PRACTICE 2. CULTIVATE PSYCHOLOGICAL SAFETY.

Harvard Business School professor Dr. Amy Edmondson describes psychological safety as a work environment where staff believe they can be honest, disagree, and even fail without fear of retribution. Create a space where perspectives, feedback, and failure are welcomed. To help people from underrepresented backgrounds feel safe at work, ensure that your organization has clear and enforced policies against harassment and discrimination. Ruchika Tulshyan, author of *Inclusion on Purpose: An Intersectional Approach to Creating a Culture of Belonging at Work*, found that when women of color experience psychological safety, they experience greater inclusion in their workplace. Creating a culture of acceptance and psychological safety benefits all staff regardless of gender or background.

PRACTICE 3. MONITOR PROGRESS.

Actively seek feedback from employees, understanding their experiences and areas for improvement. Break down this data by demographics, especially focusing on the experiences of women of color. Are they feeling valued and supported? Is their unique perspective recognized?

Keep a vigilant eye on attrition rates. Utilize exit surveys to grasp the effectiveness of DEI programs. Encourage departing employees, especially those from diverse backgrounds, to share their reasons. If discrimination played a role, take swift action to address the situation, ensuring it doesn't repeat.

PRACTICE 4. SUPPORT WORK-LIFE INTEGRATION.

Acknowledge the unique challenges women face, especially when juggling family responsibilities such as raising children or caregiving for aging parents. Craft policies that bridge the gap between family and work life, eliminating the need for women to make a difficult choice between the two. Remove any stigma surrounding non-traditional work arrangements. Support women during maternity leave and upon their return so that they can seamlessly rejoin the leadership path.

Cultivate an environment that promotes productivity both at work and home. Offer flexible work options, allowing employees to decide when, where, and how they work. Introduce tools like Villyge, providing expert support to employees throughout their career and family journey, which boosts productivity and retention.

Encourage innovative approaches like walking meetings, embracing remote work, and enabling employees to find their most productive hours. Shift the focus from rigid 9-to-5 schedules to empowering individuals to work during their peak performance times. By nurturing a workplace where both professional and personal lives harmonize, we empower women of color to ascend to leadership roles, fostering a cycle of inspiration and mentorship for future generations.

IT WILL TAKE ALL OF US TO CRACK THE CONCRETE CEILING

When we join together, we can break down not just the concrete ceiling but the whole White supremacist system. We can create new, more equitable practices that are not just good for women of color but for all of us—our organizations, our society, and our future. Let's join forces and make a difference together as we improve our workplace happiness and our bottom line. Our unity is our strength.

BOOK BONUSES

Explore the Book Bonuses for this chapter:

- Summary list of strategies for organizations to support women of color
- Articles
- List of books for further reading
- Podcasts with full interviews of women leaders spotlighted in this chapter

WHAT COMES NEXT

As you contemplate the various myths, choose one that resonates with you the most, and then focus on the corresponding action steps.

If any of these ideas hit home for you and you're hungry for more, I encourage you to work with me personally one-on-one or enroll in my Women of Color Rise: Next Level Leadership Course.

In the six-week leadership program, you'll get a career growth roadmap to perform to the next level and lead with authenticity, impact, and purpose.

This program is special because we pair an advanced curriculum with a coaching cohort of like-minded women of color leaders, so it's not just about learning—it's about creating a community of support to get you results.

This program stands out because we pair a top-notch curriculum with a coaching cohort of incredible women of color leaders. It's not just about soaking up knowledge; it's about building a supportive community to help keep you accountable. This is how we get results.

This program will be especially useful if you are a woman leader of color and:

- You are a high performer who wants to up-level your leadership and impact.
- You have received some leadership training but never focused on the unique needs of women leaders of color.

- You lack a strategic career roadmap and actionable next steps to accelerate your impact and leadership.
- You have a sense of your strengths and values but don't have a clear understanding of how to leverage them.
- You want to communicate and persuade more authentically and confidently.
- You don't have a strong network or your own personal board of directors inside and outside of the organization who you can count on.
- You wish you could stop the hamster wheel and be impactful at work while having time for yourself to have "your all" in life.

What are the benefits of the Women of Color Rise: Next Level Leadership Course?

- **Join a supportive community** of women leaders of color, receive expert-level coaching, and create your personal career success roadmap in 6 weeks.
- **Gain clarity on your ideal leadership path.** Get a plan tailored to your goals and aspirations with clear next steps to earn more opportunities at work and grow in your organization and career.
- **Clarify your authentic leadership and brand.** Conduct a deep dive into your purpose, values, talents, and strengths.
- **Build a network of support.** Implement a step by step plan to network authentically and find mentors and sponsors as yourself.
- **Communicate confidently.** Craft narratives to bring visibility to your work and impact. Learn how to persuade through stories and stand out to better position and advocate for yourself.

- **Gain a tool of reframing to overcome challenges,** reframe your perspective & build confidence. Understand your inner barriers and gain tools to overcome self-doubt and impostor syndrome.
- **Craft a blueprint of your life vision** that motivates you. Define your "all" spanning work, life, family, relationships, health, wealth, and community.
- **Develop a self-care practice.** Reflect on your daily habits and understand your energizers, motivators, and de-motivators to create an individualized and sustaining restorative practice.

If this feels like a good fit for you, and you're ready to take everything you've learned in this book to the next level, sign up today using the QR code below.

The coaching strategies in this program have empowered hundreds of women leaders of color to advance in their careers with impact, authenticity, and purpose. Let's work together and become the change we wish to see in the world.

Women of Color Rise: Next Level Leadership Course

Join My Email List

If you're not quite ready to take this leap, I recommend joining my email list. I share resources weekly, featuring interviews with women of color leaders, mostly CEOs. They talk about their journeys to the top, the mistakes they made, and the wisdom they wish they had known earlier. You'll find plenty of valuable advice on climbing the ranks.

Connect With Me On LinkedIn

For other useful resources, connect with me on LinkedIn. You can scan the QR code below to find my page. However you decide to connect, I'm thrilled to be of support. If you need further guidance on these topics, don't hesitate to reach out. Together, we can navigate the next steps in your leadership and impact journey. Best of luck, and I look forward to celebrating your successes!

ACKNOWLEDGMENTS

I am grateful to the many people who made this book possible. My family, friends, mentors, and community. Thank you for supporting me on this journey and allowing me to share your stories. Thank you for your belief that more women of color in leadership make the world a better and fairer place for all of us.

Most ideas in this book are from others. First, thank you to the women who were generous enough to share their stories. Gratitude for modeling and motivating us to show up in our authentic genius.

Thank you to my editors who kindly shared their feedback, especially Virginia Vitzthum, Lynn Mandujano, Jill MacFayden, Simmons Lettre, Loretta Chan, Sunita Arora, Courtney Dastis-Galvin, Katerina Manoff, and Sarah Filipovitz. Also, thanks to Andreea Chele, my fantastic illustrator and designer, who has worked with me on multiple projects and continues to wow us with her talent.

Thank you, too, to my squad of clients and Boss Mamas. Thank you to my community at Pahara, Education Leaders of Color, Broad, and APIA Education Equity. Thank you to my Basecamp group, including James Price and Jeff Baietto who have helped ground us in love, curiosity, surrender, and gratitude.

Thank you to my mentors who have invested in me and opened doors to opportunities and guidance throughout my career. Bill Sharpe and Darrell Duffie supported me in my final year at Stanford University. "Tito" Louie Faustino taught me by example how to lead a life of service. Colonel Schiefer, my first boss, saw something in me that I could not see, a future of leadership and impact. Scott Conner greeted me with sincere care at the airport along with my team in Guam. Jon Webb modeled leadership at work and at home. Colonel Joe Smyth and Tony Monaco provided counsel. "Ate" Lumen Abad sponsored my Fulbright project and helped me get in touch with my roots. Wally Scott mentored me at Northwestern University. David Nelson gave wise advice during my many career pivots. James Willcox modeled servant leadership and how to live a values-aligned life. Mary Tan offered mentorship and an example of authenticity. Chris Smiros helped me navigate the world of brand management. Marc Somnolet was my Fabuloso teacher even before he became a NYU professor. John King Jr. helped me realize my dream of building schools for low-income children. Brett Peiser challenged me to lead with prioritization and high standards. Jeff Ginsburg strengthened my conviction to lead. Patti Soussloff shared my goal of serving children. Jerry Posman modeled real commitment and investment in women of color.

Thank you, Vanessa Rodriguez, for your mentorship and friendship. Tammy Ven Dange for our shared Filipino pride and guidance since my Stanford ROTC days. Ilene Lang for modeling service and commitment to equity throughout your career. Roosevelt Giles and the Stakeholder Leadership and Governance Institute board for your belief in diverse leaders being at the table.

Fiscal sponsorship was provided by Unique Projects, Inc., a nonprofit organization administered by Pentacle (Dance-

Works, Inc.). Pentacle is a nonprofit management support organization for the performing arts. www.Pentacle.org.

Thank you to my mother for believing in me and helping me believe in myself. Thank you to my father for teaching me discipline and respect and encouraging me to join the military, one of my best career decisions. Thank you to my brother who is modeling for me what it means to learn and grow, even when it is hard.

My husband, Alex, is my best friend, closest advisor, and love of my life. He has supported my independence yet given me a Basecamp to come back to. Thank you to my sweet, smart, and silly children, Bryson and Scarlet, who model for me what it means to be present and enjoy life now. Thank you for inspiring me to write this book.

I have so much gratitude to each and every one of you who has joined me in this journey.

Thank you.

Women of Color Rise is dedicated to helping leaders more effectively lead their organizations through better leadership, teamwork, and integration of DEI practices.

Visit our website and explore:

Coaching and Consulting: Women of Color Rise provides 1:1 and group coaching, practical consulting, and training sessions to leaders and their teams.

Speaking: Analiza Quiroz Wolf has shared her work on leadership, DEI, and organizational health with hundreds of leaders as well as schools, universities, non-profits, the military, and businesses.

Books: In addition to *The Myths of Success: A Woman of Color's Guide to Leadership*, Analiza's books include

- *Balikbayan: A Filipino Homecoming*
- *Native Americans Who Inspire Us*
- *Latin Americans Who Inspire Us*
- *Asian Americans Who Inspire Us* (named to the Gold House Book List)

Podcast: Analiza leads a podcast for women leaders of color called *Women of Color Rise*.

www.analizawolf.com

Analiza Quiroz Wolf is the founder of Women of Color Rise, a firm dedicated to helping women of color get a seat at the table. As an executive coach, facilitator, and keynote speaker, she has worked with hundreds of senior executives in organizations ranging from Fortune 500 companies to start-ups and nonprofits. She has also consulted with organizations on diversity, equity, and inclusion projects.

Prior to founding Women of Color Rise, Analiza served as the CEO of a charter network in New York City. She started her career as a captain in the US Air Force and was also a brand manager at a Fortune 200 company.

Analiza graduated with her BA and BS from Stanford University, MBA from Northwestern University Kellogg

School of Management, and Master of Educational Leadership from the Broad Center (now at Yale). A Fulbright Scholar and Pahara Fellow, Analiza is also an acclaimed author with books including: *Balikbayan: A Filipino Homecoming*, *Native Americans Who Inspire Us*, *Latin Americans Who Inspire Us*, and *Asian Americans Who Inspire Us*, which was named to the Gold House Book List. Analiza leads women's leadership programs and a podcast for women leaders of color called *Women of Color Rise*.

Analiza enjoys languages and speaks Tagalog, Chinese, and Spanish. She also enjoys adventures and has climbed Everest Base Camp and Kilimanjaro, ran 13 marathons, scuba dived with sharks, and wrestled with alligators. She, her husband, and two kids live in New York City and enjoy rock climbing and skiing together.

To learn more about Analiza and Women of Color Rise, please visit **www.analizawolf.com**

WORKS CITED

BACK COVER

1 percent
Emma Hinchliffe, "Women CEOs run 10.4% of Fortune 500 companies. A quarter of the 52 leaders became CEO in the last year," June 5, 2023, fortune.com, fortune.com/2023/06/05/fortune-500-companies-2023-women-10-percent/.
6 percent, 56 percent, 22 percent
McKinsey & Company and LeanIn.org, "Women in the Workplace Report," 2023, leanIn.org, sgff-media.s3.amazonaws.com/sgff_r1eHetbDYb/Women+in+the+Workplace+2023_+Designed+Report.pdf.

PREFACE

9   **Despite representing about 20 percent of the US population, women of color represented only 6 percent of C-Level positions in 2023, falling far below White men (56 percent) and White women (22 percent).**
McKinsey & Company and LeanIn.org, "Women in the Workplace Report," 2023, leanin.org, 2023, sgff-media.s3.amazonaws.com/sgff_r1eHetbDYb/Women+in+the+Workplace+2023_+Designed+Report.pdf.

9   **But only 13 percent of managers, 9 percent of senior managers, and 6 percent of top C-Suite leaders (such as Chief Operations Officer, Chief Financial Officer, and Chief Executive Officer) are women of color.**
McKinsey & Company and LeanIn.org, "Women in the Workplace Report," 2023, leanIn.org, sgff-media.s3.amazonaws.com/sgff_r1eHetbDYb/Women+in+the+Workplace+2023_+Designed+Report.pdf.

9   **One study**
McKinsey & Company and LeanIn.org, "Women in the Workplace Report," LeanIn.org, 2020, https://wiw-report.s3.amazonaws.com/Women_in_the_Workplace_2020.pdf.

9   **96 percent**
McKinsey & Company and LeanIn.org, "Women in the Workplace Report," 2023, leanIn.org, sgff-media.s3.amazonaws.com/sgff_r1eHetbDYb/Women+in+the+Workplace+2023_+Designed+Report.pdf.

10   **lack of women at the highest level**
Chiefs for Change, "Breaking Through: Shattering the Glass Ceiling for Women Leaders," April 23, 2019, chiefsforchange.org, chiefsforchange.org/wp-content/uploads/2019/04/CFC-WomenLeaders-Final-April-23-2019.pdf.

10   **Research**
Anna Powers, "A Study Finds That Diverse Companies Produce 19% More Revenue," forbes.com, Jun 27, 2018, forbes.com/sites/annapowers/2018/06/27/a-study-finds-that-diverse-companies-produce-19-more-revenue/#1e41881b506f.

11   **Catalyst report**
Catalyst, "The Bottom Line: Connecting Corporate Performance and Gender Diversity," 2004, catalyst.org, catalyst.org/wp-content/uploads/2019/01/The_Bottom_Line_Connecting_Corporate_Performance_and_Gender_Diversity.pdf

11   **Companies with female board representation outperform**
Vivian Hunt, Dennis Layton, and Sara Prince, "Why Diversity Matters," mckinsey.com, January 1, 2015, mckinsey.com/capabilities/people-and-organizational-performance/our-insights/why-diversity-matters.

11 **higher than men by 10 percent**
Richard Reeves and Ember Smith, "The Male College Crisis is Not Just in Enrollment but Completion," October 8, 2021, brookings.edu, brookings.edu/blog/up-front/2021/10/08/the-male-college-crisis-is-not-just-in-enrollment-but-completion/.

11 **learning and effectiveness paradigm**
David Thomas and Robin Ely. "Making Differences Matter: A New Paradigm for Managing Diversity." Harvard Business Review 74, no. 5 (September–October 1996): 79–90, hbr.org/1996/09/making-differences-matter-a-new-paradigm-for-managing-diversity.

12 **thesis**
Victoria Sepand, "The Black Ceiling: Barriers to Career Advancement for African American Women in the US," 2015, Scripps, 639, scholarship.claremont.edu/scripps_theses/639.

13 **phrase**
Frances Beal, "Double Jeopardy: To Be Black and Female," Meridians 8, no. 2 (2008): 166–76, jstor.org/stable/40338758.

13 **lack of management support**
Zuhairah Washington and Laura Morgan Roberts, "Women of Color Get Less Support at Work. Here's How Managers Can Change That," hbr.org, March 4, 2019, hbr.org/2019/03/women-of-color-get-less-support-at-work-heres-how-managers-can-change-that.

13 **feeling invisible**
Amanda Sesko and Monica Biernat, "Prototypes of Race and Gender: The Invisibility of Black Women," Journal of Experimental Psychology, 46, no. 2 (2010): 356-360, sciencedirect.com/science/article/pii/S0022103109002698?via%3Dihub.

13 **asked to do more office work and penalized when we don't**
Ruchika Tulshyan, "Women of Color Get Asked to Do More Office Housework," hbr.org, April 6, 2018, hbr.org/2018/04/women-of-color-get-asked-to-do-more-office-housework-heres-how-they-can-say-no.

13 **impacts women**
Alice Eagly and Steven Karau, "Role Congruity Theory of Prejudice Toward Female Leaders," Psychological Review 109, no. 2 (2002): 573-598, web.pdx.edu/~mev/pdf/Eagley_Karau.pdf.

13 **study**
Ashleigh Rosette, Geoffrey Leonardelli, and Katherine Philipps, "The White Standard: Racial Bias in Leader Categorization." Journal of Applied Psychology, 93, no. 4 (2008): 758-777, doi.org/10.1037/0021-9010.93.4.758.

14 **Alicia Garza shared**
Alicia Garza, The Purpose of Power: How We Come Together When We Fall Apart (New York: Random House Publishing Group, 2020), 199.

20 **Heather McGhee shared**
Heather McGhee, Sum of Us (New York: One World, 2021), 284.

20 **second Black woman**
Emma Hinchliffe, "Thasunda Brown Duckett Will Become the Second Black Female CEO Currently in the Fortune 500," February 25, 2021, fortune.com, fortune.com/2021/02/25/thasunda-brown-duckett-tiaa-ceo-black-women-ceos-fortune-500/amp/.

20 **Thasunda Brown Ducket wrote**
"Thasunda Brown Duckett," 2021, worth.com, worth.com/women/thasunda-brown-duckett/.

28 **only 40**
Timothy Wilson, Strangers to Ourselves: Discovering the Adaptive Unconscious (Cambridge: Harvard University Press, 2004), 24.

28 **shortcuts often uses instinct, not analysis, and introduces unconscious bias**
Anthony Greenwald and Mahzarin Banaji, "Implicit Social Cognition: Attitudes, Self-esteem, and Stereotypes." Psychological Review, 102, no. 41: 4-27, faculty. washington.edu/agg/pdf/Greenwald_Banaji_PsychRev_1995.OCR.pdf.

29 **why do we picture a male?**
Heather Murphy, "Picture a Leader: Is She a Woman?," March 16, 2018, nytimes. org, nytimes.com/2018/03/16/health/women-leadership-workplace.html.

29 **supporting-role qualities**
Kark, Ronit & Eagly, Alice. (2010). Gender and Leadership: Negotiating the Labyrinth. 10.1007/978-1-4419-1467-5_19, researchgate.net/ publication/226699862_Gender_and_Leadership_Negotiating_the_Labyrinth.

30 **unlikely to reach a top leadership role**
Catalyst, "The Double-Bind Dilemma for Women in Leadership," July 15, 2007, catalyst.org, catalyst.org/research/the-double-bind-dilemma-for-women-in-leadership-damned-if-you-do-doomed-if-you-dont.

30 **she blamed sexism**
Andrew Clark, "New technology, old sexism, says ousted HP executive," October 9, 2006, theguardian.com,theguardian.com/technology/2006/oct/10/news. genderissues.

31 **research**
Madeline E. Heilman and Suzette Caleo, "Gender Stereotypes and Their Implications for Women's Career Progress," Handbook of Research on Promoting Women's Careers (2013): 143–161.

31 **"intimidating" or "angry"**
Bianca Barratt, "The Microaggressions Towards Black Women You Might Be Complicit In At Work," June 19, 2020, forbes.com, forbes.com/sites/ biancabarratt/2020/06/19/the-microaggressions-towards-black-women-you-might-be-complicit-in-at-work/.

31 **illegally in the country**
Gladys García-López, "Nunca Te Toman En Cuenta [They Never Take You Into Account]: The Challenges of Inclusion and Strategies for Success of Chicana Attorneys," Gender & Society, 22, no. 5 (2008): 590-612, journals.sagepub.com/ doi/10.1177/0891243208321120

32 **not "leader" material**
James Jones, Prejudice and Racism (New York: McGraw-Hill Companies, 1997), 17.

32 **twice as good and work twice as hard**
Gillian White, "Black Workers Really Do Need to Be Twice as Good," October 7, 2015, atlantic.com, theatlantic.com/business/archive/2015/10/why-black-workers-really-do-need-to-be-twice-as-good/409276/.

44 **investigate what strategies**
Wei Zheng, Wei, Ronit Kark, and Alyson Meister, "How Women Manage the Gendered Norms of Leadership," hbr.org, November 28 2018, hbr.org/2018/11/ how-women-manage-the-gendered-norms-of-leadership.

54 **study**
Jane Stevenson, "Women CEOs Speak," November 9, 2017, kornferry.com, kornferry.com/content/dam/kornferry/docs/pdfs/kf-rockefeller-women-ceos-speak.pdf

54 **"different from peers at work because of gender, race, and/or ethnicity and the associated effects on health, well-being, and ability to thrive at work"**
Dnika Travis and Jennifer Thorpe-Moscon, "Day-to-Day Experiences of Emotional Tax Among Women and Men of Color in the Workplace," February 15, 2018, catatylst.org, catalyst.org/knowledge/day-day-experiences-emotional-tax-among-women-and-men-color-workplace.

67 **article**
Leslie Jamison, "The Dubious Rise of Impostor Syndrome," February 6, 2023, newyorker.com, newyorker.com/magazine/2023/02/13/the-dubious-rise-of-impostor-syndrome.

68 **"It's never about whether we're qualified .... And I can lead too."**
Reshma Saujani, "E149: How I Taught Millions Of Women The Most Important Skill: Girls Who Code Founder: Reshma Saujani," The Diary Of A CEO with Steven Bartlett, June 6, 2022, podcast, podcasts.apple.com/gb/podcast/e149-how-i-taught-millions-of-women-the-most/id1291423644?i=1000565326705.

69 **We tend to be more compassionate toward others and more critical of ourselves.**
Angélica López, Robbert Sanderman, Adelita V. Ranchor, and Maya J. Schroevers, "Compassion for Others and Self-Compassion: Levels, Correlates, and Relationship with Psychological Well-being," Mindfulness, 9, no. 1 (2017): 325–331, ncbi.nlm.nih.gov/pmc/articles/PMC5770484/.

70 **steps**
Adia Gooden, "Cultivating Unconditional Self Worth," filmed at TEDxDePaulUniversity 2018, May 30, 2018, Chicago, IL, video, ted.com/talks/adia_gooden_cultivating_unconditional_self_worth.

70 **118**
SWNS Digital, "Here's Your Worst Work Fears Coming True, According to a New Survey," 2021, Sep 6, swnsdigital.com/us/2017/10/heres-your-worst-work-fears-come-true-according-to-a-new-survey.

72 **research**
Roy Baumeister, Ellen Bratslavsky, Catrin Finkenauer, Kathleen D. Vohs, "Bad is Stronger Than Good," Review of General Psychology 5, no. 4 (2001): 323-370, journals.sagepub.com/doi/10.1037/1089-2680.5.4.323.

78 **"The day and night before competitions, I would visualize my performance. I would run it through in my mind and watch the routine on the floor. I'd tell myself I'd trained and I was ready. Still, every single time, I'd be nervous, no matter what competition it was."**
Suzanne Riss, "'92 Olympian Yamaguchi Balances Road, Family," February 23, 2010, cnn.com, edition.cnn.com/2010/LIVING/worklife/02/23/working.mother.olympics.yamaguchi/index.html.

MYTH THREE: Women are too emotional to be good leaders

84 **"Without [EQ] a person can have the best training in the world, an incisive, analytical mind, and an endless supply of smart ideas, but he still won't make a great leader."**
Daniel Goleman, "What Makes a Leader?," Harvard Business Review, 82 (2004): 82-91, hbr.org/2004/01/what-makes-a-leader.

86   Catalyst's research
Women Business Collaborative, "Women CEOs in America," September 9, 2022, wbcollaborative.org, wbcollaborative.org/wp-content/uploads/2022/09/Women-CEOS-in-America_2022-0920221847.pdf.

99   Research
Claude Werder, "Empower Your Employees to Take Charge of Their Own Career Development," May 14, 2021, brandonhall.com, brandonhall.com/blogs/empower-your-employees-to-take-charge-of-their-own-career-development/.

99   "So much of our efforts for social change …. the two cannot be separated."
Shawn Ginwright, The Four Pivots: Reimagining Justice, Reimagining Ourselves (Berkeley: North Atlantic Books, 2022), 59.

101   "Our mind can be pictured as a bicycle wheel …. Our awareness resides in the hub, and from here we can focus on the various points on the rim of our wheel."
Daniel Siegel, Tina Payne Bryson, Whole Brain Child (New York: Random House Publishing Group, 2011), 122.

103   exercise
Martha Beck, "Body Truth, Mind Lie: How to Make the Right Decision," July 2015, marthabeck.com/2015/07/make-right-decision/.

107   research finding
Center for Creative Leadership, "Keep a Promising Career on Track & Prevent Derailment," Feb 16, 2020, ccl.org, ccl.org/articles/leading-effectively-articles/5-ways-avoid-derailing-career/.

109   good at relationships
Jack Zenger and Joseph Folkman, "Women Score Higher Than Men in Most Leadership Skills," June 25, 2019, hbr.org, hbr.org/2019/06/research-women-score-higher-than-men-in-most-leadership-skills.

110   Research
Bill J. Bonnstetter, "New Research: The Skills That Make an Entrepreneur," December 7, 2012, hbr.org, hbr.org/2012/12/new-research-the-skills-that-m

MYTH FOUR: Be humble. Our work will speak for itself

115   Research
Deborah Tannen, "Who Gets Heard and Why," September 1, 1995, hbr.org, hbr.org/1995/09/the-power-of-talk-who-gets-heard-and-why.

116   research
Carol Gilligan, In a Different Voice (Cambridge: Harvard University Press, 1993), 65.

116   tendency to plant roots
Ashley Milne-Tyte, "Women Stay in Jobs Longer Than They Should," July 17, 2013, marketplace.org, www.marketplace.org/2013/07/17/women-stay-jobs-longer-they-should/.

116   study
Nancy Carter and Christine Silva, "The Myth of the Ideal Worker: Does Doing All the Right Things Really Get Women Ahead?," October 1, 2011, catalyst.org, catalyst.org/knowledge/myth-ideal-worker-does-doing-all-right-things-really-get-women-ahead.

117   survey
Lou Adler, "New Survey Reveals 85% of All Jobs are Filled Via Networking," LinkedIn, February 26, 2016, June 16, 2022, linkedin.com/pulse/new-survey-reveals-85-all-jobs-filled-via-networking-lou-adler.

117 **article**
Kathy Lockwood, "Quietly Competent: Why You Need To Promote
Yourself To Get Noticed," March 6, 2018, forbes.com, forbes.com/sites/
forbescoachescouncil/2018/03/06/quietly-competent-why-you-need-to-promote-
yourself-to-get-noticed/.

129 **Take-12**
Peggy Klaus, BRAG! The Art of Tooting Your Own Horn Without Blowing It
(New York: Warner Books, 2003).

MYTH FIVE: Women who negotiate are greedy

138 **79 cents... 64 cents... 57 cents**
Ariane Hegewisch and Eve Mefferd, "Lost Jobs, Stalled Progress: The Impact of
the 'She-Cession' on Equal Pay," September 2021, iwpr.org, iwpr.org/wp-content/
uploads/2021/09/Gender-Wage-Gap-in-2020-Fact-Sheet_FINAL.pdf.

139 **"disheartening but not surprising .... It's not about something inherent to
women or people of color, but how they are treated."**
Kim Elsesser, "Women Of Color Set Lower Salary Requirements Than White
Men, According To Job Search Site," February 6, 2023, forbes.com, forbes.com/
sites/kimelsesser/2023/02/06/women-of-color-set-lower-salary-requirements-than-
white-men-according-to-job-search-site.

139 **study**
Janet Nguyen, "Men and Women Ask for Pay Raises at the Same Rate – But
Men Get Them More Often," June 10, 2019, marketplace.org, marketplace.
org/2019/06/10/men-and-women-ask-for-pay-raises-at-the-same-rate-but-men-get-
them-more-often/.

139 **study**
Hannah Bowles, "Why Women Don't Negotiate Their Job Offers," June 19, 2014,
hbr.org, hbr.org/2014/06/why-women-dont-negotiate-their-job-offers.

140 **7.6% higher**
Linda Babcock, "Nice Girls Don't Ask," October 2003, hbr.org, hbr.org/2003/10/
nice-girls-dont-ask.

140 **"Men are four times more likely than women to negotiate the first offer."**
Tory Johnson and Robyn Freedman Spizman, Take this Book to Work: How to
Ask for (and Get) Money, Fulfillment and Advancement (New York: St. Martin's
Griffin, 2007), 14.

140 **study**
Jeff Haden, "Research Shows Not Negotiating Your Salary Could Cost You $1
Million (Especially Women)," December 19, 2016, inc.com, https://www.inc.
com/jeff-haden/research-shows-not-negotiating-your-salary-could-cost-you-1-million-
especially-.html.

140 **internal report**
Tara Mohr, "Why Women Don't Apply for Jobs Unless They're 100% Qualified,"
August 25, 2014, hbr.org, hbr.org/2014/08/why-women-dont-apply-for-jobs-unless-
theyre-100-qualified.

140 **research study**
Mary Sigmond, "Women Leaders in Construction: Bringing Grit and Guts to
A Male-Dominated Industry," December 17, 2021, ypo.org, ypo.org/2021/12/
women-leaders-in-construction-bringing-grit-and-guts-to-a-male-dominated-industry.

140 **top spot earlier**
Jane Stevenson, "Women CEOs Speak," November 9, 2017, kornferry.com,
kornferry.com/content/dam/kornferry/docs/pdfs/kf-rockefeller-women-ceos-
speak.pdf.

150 **60 percent**
Kaila Kea-Lewis, "Why 60% Qualified is Enough," November 14, 2019, inhersight.com, inhersight.com/blog/insight-commentary/why-60-percent-qualified-is-enough.

150 **TalentWorks study**
TalentWorks, "The Science of the Job Search," November 27, 2018, talent-works.com, talent.works/blog/2018/11/27/the-science-of-the-job-search-part-vii-you-only-need-50-of-job-requirements/.

152 **two months and $4,000**
Glassdoor, "How to Calculate Cost Per Hire," July 5, 2019, glassdoor.com, glassdoor.com/employers/blog/calculate-cost-per-hire/.

156 **Do you want to be in this job on your next work anniversary?**
Jon Bishcke, "Entelo Study Shows When Employees Are Likely to Leave Their Jobs," October 6, 2014, blog.entelo.com\new-entelo-study-shows-when-employees-are-liekly-to-leave-their-jobs.

157 **three to five years**
Patrick Gillespie, "The Best Time to Leave Your Job is...," May 12, 2016, money.cnn.com, money.cnn.com\2016\05\12\news\economy\best-time-to-leave-your-job\.

157 **Research**
Peter Boxall, "Mutuality in the Management of Human Resources: Assessing the Quality of Alignment in Employment Relationships," Human Resource Management Journal 23, no. 1 (2013): 3-17.

MYTH SIX: Networking is an exhausting and fake way to make connections

163 **more effective**
Anna Powers, "Women Need to Network Differently to Advance, New Research Suggests," March 31, 2019, forbes.com, forbes.com/sites/annapowers/2019/03/31/women-need-to-network-differently-to-advance-new-research-suggests/?sh=75efe84419b2.

164 **23 percent more likely**
Nancy Wang, "Women Execs Find Your Tribe and Tap Into Success," October 22, 2019, forbes.com, forbes.com/sites/nancywang/2019/10/22/women-execs-find-your-tribe-and-tap-into-success/

164 **Research**
Herminia Ibarra, Nancy Carter, and Christine, "Why Men Still Get More Promotions Than Women," September 2010, hbr.org, hbr.org/2010/09/why-men-still-get-more-promotions-than-women.

164 **45 percent more likely**
Catalyst, "Women and Opportunity Initiative," 2016. catalyst.org, catalyst.org/knowledge/gap-inc-women-and-opportunity.

164 **38 percent sponsored vs 30 percent unsponsored, 68 percent of sponsored women vs 57 percent of unsponsored women**
Sheri Newman and Kala McDonald, "Women in Industry," digital.bnpmedia.com/publication/frame.php?i=638754&p=&pn=&ver=html5&view=articleBrowser&article_id=3548532.

165 **Catalyst**
Catalyst, "Women of Color in Corporate Management: Opportunities and Barriers," July 13, 1999, catalyst.org, catalyst.org/research/women-of-color-in-corporate-management-opportunities-and-barriers/.

165 **have few senior leaders of the same race or gender**
Catalyst, "Connections that Count: The Informal Networks of Women of
Color in the United States," 2006, catalyst.org, catalyst.org/wp-content/
uploads/2019/01/Connections_that_Count_The_Informal_Networks_of_
Women_of_Color_in_the_United_States.pdf.

175 **research**
Yang, Nitesh Chawla, Brian Uzzi, "A Network's Gender Composition and
Communication Pattern Predict Women's Leadership Success," pnas.org,
November 2018, doi.org/10.1073/pnas.1721438116.

176 **Catalyst survey**
Catalyst, "Women of Color in Corporate Management: Opportunities and
Barriers," July 13, 1999, catalyst.org, catalyst.org/research/women-of-color-in-
corporate-management-opportunities-and-barriers/.

179 **"the relationships people have with each other .... reciprocity."**
Claire Boyte-White, "What are Some Examples of Different Types of Capital?,"
December 4, 2022, investopedia.com, investopedia.com/ask/answers/032715/
what-are-some-examples-different-types-capital.asp.

179 **Benjamin Franklin effect**
Benjamin Franklin, The Autobiography of Benjamin Franklin (New York: Simon
& Schuster, 2004).

MYTH SEVEN: Women need to act like men to be successful in leadership

180 **opt out of happy hours**
Katherine W. Phillips, Tracy L. Dumas, and Nancy Rothbard, "Diversity and
Authenticity," March, 2018, hbr.org, hbr.org/2018/03/diversity-and-authenticity.

186 **Pew Research Center report**
Pew Research Center, " What Makes a Good Leader, and Does Gender
Matter?," January 14, 2015, pewresearch.org, www.pewresearch.org/social-
trends/2015/01/14/chapter-2-what-makes-a-good-leader-and-does-gender-matter/.

187 **study**
Alice Eagly, "Gender & Work: Challenging Conventional Wisdom," March 2018,
hbs.edu, hbs.edu/faculty/Shared%20Documents/conferences/2013-w50-research-
symposium/eagly.pdf

202 **Research**
Herminia Ibarra, "Women Rising: the Unseen Barriers," September 2013, hbr.org,
hbr.org/2013/09/women-rising-the-unseen-barriers.

203 **research**
Bill J. Bonnstetter, "New Research: The Skills That Make an Entrepreneur,"
December 7, 2012, hbr.org, hbr.org/2012/12/new-research-the-skills-that-m.

208 **Research**
Elena Doldor, Madeleine Wyatt, and Jo Silvester, "Research: Men Get More
Actionable Feedback Than Women," February 10, 2021, hbr.org, hbr-org.cdn.
ampproject.org/c/s/hbr.org/amp/2021/02/research-men-get-more-actionable-
feedback-than-women.

208 **vague feedback**
Shelley Correll, Shelley J Correll, and Caroline Simard, "Research: Vague
Feedback is Holding Women Back," April 29, 2016, hbr.org, hbr.org/2016/04/
research-vague-feedback-is-holding-women-back.

208 **not connected to outcomes and goals**
Paola Cecchi Dimeglio, "How Gender Bias Corrupts Performance Reviews and

What to Do About It," April 12, 2017, hbr.org, hbr.org/2017/04/how-gender-bias-corrupts-performance-reviews-and-what-to-do-about-it.

210 **79 percent**
Joan C. Williams, Olivia Andrews, Mikayla Boginsky, "Why Many Women of Color Don't Want to Return to the Office," May 12, 2022, hbr.org, hbr.org/2022/05/why-many-women-of-color-dont-want-to-return-to-the-office.

MYTH EIGHT: We can have it all

215 **article**
Anne-Marie Slaughter, "Why Women Still Can't Have It All," July/August 2012, atlantic.com, theatlantic.com/magazine/archive/2012/07/why-women-still-cant-have-it-all/309020/.

234 **And we're winning!**
Rina Raphael, Netflix CEO Reed Hastings: Sleep Is Our Competition," November 6, 2017, fastcompany.com, fastcompany.com/40491939/netflix-ceo-reed-hastings-sleep-is-our-competition.

236 **three strategies**
Connie Gersick, "Having It All, Having Too Much, Having Too Little: How Women Manage Trade-Offs Through Adulthood," SSRN Electronic Journal (2013), researchgate.net/publication/251347595_Having_It_All_Having_Too_Much_Having_Too_Little_How_Women_Manage_Trade-Offs_Through_Adulthood.

241 **Data**
Charles Kenny and George Yang, "The Global Childcare Workload from School and Preschool Closures During the COVID-19 Pandemic," June 25, 2021, cgdev.org, cgdev.org/publication/global-childcare-workload-school-and-preschool-closures-during-covid-19-pandemic.

242 **"As we become the growing majority of the educated workforce, we have an opportunity to be the change the world needs right now. We can come together and push against a system that was not constructed with our voices and truths in mind."**
Deepa Purushothaman, The First, The Few, The Only: How Women of Color Can Redefine Power in Corporate America (New York: Harper Business, 2022), 197.

MYTH NINE: There is one path to success

248 **having workers who want to be there**
Gallup, "What is Employee Engagement and How Do You Improve It?," gallup.com/workplace/285674/improve-employee-engagement-workplace.aspx.

248 **PERMA model**
Martin Seligman, "PERMA Theory of Well-Being," ppc.sas.upenn.edu/learn-more/perma-theory-well-being-and-perma-workshops.

249 **A 2013 study examining 860 US managerial women**
Regina O'Neill, Mary Shapiro, Cynthia Ingols, Stacy Blake-Beard, "Understanding Women's Career Goals across Ethnic Identities," Advancing Women in Leadership Vol. 33, pp. 196-214, 226, June 16, 2017, doi.org/10.21423/awlj-v33.a111.

250 **A study with first generation low-income students of color**
Rashné Jehangir, Arien Telles, Veronica Deenanath, "Using Photovoice to Bring Career into a New Focus for First-Generation College Students," Journal of Career Development, 47(1), 59-79, February 25, 2019, doi.org/10.1177/0894845318824746.

276 **"You can't run the company until you get some broader set of experiences"**
Taylor Dunn, "Record 41 female CEOs among Fortune 500 includes
2 Black women for 1st time," June 2, 2021, goodmorningamerica.com,
goodmorningamerica.com/news/story/record-41-female-ceos-fortune-500-includes-
black-78046013.

**MYTH 10 : We will get the workplaces we want through
incremental change led by DEI officers**

282 **three of four companies**
Te-Ping Chen, "The Rise and Fall of Chief Diversity Officers," July 23, 2023, wsj.
com, wsj.com/articles/chief-diversity-officer-cdo-business-corporations-e110a82f.

291 **Harvard Business Review had an article**
Jeremie Brecheisen, "Research: Where Employees Think Companies' DEIB Efforts
Are Failing," March 9, 2023, hbr.org, hbr.org/2023/03/research-where-employees-
think-companies-deib-efforts-are-failing.

303 **researchers**
Francine Blau, Jed DeVaro, "New Evidence on Gender Difference in Promotion
Rates: An Empirical Analysis of a Sample of New Hires," National Bureau of
Economic Research, June 2006, doi:10.3386/w12321.

303 **study**
Cristian L. Dezsö, David Gaddis Ross, Jose Uribe, "Is there an implicit quota on
women in top management? A large-sample statistical analysis," November 15,
2015,onlinelibrary.wiley.com/doi/abs/10.1002/smj.2461.

305 **Report**
Sundiatu Dixon-Fyle, Kevin Dolan, Dame Vivian Hunt, and Sara Prince,
"Diversity Wins and How Inclusion Matters," May 19, 2020, mckinsey.com,
mckinsey.com/featured-insights/diversity-and-inclusion/diversity-wins-how-
inclusion-matters.

306 **ranks second in their industry**
"How 3M performs on the issues that matter," Just Capital Rankings.justcapital.
com/companies/3m-company. Accessed October 7, 2023.

306 **3M plans**
"3M to invest $50 million over 5 years to address racial opportunity gaps,"
September 14, 2020, news.3m.com, news.3m.com/3M-to-invest-50-million-over-5-
years-to-address-racial-opportunity-gaps.

307 **51 percent**
Meryl Spierings, "Linking Executive Compensation to ESG Performance,"
November 27, 2022, corpgov.law.harvard.edu, corpgov.law.harvard.
edu/2022/11/27/linking-executive-compensation-to-esg-performance.

307 **30% Club**
"About Us," (n.d.), 30percentclub.org, 30percentclub.org/about-us.

307 **14 percent**
Lindsey White and Gaurang Dholakia, "Ranks of US gender-diverse boards
grow, but less than 25% of directors are women," September 17, 2018, Ranks
S&P Global, spglobal.com/marketintelligence/en/news-insights/latest-news-
headlines/ranks-of-us-gender-diverse-boards-grow-but-less-than-25-of-directors-are-
women-45712062.

308 **evaluated based on their progress**
"Wells Fargo Q2 2020 Earnings Call Transcript," July 14, 2020, rev.com, rev.com/
blog/transcripts/wells-fargo-wfc-q2-2020-earnings-call-transcript.

308 **30 percent**
Amelia Lucas, "Starbucks pledges to have 30% of corporate workforce identify as minority by 2025," October 14, 2020, cnbc.com, cnbc.com/2020/10/14/starbucks-to-have-30percent-of-corporate-staff-identify-as-a-minority-by-2025.html.

308 **program**
Allen Smith, "More Companies Use DEI as Executive Compensation Metric," July 12, 2021, shrm.org, shrm.org/resourcesandtools/legal-and-compliance/employment-law/pages/dei-as-executive-compensation-metric.aspx.

310 **Implicit Association Test**
Project Implicit, Implicit.Harvard.edu/implicit/takeatest.html.

311 **85 percent**
Aja Frost, "15 Surprising Stats on Networking and Face-to-Face Communication," June 25, 2019, hubspot.com, blog.hubspot.com/sales/face-to-face-networking-stats.

311 **Research**
Stefanie K Johnson, David R. Hekman, and Elsa Chan, "If There's Only One Woman in Your Candidate Pool, There's Statistically No Chance She'll Be Hired," April 2016, hbr.org, hbr.org/2016/04/if-theres-only-one-woman-in-your-candidate-pool-theres-statistically-no-chance-shell-be-hired.

311 **Rooney Rule**
Office of the Press Secretary, "Fact Sheet: President Obama Announces New Commitments from Investors, Companies, Universities, and Cities to Advance Inclusive Entrepreneurship at First-Ever White House Demo Day," August 4, 2015, obamawhitehouse.archives.gov/the-press-office/2015/08/04/fact-sheet-president-obama-announces-new-commitments-investors-companies?itid=lk_inline_enhanced-template.

312 **Confirmation bias**
Raymond Nickerson, "Confirmation Bias: A Ubiquitous Phenomenon in Many Guises," Review of General Psychology, 2, no. 2 (1998): 175-220, uvm.edu/~pdodds/teaching/courses/2009-08UVM-300/docs/others/1998/nickerson1998a.pdf.

312 **confirm this belief**
Thomas Dougherty, Daniel Turban, and John Callender, "Confirming First Impressions in the Employment Interview: A Field Study of Interviewer Behavior," Journal of Applied Psychology, 79, no. 5 (2014): 659-665, business.missouri.edu/sites/default/ files/publication/dougherty_turban_callender_1994_jap.pdf.

312 **tendency to favor people**
Anthony Greenwald and Thomas Pettigrew, "With Malice Toward None and Charity for Some: Ingroup Favoritism Enables Discrimination," American Psychologist, 69, no. 7 (2014): 669-684, faculty.washington.edu/agg//pdf/AGG&TFP.With%20mal ice%20toward%20none.AP_online.24Mar2014.pdf.

312 **name on a resume**
Marianne Bertrand, and Sendhil Mullainathan, "Are Emily and Greg More Employable than Lakisha and Jamal? A Field Experiment on Labor Market Discrimination," The American Economic Review, 94, no. 4 (2004): 991-1013, www2.econ.iastate.edu/classes/ econ521/orazem/Papers/bertrand_emily.pdf.

313 **effective hiring decisions**
Ellyn Brecher, Jennifer Bragger, and Eugene Kutcher, "The Structured Interview: Reducing Biases Toward Job Applicants with Physical Disabilities," Employee Responsibilities and Rights Journal, 18, no. 3 (2006): 155-170, link.springer.com/article/10.1007%2Fs10672-006-9014-y#page-1.

314   **avoids the backlash**
Riley Bowers, "Why Women Don't Negotiate Their Job Offers." June 2014, hbr.
org, hbr.org/2014/06/ why-women-dont-negotiate-their-job-offers/.

314   **2023 study**
McKinsey & Company and LeanIn.org, "Women in the Workplace Report,"
2023, leanIn.org, sgff-media.s3.amazonaws.com/sgff_r1eHetbDYb/
Women+in+the+Workplace+2023_+Designed+Report.pdf.

314   **Research**
Alan Benson, Danielle Li, and Kelly Shue, "Potential and the
Gender Promotion Gap," 2021, danielle-li.github.io/assets/docs/
PotentialAndTheGenderPromotionGap.pdf.

315   **61 percent and 28 percent**
McKinsey & Company and LeanIn.org, "Women in the Workplace
Report," 2023, leanin.org, sgff-media.s3.amazonaws.com/sgff_r1eHetbDYb/
Women+in+the+Workplace+2023_+Designed+Report.pdf.

316   **Research**
Korn Ferry, "Korn Ferry Study Reveals United States Black P&L Leaders are Some
of the Highest Performing Executives in the US, C-Suite," October 10, 2019,
kornferry.com, kornferry.com/content/dam/kornferry/docs/pdfs/korn-ferry_
theblack-pl-leader.pdf.

316   **Prove their credibility**
Michelle Ryan and S. Alexander Haslam, "The Glass Cliff: Evidence that Women
are Over-Represented in Precarious Leadership Positions," British Journal of
Management, 16, (2005): 81–90, onlinelibrary.wiley.com/doi/abs/10.1111/j.1467-
8551.2005.00433.x.

318   **create a culture of sponsorship**
SheWorks, "SheWorks: Putting Gender-Smart Commitments into Practice,"
March 8, 2012, ifc.org, ifc.org/wps/wcm/connect/de9a7ee8-940a-450a-bb19-
eb452f9fa08e/SheWorks+Final+Report.pdf?MOD=AJPERES&CVID=lDhiP4z.

319   **more successful**
Dame Vivian Hunt, Lareina Yee, Sara Prince, Sundiatu Dixon-Fyle, "Delivering
Through Diversity," January 2018, mckinsey.com, mckinsey.com/~/media/
mckinsey/business%20functions/people%20and%20organizational%20
performance/our%20insights/delivering%20through%20diversity/delivering-
through-diversity_full-report.pdf

320   **study**
Jane Stevenson and Evelyn Orr, "We Interviewed 57 Female CEOs to Find Out
How More Women of Color Can Get to the Top," November 8, 2017, hbr.org,
hbr.org/2017/11/we-interviewed-57-female-ceos-to-find-out-how-more-women-can-
get-to-the-top.

321   **more flexibility**
Jane Stevenson, "Women CEOs Speak," November 9, 2017, kornferry.com,
kornferry.com/content/dam/kornferry/docs/pdfs/kf-rockefeller-women-ceos-
speak.pdf.

321   **Dr. Amy Edmonson describes psychological safety**
Amy Edmonson, "Leading in Tough Times: HBS Faculty Member Amy C.
Edmondson on Psychological Safety," November 22, 2022, hbs.edu, hbs.edu/
recruiting/insights-and-advice/blog/post/leading-in-tou